ACKNOWLEDGMENTS

A special thanks to The Berkley Publishing Group and my editor, Judith Palais, along with my agent, Alison Picard, for presenting the idea for this book to me and then letting me care for its soul.

CARING FOR THE
FAMILY SOUL

CARING FOR THE
FAMILY SOUL

Amy E. Dean

Berkley Books, New York

To Helena, Sissy, Kim, Betsy, Linda, Joellyn, and Kathy—my "college family"

CONTENTS

"As to the family, I have never understood how that fits in with the other ideals—or, indeed, why it should be an ideal at all. A group of closely related persons living under one roof; it is a convenience, often a necessity, sometimes a pleasure, sometimes the reverse; but who first exalted it as admirable, an almost religious ideal?"
—*Rose Macaulay*
from The World My Wilderness *(1950)*

INTRODUCTION

∽∞∾

The Family Matters

I have been forced all my life to think about family—what it is, what it means, what it stands for—because my experience of family did not fit in with the ideal that was commonly accepted at the time of my childhood. I was born out of wedlock to a seventeen-year-old high school girl and then turned over to a temporary foster home prior to adoption. A short time later, I was placed in the home of adoptive parents, not only because I was available, but also because my physical appearance and nationality closely matched theirs. Unfortunately my adoptive mother had a drinking problem that resulted in times of neglect and placed my life in jeopardy when she took me for rides in the car. So state social workers intervened. I was removed from my adoptive home and placed in foster care for a period of five years. During this time, my adoptive parents divorced. My adoptive father gained custody, and every weekend he and I would spend time together outside the foster home. When I was seven years old, he remarried; by that time, I had had four different mothers.

For many years, I was both ashamed and saddened about my family experiences. In ways both subtle and blatant, I was led to believe that there was only one "right" family in which to grow up—one in which a birth mother and birth father lived with their birth child. Since that was not my experience of family, imagine the impact such a single-minded, exclusive view had upon me. All around me there was no validation, acceptance, respect, tolerance, compassion, or understanding for my unique experience of family. Adoption was a word spoken in hushed tones at that time; it was not celebrated or embraced but often treated as a family secret—like alcoholism, disease, illness, job loss, criminal activity, and homosexuality. Even though my parents told me I was special because I was adopted ("We *chose* you"), I never felt special outside the home. Neither public school teachers nor Sunday school teachers acknowledged that adoption was a legitimate part of the experience of family. My peers viewed my adoption either as a cool alternative to being stuck with their particular set of "real" parents or as a cruel outcome of not being wanted. Adults alternately expressed sympathy to my parents for their inability to have "one of their own" or marveled at how much I looked like my stepmother (amazingly, I look more like her than I do my adoptive mother, whom I was intended to "match").

When I reflect upon my early childhood, it still astounds me that during the most formative years of my life I went through an adoption, grew up with alcoholism, experienced parental separation and divorce, received years of care from foster parents, was raised for a short time by a single parent, and was then brought up by my adoptive father and a stepmother who immigrated to this country as a child and whose nationality I did not share—experiences that have become the norm for many children today. Did growing up in such a "nontraditional" family—without biological parents, without consistent parenting from a father and a mother, with caretaking often provided by those outside the family (a family that included my adoptive father's family, my adoptive mother's family, my stepmother's family, my biological mother's family, and my foster parents and their children)—create disastrous results? On the contrary; my particular experience of family and my relationship with many members of this rather large family is rich with love, bound by deep connections, nurtured by acceptance and respect, founded upon and honored by rituals and traditions, filled with trust and spiritual values, and connected to its past, present, and future with shared goals and dreams.

In sum my experience of family, although it is not one that ever fit or will ever fit "the norm," "the ideal," or the "perfect image," has provided me and still provides me with everything I need as a member of a family. My family makes me feel safe and secure, loved and accepted, nurtured and respected; they make me feel connected not only to myself, but to every other member of the family; my family gives me a sense of belonging, a firm foundation upon which I can build myself and my future. They are connected to me and I am connected to them; in short, my family has soul. And because it has soul—a heartfelt bonding that will be explored in greater detail in Chapters 3 and 4—it does not matter to me (nor should it matter to any other person, group, or institution) what my particular experience of family is. As Gloria Steinem writes in her foreword to Marlo Thomas's book *Free to Be . . . a Family,* after she discusses how odd she felt as a child because her family lived and traveled in a house trailer most winters before she was ten, her parents separated and divorced when she was about eleven, and her sickly mother needed her caretaking:

> Years later, I talked to my now grown-up friends and realized something very interesting. Linda said she had felt funny because her mother was a widow and they didn't live in a real house. Carol had been a little ashamed because her father went to work in overalls and didn't speak English very well. Both of them envied me. . . . All of us felt a little bad because we didn't live the way that kids did in the movies. . . . [But] movies and other made-up images aren't always right or real.
>
> Neither are all of our ideas about what a "real family" is. If we feel loved and supported for being special and unique, if we have enough food and a warm, dry place to live, if we have people we love and feel close to, then we are probably in a real family. It doesn't matter whether it is one we got born into, or one we chose, or one that chose us, or one that came together because people who already had families

loved each other and decided to blend them into one. . . . no one way of living can be right for everybody.[1]

Yet there are many forces in society today that want to convince you that there is only one "legitimate" family structure and only one way of living together as a household. Such a view is, at best, dated and myopic, and, at worst, destructive, discriminatory, and devaluing to many of today's family structures and households. For some, this view harkens back to a time in the 1800s in America when the family was initially being threatened by the new industrial age and the household was purportedly epitomized by the popular sampler saying, "Home Sweet Home." But the American family in the 1800s was more like what families were like in the 1700s than what they would eventually become in the 1900s. A typical 1800s family was rural; their households were the center of economic activity. The village blacksmith plied his highly regarded trade in a shop adjacent to his living quarters; food and clothing for the family were produced in one's own household, and patriarchal family relations were the norm, where the father ruled and everyone else obeyed.[2] It was a time in which, upon examination, we see that family structures and values were so out-of-step with present-day standards as to be absurd as a viable option for today's families.

The 1800s in America were also a time in which change and progress were occurring both from within the family structure and without. The charming hominess attributed to that era was, in reality, being reforged, as is evident in this report from an October 1857 issue of *Harpers Weekly:* "It is a gloomy moment in the history of our country . . . never has the future seemed so incalculable as at this time. The domestic situation is in chaos. . . . Prices are so high as to be utterly impossible. The political cauldron seethes and bubbles with uncertainty. Russia hangs as usual, like a cloud, dark and silent upon the horizon. It is a solemn moment. Of our troubles no man can see the end."[3] So the concept of the 1800s being a sweeter, gentler time for families and the notion that a charming hominess existed in households that embodied old, eternal values simply does not follow the true, changing nature of families that was occurring at that time in this country's history. Factory production was eliminating time-consuming household production of goods, the creation of a middle class was beginning to diminish the advantages status-laden aristocratic families had over the lower-class families, and urbanization was helping to form communities of families that participated with one another in a more social context rather than in the privacy of an inherited homestead in a rural location.

Others today long for a return to more "traditional" family values and view such "happy days" for families as being comfortably nestled in the 1950s. They may point to the 1950s as the "last gasp of time-honored family life before the sixties generation made a major break from the past. But the comparison is short-sighted,"comments Elaine Tyler May in her book *Homeward Bound: American Families in the Cold War Era:*

> In many ways, the youths of the sixties resembled their grandparents, who came of age in the first decades of the twentieth century. Like many of their baby-boom grandchildren, the grandparents had challenged the sexual norms of their day, pushed the divorce rate up and the birth rate down, and created a unique youth culture, complete with music, dancing, movies, and other new forms of urban amusements. They also behaved in similar ways politically, developing a powerful feminist movement, strong grass-roots activism on behalf of social justice, and a proliferation of radical movements to change the status quo.[4]

From the colonization of America to present times, families have always been in flux and in crisis; they have rarely lived up to the nostalgic notions about the way things should be, except in the images created through television, cinema, and print media such as advertising. Following this evolution of family in America from the 1600s to the 1900s makes for a fascinating journey of discovery and, additionally, encourages reevaluation of the actual historical, sociological, pyschological, and spiritual formation and reformation of the American family. Chapter 1 of this book provides a historical exploration of families that begins in ancient civilizations before moving to America, while Chapter 2 explores the ways in which the image of family has changed drastically from that of "a man, woman, and children living blissfully in a mortgaged house on a quiet neighborhood street"[5] to that of a more diverse group of individuals of all ages, backgrounds, and lifestyles who may live for the most part in one location, spend alternating periods of time apart, or may come together only on special occasions.

This book recommends and supports the proposition that a family needs to be seen as a constantly changing, fluid unit that has simply developed new functions over the years and incorporated them into the foundation of family life as it is today. Accepting the family's fluidity and then striving to strengthen the foundations of family life is the first step in caring for the family's soul; refusing to let go of myths and misconceptions and seeking to resculpt the family into some sort of ideal image destroys the possibility of developing and then nurturing a family's soul.

There are two schools of thought regarding what can "save" today's family. One school says that in order to have strong families, the functions of the earlier family unit must be adopted: Dad must once again become the breadwinner, Mom needs to be content fulfilling the role of the at-home nurturer, and the children ought to do their chores. Then, and only then, can the order and solidarity of the traditional family be restored. But respected family specialist Dr. Ashley Montagu writes that "This reaction indicates that the problem may lie not so much with the family itself as with the excessive demands that Americans have made upon it—in the form of myths and misconceptions which, in fantasy but not in fact, have converted the home into a shrine and the family into a band of angels."[6] Those today who believe that if families returned to the old functions of yesteryear the breakdowns in society would be repaired and so-called "good" families would return once again—families that are close, loving, and problem-free—forget that living according to those functions never did guarantee a "perfect" or good family or create a more perfect world in which to live. Many of today's family problems are no different than yesterday's, but professionals, politicians, and preachers still proclaim that family structures have evolved in a more socially damaging direction. For example, even though a large percentage of American children live in poverty today, at the turn of the century the same proportion lived in orphanages—not because they lacked both parents but because one or both parents could not afford them. Women and children bore the brunt of poverty within so-called "traditional" two-parent families years ago; budget studies and medical records from that time reveal that women and children in poor families were far more likely to go without needed nutrients than were male heads of families.[7] While overpermissiveness may be seen as creating problems among today's youth, overwork was responsible for the prevalence of delinquency and runaways in the nineteenth century. Today's high school dropout rates are shocking, but as late as the 1940s less than half the youths entering high school managed to finish. Violence is reaching new highs in America, but before the Civil War New York City was already considered the most dangerous place to live in the world.[8] Alcohol and drug abuse were widespread long before modern rearrangements of family life; in the 1820s, per capita consumption of alcohol was almost three times higher than it is today, and there was a major epidemic of opium and cocaine addiction in the nineteenth century. "On a per capita basis, narcotic abuse was certainly as bad and probably worse" than it is today, with pharmacists routinely dispatching young messenger boys with vials of morphine to the homes of middle-class women.[9] While modern statistics on child-support evasion are appalling, prior to the 1920s a divorced father did not even have a legal child-support obligation to evade; until that time, children were considered assets of the family head, and the father's duty to support them ended if he was not in the home to receive the wages the children could earn. And child abuse—verbal, physical, and sexual—has had such a long and brutal history that it cannot be blamed on recent family innovations.[10]

Thus, the historical record on families is clear on one major point: although there have been some wonderful influences that so-called traditional families have had upon their members and society, there is no one family form that has been proven to protect its members from poverty, violence, abuse, addiction, social disruption, or any of the other number of current ills that are being blamed on the erosion of the family. Each of the many transformations in family life and social relations in American history has influenced family members and society in important ways, both good and bad. Such transformations should not and cannot be referred to as the sole causes of the current state of society or the creation of "children at risk." There have been undeniable gains and positive outcomes associated with many of the changes in family structures, a number of which were once considered radical. The expansion of women's options outside the family, for example, has led to the reformation of men's responsibilities within the family in ways that create more equal partnerships, provide more accurate and well-rounded role models for both boys and girls, and enable children to form profound connections and spend quality time with their fathers—benefits that cannot be elicited from the "traditional" family image of an at-home, full-time female caretaker and an out-of-home male provider and ultimate authority.

This book rejects the notion that the answer to this country's problems lies in recapturing family arrangements that either never truly existed (except in Norman Rockwell paintings) or existed in a totally different context (for example, when this country was agrarian rather than urban). Such views of families are based on myths that create unrealistic expectations about what families can or should do, such as urging mothers to stay at home when the family clearly cannot survive solely on the father's salary. They erode confidence in a family structure that falls short of the ideal, particularly in the use of terms such as "broken home" to describe a single mother and her children who, in reality, feel far from being in need of repair. And they distort the diverse experiences of other groups in America, for most often the call to return to such unrealistic family structures goes hand-in-hand with one rigid model view of "the right family"—one that typically abides by white, middle-class expectations. This Ward-and-June *Leave It to Beaver* ideal was an invention of the 1950s, not an example of tradition; families of that time period were far more diverse and less idyllic than what was portrayed. As Tom Brokaw, anchorman of the *NBC Nightly News* comments:[11]

> The other America —African-American, Native American, Latino, Asian—the people of color, whatever color, were invisible to most of white America forty years ago, except when they were celebrated as entertainers or athletes. Forty years ago, the face of the American political, economic, and cultural establishment was white only. Four decades later all the primary colors are vivid and visible in the mosaic of America. We still have far to go in resolving our complex feeling about race, but the fact of a multiracial society is no longer denied.

The other school of thought regarding what can "save" today's family holds that the needs of today's families cannot be met with yesterday's structures. Instead new solutions must be created, cultivated, nurtured, and accepted. These new solutions need to be relational; that is, they need to be based on the quality of the relationships within the family unit, no matter what the age, background, or lifestyle of each individual member. This means that families need to join together for reasons such as to love and be loved (rather than feed and be fed), to search for intimacy (and not protection), to have children (if they desire) in order to give and be given to, to share the joys of connecting with one another as well as with a community (perhaps by extending their family circle to include friends and neighbors, adoptive parents as well as birth parents, church or civic organizations, and so on), to instill religious and spiritual values in order to create attitudes of acceptance and tolerance within the family and within the world around them, to develop and celebrate unique and individual family traditions and rituals, and to contribute in a profound way to each individual's personal development. In effect, the family needs to be given a soul—

> a felt network of relationship, an evocation of a certain kind of interconnection that grounds, roots, and nestles. This connectedness doesn't have to be perfect or whole in order to do its business and give its gifts, but it has to be able to stir the imagination and move the emotions in a way that is particular to the family.[12]

Part III of this book, which includes Chapters 5 through 10, explores ways in which to grow a family's soul: to plant the seeds needed to create the family's soul, and then to cultivate and nurture this soul through the shared experience of family, so each individual within the family, the family as a unit, and the family as a member and participant in society can benefit from its creation and ongoing growth.

The current conservative rallying cry for a return to "traditional" family values is based on the nineteenth-century myth of the traditional family—an image in which family was isolated from the rest of society. But, in reality, the family is a basic social institution, simply one of the major institutions in America, which also include the government, the economic system, educational structures, and religious organizations.[13] Because of this, the family can only be understood in the context of its relations with other institutions. There was a time in this country's history when there was relatively little differentiation among the major institutions; when, for example, the family performed many of what today are functions of the economy, government, religion, and the schools. But the impact of scientific and technological developments, of a work world that has evolved from households as primary economic units to factories and office buildings as economic bases, of changes in the physical settings in which the family exists, and of various governmental, legal, and social forces have completely integrated the family as a social unit within the other institutions.

The legacy of the American family is long and complex, but the actual complexity of its history—even of your own personal experience—may often get buried under the weight of an idealized image or a need to remember things as you would have liked them to be, rather than as they really were. Just as people suffer from sexism, racism, and other forms of discrimination and denial, so too are families hurt whenever their particular experience of family is discredited, either directly or by inference. There was no "golden age" of the family; things were not always right in families of the past. But the 1990s marks a time of confusion about family. When Republican House Speaker Newt Gingrich announced in January 1995 that he planned to hold hearings on a measure to discourage school districts from adopting gay-friendly curricula, his lesbian half-sister Candace imagined what she would tell the House were she permitted to testify, for her brother's comments are in sharp contrast to his personal family relationship with her. "I can't believe that Newt would really want gay and lesbian kids denied information that there are others like them out there and that they can live a happy life and be gay at the same time," she responded. And when her brother said in an interview that "it would be madness to pretend that families are anything other than heterosexual couples" and that "over time we want to have an explicit bias in favor of heterosexual marriage," such views were inconsistent with his own experience of family, raising serious questions about the conflict between public and private views of what makes a family a family.[14]

The expanded tolerance for alternative family forms and reproductive arrangements has created difficulties when boundary disputes accompany new family definitions (for example, how should child custody disputes be resolved between lesbian and gay partners or who has a higher right to a child: the child's adoptive parents or the child's biological parents) and when the institutions with whom a family must interact (schools, government, churches, and so on) deny rights afforded to other families. But, on the whole, there are the beginnings of legal recognition of families that are not always based on marriage or conventional heterosexual arrangements.

To find effective answers to the dilemmas facing modern families, this book rejects attempts to "recapture" family traditions and relations that either never existed or existed in another context, and instead attempts to define how to strengthen and support families in the present so they can improve their future prospects. And, since this book is founded on the premise that the soul needs a felt experience of family, the book seeks to define family more as the "shaping unit" for fashioning the enrichment of all of its members.

The family today is not all newness and modernity; it is simply the outcome of a gradual, natural, and logical evolutionary process. Today whatever a family looks like, wherever it resides, and whomever it contains is very real and precious to the people in it. In this country you may live in a "traditional" family (a stay-at-home mother, an employed father, and their biological children), a two-paycheck family, a stepfamily, a blended family, an extended family, an adoptive family, a single-parent family, a gay or lesbian family, a multicultural family, a foster family, or some other family that has no label at all. This book has been written on the premise that all of these families are the "right" kinds of families. *All families matter.*

NOTES

1. Thomas, Marlo & Friends. *Free to Be . . . A Family: A Book About All Kinds of Belonging.* Bantam Books, New York, 1987, p. 10.
2. Gottlieb, Beatrice. *The Family in the Western World: From the Black Death to the Industrial Age.* Oxford University Press, New York, 1993, p. 270.
3. Kirkendall, Lester A. and Gravatt, Arthur E., eds. *Marriage and the Family in the Year 2020.* Prometheus Books, Buffalo, NY, 1984, p. 7.
4. May, Elaine Tyler. *Homeward Bound: American Families in the Cold War Era.* Basic Books, Inc., New York, 1988, p. 9.
5. Moore, Thomas. *SoulMates.* HarperCollins Publishers, New York, 1994, p. 71.
6. Montagu, Dr. Ashley. "Can the Family Survive Free Love?" *Empire Magazine,* 4 November 1979.
7. Coontz, Stephanie. *The Way We Never Were: American Families and the Nostalgia Trap.* Basic Books, New York, 1992, p. 4.
8. *Ibid.,* p. 5.
9. *Ibid.*
10. *Ibid.*
11. Brokaw, Tom, contributor. *American Heritage,* 40th Anniversary Issue, December 1994, pp. 62–63.
12. Moore, p. 71.
13. Leslie, Gerald. *The Family in Social Context,* 4th ed. Oxford University Press, Inc., New York, 1979, p. 6.
14. Bull, Chris. "Family Matters," *The Advocate,* 7 March 1995, pp. 27–31.

PART I

A Family Perspective

"Call it a clan, call it a network, call it a tribe, call it a family. Whatever you call it, whoever you are, you need one."
—Margaret Mead

CHAPTER 1

∞

From Homestead to Hearth to Heart

Many perceive the 1990s to be an evolutionary time for family. Determining what does or should qualify today as a family can be confusing and conflicting, especially when compared to yesterday's ideals and traditional notions. Yet throughout the history of the world family has taken many different forms in all human societies, from primitive nomads to Western industrial nations. The family in the United States, in particular, has always been an institution remarkably affected by a way of life that was founded upon the pursuit of personal freedom; therefore, it respects the ability to make choices. For example, the selection of a life partner in this country may be out of love, for economic reasons, or to "win" a mate from a rival, but the person whom someone marries or with whom someone chooses to enter into a long-term relationship is based on a personal choice and not arranged by family or command from an authoritarian figure. Additionally, the American family has been and continues to be blessed by its right to privacy and by its development of independence in its children; in contrast, in many countries, after a couple marries, they may have to provide a home to their parents and siblings or share one with them for the duration of their marriage, while the husband is expected to work in the same profession or trade as the father or father-in-law. The right to terminate an unhappy marriage is also a great freedom in this country, even though there are some who would point to separation and divorce as the original destroyers of families. In actuality, what divorce and its resulting coparenting and stepparenting options have done is recreate what has historically been an integral part of family traditions; that is, an extended family (which includes blood relatives as well as nonrelatives) rather than a nuclear family (which consists of mother, father, and children), which increases, rather than decreases, each family member's ability to learn from and be nurtured by a diversity of intimate relationships.

Just how different from other time periods the 1990s are in regards to the American family bears close examination, for much of what you may perceive as "real" or "traditional" is based upon myth, media manipulation, or misinterpretation of the past. To illustrate this, try to determine when the following opinion was expressed by an American anthropologist:

> A great many people today speak as if the family were in some special sort of danger in our times. We hear a great deal about "saving the family" and about "preserving the home." Authors and lecturers describe how the family is threatened by divorce, or by mothers who work outside of the home, or by unemployment, or by lack of religious training of children. Each of them, depending on his experience in his own home and on his observations in the families he knows, selects something he thinks should be changed—or should be preserved—and says that, if this or that were done, the family would be "saved."[1]

Or when were the next comments made regarding the effects of war on the American woman and family life?

> It must not be supposed that the war was the sole cause of the invasion by woman of the industries and professions. The movement was not a new one; and other causes contributed, as for example the ordinary desire of the capitalists for cheap labor. Moreover the higher education of woman was bearing fruit. The whole movement signifies an exten-

sion of woman's economic independence of man, and the breaking down of that barrier of inequality that had so long served to keep woman in a subordinate place in the household. While the [war] did not start the movement, it did greatly stimulate it, and thus . . . helped to unsettle the foundations of the "mediaeval" family which was now passing out and through a transition of storm and stress yielding to the new family of equality and comradeship.[2]

Anthropologist Ruth Benedict contributed the first opinion in *The Family: Its Function and Destiny,* published in 1949; Arthur W. Calhoun reflected on the effects of the Civil War on women and family in the second, an excerpt from his 1945 book *A Social History of the American Family from Colonial Times to Present.*

Change in the American family has not only been rapid and continuous throughout history but also cyclical in its nature, affecting not only the family as a whole but also its individual members—women, men, and children. To see the complete evolution of the American family system, its roots first need to be traced back three thousand years or more to the earliest family forms—long before the first settlers arrived in Jamestown—in order to provide a basis for the many shifts in the family's focus and the variety of changes in its structure and function.

History of the Western Family

The ancient Hebrew family system was the earliest direct antecedent of the American family system. The Hebrews were a nomadic desert people who depended upon a pastoral economy. Because of this, they roamed the countryside seeking pasture for their herds and maintained a kinship organization. Beyond the nuclear family there was the *sib,* a group of kinsmen related through males, and a *clan,* which included the wives as well. Several related clans made up a *tribe;* twelve tribes constituted the nation of Israel. The Hebrew family was based on a strong patriarchy; the authority of the father was nearly absolute, and he could have several wives through the practice of polygamy and concubinage. Women were under the control of one or more males, even though it was common for each wife and her children to live in and maintain a separate dwelling. Up until the time of Christ, the Hebrew husband had almost unlimited power to divorce his wife. The Mosaic law allowed the husband to simply hand his wife a piece of paper that stated "Be thou divorced from me" and then send her out of her house. Most of the women who were divorced for "just reasons"—such as adultery or another similar cause—became "free agents"; no longer under the power of their husbands, they were entitled to have their dowries returned.

Hebrew children were expected to be obedient and respectful; Mosaic law indicated that persistently disobedient children could even be put to death. The father could marry off his children as early as the age of thirteen for boys and twelve for girls; in addition, he could sell their labor. However, as an increasing interest in pursuing trades and settling towns developed, a class of religious functionaries—the rabbis—emerged. These men took control of marriages, elevated women to a more equal status—complete with legal rights and greater responsibilities—and limited the power of both husbands and wives over their children. Rabbinical law then became the foundation for marriage and family life as Israel was first conquered by the Assyrians, then the Babylonians, and finally the Romans.[3]

Similar to the original Hebrew way of life, the Greek family was dependent upon agriculture. The family was essentially a strong patriarchy in which divorce was uncommon, wives were dominated by essentially monogamous husbands (who supplemented their monogamy with concubinage and prostitution), and extreme paternal power was exerted over children. Fathers could desert their infants (literally expose them to the elements to determine whether they were strong enough to survive, inherit property, and carry on the family line), sell their labor into indentured servitude, and arrange their marriages. During "the golden age" in Greece, the family became urban, having evolved from its patriarchal, land-oriented precursor; during this time, women earned limited rights to divorce—not for flagrant adultery, but if the husband was physically cruel or neglected his family.[4]

The development of the Roman family system was more progressive than that of the Hebrews and Greeks. The early Roman family was the strongest patriarchy known in the history of family. The father was the only "legal" person in the family; he held ownership of all property and power over his children throughout his lifetime—from birth, when he could choose whether they would live or die through exposure; through childhood, when he could sell them into slavery, banish them from the country, or kill them; and into adulthood, when he could marry them off and have them divorce against their will. The only way for a male child to escape a father's control, aside from the father's death, was through emancipation, which was rarely granted. Marriage was monogamous, descent was patrilineal, and a three-generation extended family was quite common. Girls were married young; it was not unusual for girls of ten or twelve to enter into marriages and then be encouraged to engage in sexual intercourse. The Roman husband could divorce his wife for adultery, drinking wine, or preparing poisons (most likely for her husband's consumption).

During the Punic Wars, however, the men went off to battle and left their wives, by default, with increasing power. Inevitably a shift in the power relations between the sexes occurred. When the husbands returned, they found wives unwilling to submit to their power and return to the old ways. But the women's desires were soon accepted. Because Rome had emerged victorious, the wealth of the provinces and Rome's control over the entire Mediterranean region encouraged more egalitarian and relaxed family interactions. Within the leisure class marriage ceased to be a sacred obligation and instead became a matter of personal satisfaction and convenience; both the marriage and the birth rate dropped as a result of personal preference. Abortion was widely practiced. Prostitution increased. Concerned officials wrote and passed laws that penalized the single or divorced; the inheritances of childless couples were taxed at 50 percent. The laws exempted children who were adopted, however; it therefore became fashionable to adopt children, if solely for the purpose of protecting inheritances.[5]

At the same time the Christians were gaining in strength and numbers; they battled with the Roman government for control of marriage and other family matters. The Christians taught that the power of the church was superior to that of the state. While Roman emperors, concerned with the decreasing birth rate, were passing laws that penalized celibacy, the Christians were teaching that the virginal state was exalted. In many ways the Christians sought to resurrect the stern morality of the earlier Hebrew, Greek, and Roman periods; in effect, they were striving to create a movement toward the reestablishment of former "family values"—values that saw the demands of the spirit and of the flesh as being diametrically opposed. By A.D. 311 the Christians had grown so numerous and powerful that they could not be suppressed; by 313 Christianity had become an officially tolerated religion in Rome. Ironically, under Christian influence marriage and the family were more lowly regarded than ever before. While the church attacked abortion, adultery, infanticide, and child exposure, it also fostered the attitude that marriage was purely for sexual union—"a slightly more desirable alternative than fornication."[6]

For over a thousand years after the fall of Rome and through the various settlements in the area that was to become Great Britain, the Roman Catholic Church was the most powerful and influential family institution in Europe. What the church taught about sexuality, about male and female roles, and about marriage and divorce shaped the personal understanding and daily lives of millions of people. Catholics were taught the sinful nature of sex; premarital and extramarital sex were forbidden. Marriages were usually arranged; people did not marry for love and were not expected to love their spouses; birth control, abortion, and divorce were prohibited.

But the role religion would play in the formation of early American families would evolve from a church that was eventually plagued by numerous scandals and against which Martin Luther led a revolt at the end of the fifteenth century. Luther was influential in reintroducing the concept of a civil marriage and state regulation of marriage and divorce. Even though the Christian church fragmented into Catholic and Protestant factions following Luther's Reformation, while civil authorities gradually assumed control of family matters, the church still had power over many components of marriage and family life, including performing marriage ceremonies and prohibiting divorce.

But the Protestant Reformation ended the virtual monopoly the Roman Catholic Church had enjoyed in Europe. Some of the new Protestant religious groups developed less restrictive understandings of sex, love, marriage, and family, including the English-speaking Calvinists, also known as the Puritans. The Puritans embraced sexual pleasure within marriage as good; they considered it God's way of encouraging a harmonious and companionable relationship between husband and wife. This belief contributed to a strengthening of the nuclear family, a strengthening that helped the Puritans survive religious wars and persecution in England as well as an arduous journey to America.

The Family in the American Colonies

When the English colonists came to America in the seventeenth and eighteenth centuries in pursuit of religious freedom, they traveled not in extended families but in nuclear families or, for the most part, as single persons. They brought with them some of the customs, traditions, and laws regarding family life they had learned in their mother country, but because of the great risk they were undertaking, the pioneer conditions they had to endure, and the incredible freedom they were able to experience after they arrived, many of the familiar familial ways were altered to make life easier in the early colonial settlements.

In the beginning life was hard for the colonists: houses were crude, food was scarce, the climate was severe, the Indians were sometimes hostile, possessions were minimal, medical skill and knowledge limited (disease claimed large numbers of the settlers), and the margin of survival narrow. Those who settled in New England established villages in which they could live compactly together for defense as well as for neighboring purposes; in the mid-Atlantic and southern colonies people settled less frequently in villages and more often on isolated plantations and farms, replicating in many ways the social system of English feudalism and chivalry, with stratification between elite families, indentured servants, Negro slaves, and the ordinary farmers, or "poor whites."[7]

In the New England colonies it was assumed that everyone was a member of some family group; few colonists lived outside a family. Such extended family-style groupings created independent economic units as well as households. Under the direction of the father (or, in the case of the southern colonies, the master of the plantation) many types of work were carried on: tilling the soil, raising the livestock, erecting buildings, and making and repairing vehicles and implements. The mother often supervised spinning, weaving, sewing, cooking, preserving, soapmaking, and other domestic duties. This family system functioned also as an educational agency, instilling in children a large part of their general, vocational, and religious training. Even though the religious orientation in the northern colonies was Puritan and in the southern colonies Anglican, in both cases the family was a religious unit organized around the father, who directed reading of the scriptures, family prayers, and hymn singing.

For the most part women and children were held under the power of the husband, perpetuating a patriarchal family structure, but American men were not permitted to beat their wives or even tongue-lash them too freely. "Cruelty" was a term that could be used to bring legal action against a verbally or physically abusive husband. The father could make many decisions regarding his children, but his power was not as great as it was elsewhere in the

Western world. Even though laws in Massachusetts and Connecticut, based on old Hebrew tradition, allowed that persistently disobedient youths be put to death, no colonial child was ever slain under this regulation. Treatment of children was often harsh, however. The adage "children are to be seen and not heard" was vigorously preached; in some households children were made to stand through meals, eating only when scraps of food were handed to them.

Corporal punishment was liberally employed through the use of birch rods, canes, and "flappers" (leather straps with a hole in the middle). Most often children were overworked, a response as much to the Puritan work ethic that discouraged idle time as to the severe living conditions. Boys had to rise early and do chores before school; time out of school was spent bringing in fuel, feeding pigs, watering horses, picking berries, gathering vegetables, and spooling yarn. At the age of six, girls could spin flax and were expected to work around the home.[8]

In the southern colonies families were large, with an average of ten to twelve children per household; one woman bore nineteen children to one husband! Children were set to work as early as eight years old and were oftentimes treated little better than the servants. Because of the scattered residences in the south, educational standards trailed the colonies in the north, where schoolhouses were prominent fixtures in most villages. Instead, southern children from wealthy families were sometimes educated abroad or taught at home by tutors; the rest were educated at home—the boys in the father's vocation; the girls in feminine duties.

Parents sometimes arranged marriages for their children; under common law boys could marry at fourteen and girls at twelve. Child marriages were uncommon, however; young people were given considerable freedom, and girls could refuse the young men their fathers had selected.[9] Considerable premarital freedom was given to young people; often they traveled to and from dances unescorted or from town to town together. As towns were often far apart and the journey took more than one day, the custom of "bundling" became accepted and widely practiced—a couple could retire to bed together fully clothed, with a bundling board placed between them to discourage physical contact.[10]

Women in the northern colonies usually held no property unless it was specifically given to them by their husbands; their clothing even belonged to the men. Husbands, however, were legally responsible for their wives, obligated to support them, and had to pay off their debts incurred both before and during the marriage. If the husband died first, the woman gained control of her own property; in the middle and southern colonies, where single men greatly outnumbered available women, an unmarried woman was elevated to a high status and could even hold land in her own name.[11] In general men could divorce wives for adultery, desertion, and cruelty; a woman could seek divorce on the grounds of adultery if she could also prove desertion, and some colonies granted alimony if the woman was unjustly divorced by her husband. The middle and southern colonies, however, were not so liberal in their attitudes toward divorce, preferring instead to recognize separation.[12]

In sum, the basic family units in the early American colonies were the nuclear family as well as the extended family, with the household a social unit. Some households were large, and because of ties to the land and the need for economic independence, unmarried kin and those who had lost spouses through divorce or death often had no choice but to keep their attachments to existing households. Patriarchy continued, as it had throughout history, with the wife's property for the most part belonging to the husband and women not recognized as the legal guardians of their children. Children had no rights, and their lives centered around work and contributing to the household rather than being a part of it.

The Unsettling of Old Family Foundations

Democratic independence in America and expansion westward from the eastern shore colonies set precedents that challenged and changed family life in ways that had not been experienced before in the history of families of the world. Following the American Revolution the growing population spread westward across the Appalachians, the Mississippi, and out to the Pacific Ocean. Nuclear families made the journey to seek out new opportunities; large numbers of single men also set off on their own with the intent of building families once they made their way west. Grandparents or weak or sickly family members were often left behind so they did not have to endure the arduous crossing and unknown future, thereby breaking up nuclear family households and depriving both the adult children and the grandchildren of ancestral influence.

The westward expansion changed the structure not only of America, but also of the family. Although the father was often the final authority in the family, and it would be many years before women gained legal equality, the isolation and rigors of frontier life produced a hardy breed of women who became, in many ways, equal to the men. Children also became more equal participants within the family; as extended families broke up and spread over the countryside, parents disposed of property at will so daughters, as well as sons, could inherit equally. Increased democratization within family units brought to a decline the patriarchal structure and ensured, for the first time in the history of family and marriage, a conjugal family system—one based on the concept of romance, sex, and love between two people. As one European observer noted at the time: "American homes are warmed by parental love. The relationship between parents and children harmonizing in their outward manifestations . . . [is] special to the development of American society."[13]

The abundant opportunities presented by frontier expansion and the certainty that children could seek and gain their own opportunities tended to loosen family attachments in ways that fostered independence rather than dependence upon the father and the nuclear family as an economic unit; in essence, each child could be raised to follow a calling and make his or her own way in the world without the need for parental guidance or arrangement. During the first half of the nineteenth century, the development of the public school system and the formation of Sunday schools drew more attention away from the home as the primary educational and religious instructional center; education went beyond the "three Rs" and basic vocational instruction to include more cultural, creative, and scientific fields of study.

While such changes created family conflicts, for the most part Americans had not become indifferent to fundamental family values. They were still a domestic people, and home was still home to them—a center of affection and social relationships. Family bonds had not been weakened as a result of relocation and settlement; rather, marriage had become a happy consummation marked by mutual esteem. A strong spirit of respect was instilled in such restructured families. For example, Susan B. Anthony was born into a home where there was great respect and affection between her father and mother. When her father failed in business, both she and her mother taught for next to nothing and gave Mr. Anthony all they could to help pay interest on the mortgage on factory, mills, and home. Years later, he gratefully paid them back.[14]

Home life was additionally transformed during the Civil War. As the men went off to battlefields, the women joined aid societies, maintained their households, corresponded between the homes and the tents, and managed finances; in effect, they did not only the women's work, but also the men's. At the beginning of the war women were performing one-fourth of the manufacturing of the country. They were doing more work in teaching, on industrial lines, in clerical work, in the sphere of charity and religion, and were forging ahead in the professions, particularly in medicine. As a result, education for women advanced. In 1864 between 250 and 300 women physicians were regularly graduated from medical schools; in Illinois the number of women teachers increased by four thousand.[15]

The Civil War was not the sole cause of the educational and professional advancement of women, however. In actuality the movement was not a new one; some ultra-radical women had already begun agitating for women's rights, adopting short skirts as a symbolic part of their protest. But while the education of women was clearly bearing fruit, the desire of capitalists for cheap labor was the main reason for hiring so many women into the industrial work force—war or no war. The breakdown of the barrier of inequality between men and women that had once kept women in a subordinate place in the household was eroded by the war, but it also stimulated the formation of new families that were based on equality and comradeship. The Civil War also helped to usher in a new era of city industrialization that forced the country to focus on the growth of American industries and less on the development of family life.

The Impact of the Industrial Revolution Upon Families

Industrialization in this country got under way shortly after 1800; cities rapidly sprouted and flourished around the new factories. What followed was a massive movement away from farms and into cities. This time in American history created profound effects—both positive and negative—upon the family organization as a whole and upon individual members of the family. Families ceased to be primary economic units, producing what they needed for themselves as well as for trade and bartering with others, and instead became consumer units. Rather than the father, mother, and children working together in their economic enterprise of family, the father now went out of the home to earn the family wage. This left little time to be an authoritarian figure or even a father. As well, the wives of the laboring class seldom were able to look after their children as much as when the family was economically self-sufficient. This meant that children were often allowed to run wild and do whatever they pleased or were crammed into already overcrowded school classrooms. Mothers of means, who had considerable time on their hands, often left their babies' upbringing in the care of others; among the rich, children were often treated more as pets, spoiled by material goods and sent off to boarding schools. But whether children were from rich families or poor ones, at this time in the nation's history they became neglected, either out of ignorance or out of necessity.

Yet children were positively affected by the weakening of authoritarian and harsh parental supervision. They became masters of their own thoughts and conduct, grew competent at taking care of the family, learned to take on more responsibilities (such as preparing meals while parents were working), enjoyed opportunities that their parents had lacked during their own childhoods, and moved more quickly toward maturity. Opportunities for factory employment also made children financially independent, and further weakened the authority the head of the household once had. By giving up a portion of their wages to the family, they were in effect purchasing immunity from parental control. The downside, however, was that children were greatly abused and overworked in the factories. Factory representatives often made systematic canvasses in cities and towns for small children, oftentimes pulling them from schools and into the mills. Without any laws to protect them, even parents encouraged their children to work in order to "keep the wolf from the door."

Rapid urbanization also brought about the development of hotels and rooming houses, restaurants, bakeries, groceries, laundries, and other businesses that made it possible for family members to live apart from one another (which was a good thing, since living space in the cities was often crowded and expensive). In some cases industry, particularly the mills, employed entire families, keeping them intact not only in the home, but also at the workplace. But when mills refused to hire men at higher wages and instead employed their wives or children, who would work longer hours at considerably less pay, "she towns" were created—neighborhoods where the mill hands were women and the men stayed at home as housekeepers. Sometimes the men would assist in the housework and even take in washing, but most preferred to remain idle and leave the work for their wives. This left the women exhausted, and impacted upon infants, who depended upon adequate care during pregnancy and a nutritious and steady supply of breast milk. As the cost of living rose and wages remained shockingly low, providing for children became more and more demanding. The result was a declining birthrate—not only by choice or because both parents needed to work to make ends meet, but also as a result of infant mortality—a tragic product of impoverishment, lack of adequate care during pregnancy, and tenement life.

But the economic forces of industrialization did assist women in many ways. Women gained economic opportunity outside of marriage, attained enlightenment and prestige through formal education, accumulated working experience, and learned how to develop household economics into a highly technical pursuit. Gaining these abilities made it harder for husbands to dictate to and control their wives; the pressure of business and labor, which necessitated that men needed to be increasingly absent from the home, elevated the power of women in the households. For single women, the availability of hotels and boardinghouses and the ability to pursue a career granted them freedom to delay marriage.

Because industrialization enlarged the scope of families—fewer families remained isolated on farms and in rural locations, and more formed communal groups that included urban neighbors, workplace companions, and church groups—society began to assume some of the responsibilities of parenthood: the school assumed educational responsibility as well as provided lunches, free books, medical checkups, and playground facilities; the church assumed the teaching of moral and spiritual responsibility; the juvenile courts assumed the responsibility of protecting the young and instituting guidelines to hold parents accountable for their children's behavior; baby-feeding stations with educational classes were established to take care of the children of the poor; the state assumed responsibility of setting marriage guidelines, such as the need to pass medical examinations and requiring residence and notice as preliminaries.

By the turn of the century the state of the family had become utmost in the minds of many; a diversity of publications, from daily newspapers to weekly and monthly magazines, offered their opinions and concerns about the "modern" state of family life. It was noted that families rarely ate meals together at home, preferring instead to eat downtown, at school, at restaurants, or in hotels. The only meal most families shared together was breakfast, but that was becoming disjointed and disorganized, with parents as well as children wolfing food down or skipping the meal entirely in order to dash off to begin their daily obligations. The eight-hour workdays, combined with half-day work Saturdays, left little time for family togetherness. Husbands rarely saw their wives; when they did spend time together, the men were often too tired from their jobs and the wives too fatigued from housekeeping to do much of anything.

But despite such changes, at the beginning of the twentieth century the United States was, in many ways, still very attached to its colonial roots. Comparatively speaking, a large percentage of Americans still lived on farms or in small towns. Most people lived and died at or near where they were born. Few homes had a telephone, electricity, or indoor plumbing. Trains and steamships were viewed as "luxury" forms of transportation; the horse and wagon were still the most common means of personal conveyance. In sum, the full impact of the Industrial Revolution had yet to be felt in the daily family life of the masses of people.

Family Life in the Twentieth Century

The United States changed dramatically in the decade or so following World War I, a war that was most notable because it was the last in which horses were used and the first in which tanks and airplanes combined to fight and win battles. Following the war, the United States grew prosperous and optimistic. Accelerating industrialization attracted millions of people to the cities. The automobile replaced the horse and buggy, encouraging greater mobility. The radio and early motion pictures exposed many rural people to urban values and culture. The production and consumption of alcoholic beverages, which were prohibited by constitutional amendment from 1919 to 1933, gave rise to a subculture that consumed illegal alcohol, organized crime that supplied and protected the bootleg liquor, and a lure for young people that challenged former Victorian restrictions and set new mores for social and sexual behavior. Dating and courting became as popular as the "speakeasies;" former Victorian fashions in female dress and manners were replaced by short skirts and short hair in women and a greater willingness to engage in sexual exploration and premarital sex in both men and women. For the first time, female orgasm was "discovered;" interestingly enough, shortly after this discovery the number of divorces rose.

In the 1920s the booming industrial society and the stock market were thought to be invincible and would make everyone rich. Many Americans confidently invested their earnings in the market, but their optimism was soon shattered by the crash of 1929 that marked the beginning of the Great Depression. More than one-third of the nation lost their homes and jobs. Banks collapsed and lost hard-earned savings. Businesses closed their doors. To add insult to injury, the great droughts of 1934 and 1936 burned out America's heartland, turning entire states into the Dust Bowl. Times were hard, and rampant pessimism about the future prevailed. Family breadwinners who could no longer find work sometimes abandoned their families in hopes that charities would provide some assistance to help their loved ones get by. The number of children in orphanages rose. Single as well as married men became part of an increasing population that rode in boxcars from town to town looking for work. Some found work and sent for their families to join them; others disappeared and were never heard from again.

Although the wealthy were hit first in the Depression, soon everyone began to feel its effects. The concept of extended family grew at this time, not only out of the need for economic survival, but also because pitching in and helping one another served to heal emotional and spiritual wounds. There were as many households made up of blood relatives (nuclear families) as those composed of blood relatives and unattached neighbors and friends (extended families). Some married couples moved back into their parents' homes while others delayed marriage and returned to their family homes as adult children; aunts, uncles, cousins, and grandparents often gave up their separate homes or apartments in order to live together and share in cooking, cleaning, and contributing in many other ways.

Some rural households allowed rail riders to sleep in their barns; others kept a table set up in their backyard, with a big pot of beans and piles of corn bread available for the hungry. In the cities, children hit the streets as newsboys; papers sold for three cents, and newsboys earned a penny for each one they sold. Girls and their mothers set up sidewalk stands to sell fruits and vegetables, went door to door to sell home-baked goods, or took in sewing and other piecework, contributing what they earned to the household budget. At this difficult time in the nation's history, children often grew directly from childhood into adulthood, assuming adult responsibilities without appreciating adolescence or benefiting from a higher education.

The frugality and scarcity experienced by families during the Depression continued during World War II, a time in which the lives of millions of Americans were touched by the conflict. More than sixteen million people served in the military; there were over a million battlefield casualties. The mere sight of a Western Union worker was enough to send shock waves throughout an entire neighborhood. People lost husbands, fathers, brothers, nephews, uncles, cousins, and friends. As in every war, women joined the military or worked in defense plants, but this time patriotic spirit was so high that thousands of American women joined military and civilian agencies. Thousands of marriages and promises to marry were broken by separation, death, or uncertainty about the future. People formed and then remained in extended families for emotional as well as economic support during this somber time.

For nearly two decades following World War II, the United

States was the most powerful, prosperous nation in the world, if only by default because the other major industrial powers had been destroyed or devastated in the war. Many Americans who were born during or just after the war felt entitled to share in this prosperity and security:

> Between 1945 and 1960, the gross national product grew by almost 250 percent and per capita income by 35 percent. Housing starts exploded after the war, peaking at 1.65 million in 1955 and remaining above 1.5 million a year for the rest of the decade. The increase in single-family ownership between 1946 and 1956 outstripped the increase during the entire preceding century and a half. By 1960, nearly 62 percent of American families owned their own homes, in contrast to 43 percent in 1940. Eighty-five percent of the new homes were built in the suburbs, where the nuclear family found new possibilities for privacy and togetherness. . . . The number of salaried workers increased by 61 percent between 1947 and 1957. By the mid-1950s, nearly 60 percent of the population had what was labeled a middle-class income (between $3,000 and $10,000 in constant dollars), compared to only 31 percent in the "prosperous twenties," before the Great Depression.[16]

The "traditional" family of the 1950s reestablished trends that had only once before been seen, in the early days, in America: the age of marriage and motherhood fell, fertility increased, divorce rates declined, and women's degree of educational parity with men dropped sharply. Nuclear families were encouraged; young families were urged to strike out on their own. Newlyweds established single-family homes at earlier ages and more rapid rates than ever before; they moved to the suburbs, away from the close scrutiny of the older generation. People bore their children earlier and closer together, thereby completing their families by the time they were in their late twenties and leaving them with time to experience living together as a couple after the children had left home.

But the values of the 1950s families were, in many ways, relatively new. A novel rearrangement of family ideals and male-female relations was established. For women this meant letting go of the nineteenth century belief, held by middle-class women, that housework should be the work of servants; women were encouraged to foster a cheery attitude towards the "personal service" aspect of domesticity and chores. As a result, the amount of time women spent doing housework actually *increased* during the 1950s despite the advent of convenience foods and new, labor-saving devices. And, for the first time in history, men were encouraged to root their identity in familial and parental roles. The ranch house thus became a home for all members of the family, without separate spheres for men and women; family became a focus of fun, recreation, and togetherness. Or, at least by advertising and television sitcom standards, that was the way family life *was supposed to be.* But not all Americans in the 1950s were Ward and June Cleavers or Ozzie and Harriets; in fact, many could not be.

Twenty-five percent of Americans were poor in the mid-1950s; they had to get by without the assistance of food stamps or housing programs. At the end of the 1950s, one-third of American children were poor. Sixty percent of Americans over sixty-five had incomes below $1,000 in 1958; a majority of the elderly lacked medical insurance. Only half the population had savings in 1959; one-quarter of the population had no liquid assets.[17] Women's retreat into domestic bliss was not voluntary; after World War II, management went to extraordinary lengths to purge women from assembly lines and jobs they had earned in the labor force. Many women did not want to give up the economic independence and emotional benefits that earning wages and contributing to the household had given them. In most cases women left the jobs on their own when their pay was downgraded or responsibilities were taken away from them and given to men; those who stayed on despite the pay cuts and demotions were never given opportunities to succeed. Inside the home, women were given conflicting messages by sociologists, psychologists, and popular writers about their roles; they were told that if they could not achieve happiness and fulfillment by being wife and mother, they were "unnatural," "sick," and needed help. The 1950s was a time in which women who were depressed because they were relegated to the home were labeled schizophrenic, institutionalized and controlled by electric shock treatments and/or "nerve pills" such as Valium, or made to feel worthless. They were frequently denied the right to serve on juries, own property, make contracts, take out credit cards in their own name, or establish residence.

Even men felt the pressure to find fulfillment in domesticity, as they were pushed into the fatherly role. In fact, the lack of a wife and family sometimes meant the loss of a job or promotion. Bachelors were condemned as "immature," "infantile," "narcissistic," "deviant," or even "pathological;" family advice expert Paul Landis emphatically stated that "Except for the sick, the badly crippled, the deformed, the emotionally warped, and the mentally defective, almost everyone has an opportunity [and, by clear implication, a duty] to marry."[18]

But families in the 1950s were products of even more direct repression from the government. This was a time of McCarthyism and fear of communism; it was a time when the government began to define and then regulate what it determined to be "deviant" family and sexual behavior. Cold War anxieties combined with unprecedented government intrusion into private and family lives, making neighbors suspicious of neighbors; as a result, families became important defenses against repression and investigation. Gay baiting and "red baiting" became the primary activities of the FBI and other government agencies.

Additionally, beneath the polished facades of so many "ideal" families of the 1950s were many secrets: violence, sexual and verbal abuse, alcoholism, terror, or pervasive misery and depression. Daughters and wives who reported incidents of abuse to their therapists were often told that they were "fantasizing" unconscious desires rather than relating facts. No one—not even the "experts"—believed that there could be anything wrong with such "wonderful" families who attended church together every Sunday, barbecued in their backyards, and kept their homes immaculate.

But America's youth were clearly beginning to feel the effects of such a repressive time. 1955 saw the release of the movie *Rebel Without a Cause,* which symbolized the fears youth had about parents and authority figures who had failed them, and epitomized the angry viciousness that had begun to simmer in the young in the 1950s. Crime comic books began to dominate teen leisure reading; "heavy petting" became the dating norm; teen birthrates soared. In 1957, for example, "97 out of every 1,000 girls aged fifteen to nineteen gave birth, compared to only 52 of every 1,000 in 1983 . . . there was an 80 percent increase in the number of out-of-wedlock babies placed for adoption between 1944 and 1955."[19] Sexual inequality—the familiar sexist "double standard"—was strengthened during this time period, which determined that it was natural and normal for males to be sexually aggressive and to try to go "all the way," while females bore the responsibility of "saving" themselves for marriage and had to "hold out"against such sexually charged males. Some nudity was permitted in magazines and films; *Playboy* magazine popularized the male trend toward the view of women as sex objects. To assist this new surge of male sexual energy, antibiotic drugs were invented that effectively prevented many forms of venereal disease, and an oral contraceptive was on its way to being introduced in the early 1960s.

For housewives in the 1950s "the four Bs" soon became the label of their lives: "booze, bowling, bridge, and boredom." Nearly one-third of the marriages formed in the 1950s eventually ended in divorce; two million legally married people chose to separate, while a high percentage of couples that stayed together considered their marriages unhappy. Tranquilizer consumption reached 462,000 pounds in 1958 and soared to 1.15 million a year later. By 1960 many magazines and news articles used the word "trapped" to describe the feelings of the American housewife who, when not numbed out by tranquilizers, had taken to drinking, often needing a couple of drinks prior to the dinner hour just to get through the requisite time of "family togetherness."[20]

In reality, then, rather than a time for "model" families, the 1950s was a time of familial repression, anxiety, unhappiness, and conflict; as well, it was a time in which the seeds of future problems were planted. For example, the "baby boom" generation of the 1950s overloaded most of the major social institutions that had been established during the three consecutive terms of Franklin Roosevelt and his "New Deal Democrats." For the sake of their children, many families moved out of the cities (thus beginning their decay) and into new, larger homes in the suburbs. Thousands of new schools and churches were built to accommodate the shift in geographical location. When this baby boom generation reached college age in the 1960s, their numbers triggered an expansion in university construction and gave mass to the protest movement and "cultural revolution" in the later part of the decade. As young adults, this same generation diminished the supply of available housing, thus contributing to the housing shortages later experienced; when its members began to reach retirement age, they drained Social Security and other retirement funds. The years following the 1950s motivated a "me generation" mode of thinking in which the satisfaction of the individual, rather than the nation, the community, or even the family, was utmost.

The mid-1960s and mid-1970s were also a time of protest and social turbulence. In the mid-1960s the United States went to war against North Vietnam, a socialist society in southeast Asia that was allied with the Soviet Union. The United States allied with South Vietnam, which had a government dominated by Roman Catholics who were friendly to the United States and its capitalist way of life. The Vietnam War deeply divided the country, almost as critically as the Civil War. Many supported the war at first, but by 1966 a vocal minority opposed it and were supported by some senators and presidential candidates. Hundreds of young men refused induction into the armed forces. Those who supported the war became quite hostile toward its opponents, with a resulting generational conflict. At the same time, black people—who were also fighting in Vietnam and dying by the thousands—escalated their demands for civil rights and a share of the wealth and power. Young people called for reform in universities and other government institutions. Women demanded equal pay for equal work and formed the National Organization for Women (NOW).

This decade was also marked by a dramatic liberalization of sexual attitudes and behaviors, resulting in what has been termed the "sexual revolution." Sex therapy and sex education began in the 1970s. Females engaged in premarital intercourse as willingly as males. There was less guilt about sex. Cohabitation rather than marriage became the norm for young couples. Some cohabited with many in communes. There were married couples who engaged in open marriages, renegotiated ground rules about sexual and emotional conduct outside the marriage, or exchanged mates for recreational sex at home or at "swinging" parties. Affairs were common. Sexually explicit films were readily available. The number of single adults increased dramatically. Government financial support was provided to those who wanted abortions but who could not afford them. The "youth culture" was characterized by sex, drugs, and rock and roll, as well as rebellion against any form of authority. Those from the older generation saw this time as a decline of the family and attributed the decline to the liberal attitudes of the times rather than to a backlash against past inequities and arbitrary restrictions.

The next two decades—from 1975 to 1995—were marked by stagnation, high unemployment, skyrocketing interest rates, and record inflation, compounded by numerous other financial, emotional, spiritual, and morally debilitating woes: the takeover of many American corporations by Japanese and European interests; the fear of assassins, terrorists, and extortionists, who could hold the world at bay as they performed acts of inhumanity; the small, frustrating "wars" in the Middle East, Latin America, and Africa, in which the United States participated and which were neither won nor lost; the AIDS epidemic, which was initially ignored because of its high incidence in the homosexual community but which came to be accepted as a devastating disease that affected everyone; widespread violence against children and women; poverty and homelessness; the decline of major American industries, such as shipbuilding, steel production, and electronics manufacturing; the rise of information processing and improvements in home entertainment, which impacted upon socializing skills and weakened intimate relationships; and the loss of trust by American voters due to ineffective political leadership and the indifference of elected politicians to constituents' desires and needs.

Such hard times—and the historically hard times before them—impacted on American families in ways that forced them to make changes; unfortunately some of these changes impacted upon society as a whole. For example, many middle-class parents—sensing the decline of education and wishing to protect their children from the limitations of public schools—enrolled their children in private schools; as a result, many public schools deteriorated in the quality of education and, in inner cities, became mere "holding cells" for disinterested and disenchanted youth, for whom security guards and metal detectors became part of the educational process. Debt increased in families who desperately wanted to escape from urban areas that had became huge "drug stores" and were deemed so dangerous that even police and fire departments were reluctant to enter. Neighborhoods where children once played and never had to be chastised not to talk to strangers fell into disrepute and were increasingly taken over by criminals. Libraries and social clubs closed due to lack of funding; parks and recreational facilities fell into disrepair.

Despite advances in medical technology, health care for the majority of the population deteriorated as a result of the high cost of medical services. (In fact, the United States today is the only industrial nation in which an average family can be financially destroyed by the major illness of just one family member.) Add to these changes the additional deterioration of the natural environment—in the 1980s many federal regulations for air and water pollution and contamination of water supplies were ignored—and nuclear leaks and accidents (such as the infamous Love Canal, which financially, emotionally, and physically destroyed the families living there), and what Walker Percy, in his 1971 novel *Love in the Ruins,* writes becomes true for the 1990s:

> Don't tell me the U.S.A. went down the drain because of Leftism, Knotheadism, apostasy, pornography, polarization, etcetera, etcetera. All these things may have happened, but what finally tore it was that things stopped working and nobody wanted to be a repairman.[21]

Enter the Moral Majority into the chaotic family scene in the 1980s—a group made up of fundamentalist religious leaders and other advocates of "traditional" values who called for a constitutional prohibition of abortion. They opposed women's rights and urged a return to traditional male and female roles. They condemned homosexuals, called for prayer in public schools, and sought removal of textbooks that included the theory of evolution without the Christian biblical account of creation. The responses to such strict and regulated views were that cohabitation continued to increase; more women entered occupations and professions previously dominated by men; and sexually explicit films continued to be made and shown. What the Moral Majority expected of the American people—actually, what the group was *demanding*—was out of synch with the pressures, troubles, and difficulties Americans had to face on a daily basis. Putting food on the table, staying healthy, keeping a job, and so many other basic necessities dominated the human condition. Just as in any other hard time in American history, people chose (and are still continuing to choose) what was right and best for them *based on what they were experiencing.* Because of housing shortages, high interest rates, and other economic difficulties, nuclear families combined with other nuclear families or became extended families in order to own and live in a home. Economic necessity dictated that most people marry later and have fewer children than their parents. Both the husband and wife went to work because they *had* to; two full-time jobs were needed to support one household.

In effect, what many families were discovering was that life in a crowded, congested, polluted, pessimistic nation required providing a safe haven in a heartless world—one that would provide security, warmth, hope, pride, love, and high expectations. What most families were discovering—most white families, that is—was that their families needed to be reinvented in ways that were more realistic and reflective of the times. In effect, what they were discovering was exactly what African-American families, ethnic families, gay and lesbian families, and adoptive parents had been fighting for on their own. They were fighting for the good of the family as they believed that good to be in their hearts—not as they were being told or led to believe in their heads.

A History of African-American Family Life

Black people make up the largest racial or ethnic majority in the United States; they also have the most unique history. The first blacks arrived in Virginia in 1619. Purchased from a Dutch ship, they had the same status as white indentured servants who had voyaged to America with their English families. After they worked to earn their purchase price, the blacks were then released from servitude; thus, "free Negroes" existed in the United States almost from the beginning. It was only when demands for a permanent, cheap labor supply were made that the slave status of blacks in Virginia became fixed by law in 1670. Slave traders, whose business was voyaging to Africa and selecting human cargo, gave little regard to family relationships or the culture of those they were uprooting. Men and women were packed indiscriminately in slave ships, thereby destroying social bonds and tribal distinctions. This was followed by a "breaking" process— forcibly acclimating the people into the slave system in the West

Indies before shipment to the colonies—which further erased the memories of their traditional culture.

In the colonies, full property rights of a master included the right to break up families and sell the members apart—a right that was frequently exercised. The slaves were then further scattered on many plantations, in Virginia, Maryland, the Carolinas, and Georgia. This scattering afforded little opportunity to reconnect familial bonds or recapture the African culture. Thus, the children born into slavery never learned much about their African cultural and social heritage, or their individual ancestral roots. As Booker T. Washington once wrote: "In the days of slavery not very much attention was given to . . . family records—that is, black family records. . . . Of my father I know even less than my mother. I do not even know his name."[22]

While under the ownership of white masters, slaves were often bred as livestock would be; strong, healthy males were used as "studs," and formalities of marriage were often ignored. While some slave owners treated their slaves with kindness and consideration and encouraged the development of their own stable family life, more often than not that was not the case. On some plantations, there were differences in family patterns depending on the "rank" of the slaves. Black house servants were exposed to the white family traditions; female house servants assumed much of the care and training of the white children, were taught in their owner's family, called in to worship with the family, and thus considered members of the family. The "mammy" was one of the most important members of the master's family; she often slept in the room with the white children, sometimes nursed the infants, kept the family secrets, was a confidential advisor to the older members of the household, defended the family honor, disciplined the children, and outranked even the butler and the carriage driver.

Quite often, then, the lives of owners and house slaves became intertwined, creating a racially mixed extended family. As a result, house slaves often disassociated themselves from the field hands, who formed different families. In those units, the husband and father was viewed as unimportant to the family unit, as he was to be used as breeding stock. But slave owners recognized and respected the mother-child unit—which was sometimes forged out of a fierce attachment—and reinforced the primary position of the mother in the family by assigning her a comfortable cabin in which she and her children could live, and issuing her the family's food rations. She was the mistress of the cabin, to which the father and husband made only weekly visits. Men were not encouraged to assume responsibility for their wives and children; thus, the matriarchal black family took root and continued until the post-slavery period.

By 1860 there were nearly half a million free Negroes—those who had satisfied the seven-year period of servitude as well as children born of free parents, mulatto children born of free black mothers, mulatto children born of white servants and free white women, and children of free black and Indian parentage. The free slaves formed families based on attitudes and customs of the upper-class white owners they had once served and established a family life based on a secure economic foundation. Partly on the basis of wealth and occupation, a class system emerged among the free Negroes. This led to the beginning of a familial as well as an institutional life within the free slave communities, where schools, churches, literary societies, and organizations for mutual aid were established. These families were patriarchal. But the families created by some freemen, who had purchased their wives from slavery, became extreme patriarchal unions of ownership; in fact, in cases where the marriages did not work out, husbands willingly sold their wives back into slavery.

The Civil War and emancipation created a crisis in black family life, destroying whatever stability had, to this point in time, been achieved. As the Union armies penetrated the South, the plantation regime was disrupted, and slaves were uprooted from their customary way of life. It was a time of great chaos and confusion: thousands of blacks fled to army camps and to the cities; thousands joined Sherman's march to the sea; some fathers deserted their families; some mothers deserted their children; many took their families with them in search of freedom; many went in search of relatives from whom they had become separated through sale. During this difficult time, the mother often held the family together and supported her children. When conditions became more settled in the South—slave quarters were broken up, and blacks were no longer forced to work in gangs—family groups were encouraged to move off by themselves to places where they could lead separate existences.

In the contracts freemen made with their white landlords, they found support as well as status for their position in their family relationships. The husband now assumed responsibility for the family; as the head of the family, he directed the labor of his wife and children and began to train his children to succeed him as owners of the land. His family was now thrown into competition with the poor whites, and a color caste was established in the South. The black family's personal life became oriented toward other black families rather than mimicking the behavior and ideals of white families as they had in the past. Many of the ideas concerning sex were carried over from slavery, where it was not uncommon for a girl of sixteen to have children and a woman of thirty to have grandchildren; sex outside marriage (an institution that had never been encouraged or recognized anytime during slavery) was perceived as normal behavior.

There was always a general recognition of the obligation of the mother to her child, however, and pregnancy was regarded as part of the natural phase of female maturation and fulfillment. Out-of-wedlock children were taken into the mother's family group as well as orphaned children or the children of relatives. Thus, the black family became a sort of amorphous group that was held together by feelings and common interests as the members struggled together for their existence. In this family the mother continued to enjoy a dominant position, and the grandmother enjoyed an even more important position.

But in the North, away from the plantations and the standards that were accepted in the South, life was different for black families. Although "free Negroes" had lived in small percentages in

New York, Baltimore, and other northern cities, following World War I the first large-scale migration of blacks northward got under way. This was due in large part to the serious decline of the Southern economy, as well as the major labor shortage that had developed in Northern cities with industrialization. Migration north intensified family problems. Extreme overcrowding in residential areas made normal family life difficult. In 1930, over 40 percent of the black families in New York's Harlem had from one to four lodgers living with them; by 1939 one single Harlem block had a population of 3,871 people.[23] The term "ghettoization" was coined at the time to describe the living arrangements of urban blacks.

This urbanization was accompanied by more family disorganization, higher proportions of broken marriages, more families with female heads, and larger extended families. The illegitimacy that was standard and accepted in Southern black families was not so readily accepted by whites in the North; unwed mothers and children were stigmatized by neighbors, schoolteachers, social workers, and many others; the failure of the fathers to provide for their children was a crisis and placed an economic burden upon the family group as they struggled to exist in an urban environment. A vast group of homeless men—many of whom had deserted their families—women, and children was created, and they grew dependent upon public welfare. Parents lost track of their children; children sometimes lost track of their parents. As more and more black families settled in the cities, white residents moved to the suburbs; realtors increased city rents, and businesses increased prices. The resulting discrimination and residential segregation created racial tensions that grew red-hot as the years went on, finally erupting years later in the inner city race riots.

Yet not all black families were negatively impacted from the migration north. Three well-defined classes of black families emerged from the struggle to succeed in the new locale. At the bottom was the lower class—the largest—which included the working poor (those who worked hard and steadily at their jobs as janitors, porters, and unskilled factory workers, but who were unable to earn enough money to escape poverty) as well as the working nonpoor (men who worked at steady jobs in the industrialized sector of the economy, such as factory workers, truck drivers, and so on). In this class, family life was often chaotic and uprooted, without a secure income and dependent upon incomes derived from casual employment. Most lower-class black families were matriarchal, with the mother, the maternal grandmother, or eldest daughter holding dominant influence over property, authority, and household affairs. In many families respect for a hardworking parent or parents was fostered in children; fathers who were present often shared in many of the domestic and maternal duties, and homes that included grandparents, other relatives, and nonrelatives built a strong, supportive home life.

Due to the economic improvements and greater educational opportunities in the Northern public school systems, a middle class of black families emerged that consisted of skilled blue-collar workers, clerical workers, and professionals. This class formed stable nuclear families that had roots based in Southern living. Monogamy was accepted as the proper form of marriage, and the number of family members who could be included under the roof of a single-family dwelling or apartment was limited in order to maintain privacy and to create greater living space for its members.

Upper-class families included members of the "old" upper class, or adults with parents who had been either upper class or middle class—businesspeople, executives, college presidents, judges, physicians, dentists, and so on—most of whom shared a common ancestry of either house slaves or free slaves. As well, a "new" upper class was comprised of families who had risen from obscurity to great achievement in a single generation—for example, Reverend Jesse Jackson, baseball great Hank Aaron, Mayor Thomas Bradley, and many other personalities in entertainment, sports, business, the humanities, and science and technology. Their families held deeply rooted traditions of conventional family life from an agrarian society and a former age, but also valued professional status, wealth, and material goods.

In all classes, however, if both parents were present during their children's infancy and childhood, they made up a nuclear family, even when distant employment, imprisonment, military service, temporary separation, or hospitalization occasionally removed one parent from the home. In such families husbands usually provided a disciplinarian role; mothers fulfilled an emotionally supportive role. Attenuated families, more commonly known as "broken" or one-parent families, historically constituted only a small percentage of the total number of black families; over 90 percent of attenuated families were headed by women who hired baby-sitters or used day-care facilities for their children. Many black families were also extended families—sort of variations of the typical extended white family, as they included other relatives who shared a home with a married couple, with a couple and their children, or with a single parent and his or her children. Common black family structures also included augmented families: nuclear and/or extended families who took nonrelatives such as boarders into the home on a long-term basis.

Despite ghettoization, unemployment and poverty, earning and promotion inequities, segregation and discrimination, and racism, black families created rich and thriving family subcultures rooted in unique historical traditions. But the real strengths and successes of African-American families have all but been ignored in this country. Instead, social scientists have chosen to blame African-American economic and social distress on a so-called collapse of the black family. According to them, today's black families are to blame for the rising number of childbearing teenagers, crack babies, gangs, poverty, violence, and crimes committed against the black population. This image of a black family in chaotic disarray and diametrically opposed to society as a whole has been nourished by racist stereotypes, inflamed by media distortions, and is more deeply grounded in myth than in reality. After the Civil War, blacks went to great lengths to track down family members and reunite with relatives. When job opportunities beckoned them to different locales, they strove to keep their families together.

Throughout the nineteenth century, most black children grew up in two-parent households. Because job opportunities were limited for black men and the pay was low, most households had to depend upon two incomes long before two-income families became the norm. In reality, the African-American family has thrived on its diversity, close kinship bonds, unwavering acceptance and support of its elderly and ill, strong work and achievement orientation, adaptable roles and firm religious beliefs. Even though, in many parts of America, they could not attend the same schools as whites, drink from the same fountains, eat in the same restaurants, or ride at the front of public buses, blacks used familial kinship to build high levels of solidarity in their churches and social and political organizations. They valued work and education; in the 1920s, blacks had lower unemployment rates than did whites and kept their children in school much longer than did most immigrant groups. In fact, almost twice as many black children as Italian attended school. [24]

Rather than conform to the values, traditions, and customs of white families, black families created special traditions and adapted their families in ways that are now becoming the norm. Such changes included role flexibility, with black men more willing to share in housework and so-called "female" tasks; extended-kin networks; support of cultural, religious, professional, and social organizations; racial solidarities; and a tradition of pooling economic resources within extended families. In effect, black families have been on the cutting edge of reformation and restructuring of family units in ways that are today being applied by white families, adoptive families, gay and lesbian parents, and ethnic families.

A History of Ethnic Family Life in America

In the 1930s President Franklin D. Roosevelt welcomed a convention of the Daughters of the American Revolution with the statement, "Welcome, fellow immigrants!" Beginning in 1890, migration to the United States shifted from northwestern Europe to southern and eastern Europe. Between 1890 and 1920, 22 million people arrived in America from Italy, Austria-Hungary, and Russia. To stem the flow of such overwhelming immigration, policies were created after 1920 that greatly reduced the foreign-born population, but later on, the Immigration Act of 1965 enabled about 400,000 immigrants into the United States annually.

In the 1960s, when white families were challenging their cultural, political, and social identities, various ethnic groups were going through their own struggles to preserve their cultural heritages. Previously, outside influences as well as internal conflicts had encouraged ethnic families to eradicate traits that had set them apart from the "native American" (that is, white) population. But eventually they began to endorse a "cultural pluralism" that focused on the particular contributions they could make—and could continue to make—to the American culture.

Each ethnic group that immigrated to America brought with them different family structures and customs from their homelands. The Italian family system was more patriarchal than what had been seen in America; Italians also brought with them a Roman Catholic value system that supported the authority of the father, deemphasized children's emotional needs and development, and frowned upon premarital sex, sex for pleasure, birth control, and divorce. Mexican families, on the other hand, favored extended families that included relationships from both sides of the family. Japanese families brought with them a strong, stable, and extended family system in which elders were revered. It, too, was patriarchal, and the father-son relationship was especially important.

Cuban families encouraged widespread intermarriage through the wedding of cousins once or twice removed; the families then became extended families that included aunts, uncles, and cousins who lived on adjacent estates or shared common interests in real estate, businesses, and other endeavors. Prominence in Cuban extended family relationships was given to elders, who held the family income and property and upheld the family traditions, with the most powerful head being the grandmother.

These ethnic groups, as well as many others, have brought their family patterns to the United States and then sometimes remodeled them based upon the customs and cultures of their new homeland. While the tendency for most immigrants was to assimilate themselves into their new culture and thus minimize their differences, for some it became a struggle just to find a job and a place to live, because of discrimination against their ethnicity. Most immigrants settled in cities, but each group was relegated to living all in the same area, thus turning parts of cities into "Little Italy," "Chinatown," and so on.

The children of immigrants, for whom the need to fit in became even more significant, often lost respect for their parents, their homeland, their language, their traditions—anything that detracted from their appearing to be "more American." In addition, hostility from "native" Americans, discrimination in housing and employment, wage inequities, world events (which in the case of Japanese-Americans during World War II led to extreme discrimination and even forced relocation) further restricted the acceptance of those from different cultures. As a result, in recent years, ethnic pride and the desire for diversity rather than homogenization have led to a widespread preservation and strengthening of cultural heritages in the families of those whose ancestors immigrated to America.

A History of Adoption in America

The adoption of children by foster parents—relatives and friends of the parents as well as strangers—has always had a place in society. The Greeks and Romans had well-defined policies regarding adoption that were reflected in specific laws that formed the basis for adoption laws in most countries of the modern world.

The first adoption law in America was enacted in Massachusetts in 1851. Most commonly a child was adopted by blood relatives who were motivated at least by the desire to take care of their own kin due to parental separation, war, poverty, the promise of a better life, or the death of one or both parents. But over time more and more children became available for adoption; laws were enacted to protect children from being subjected to such degrading practices as being "put up for adoption"—a term that dates to the early 1900s, when orphan trains brought children to the Midwest, where they were exhibited from platforms to be selected for adoption—or for the purposes of labor or abuse. A majority of adoptable infants were born to young, unwed mothers, who had no other option at the time but to give their babies up. Many were children who were abandoned, particularly during World War II, when fathers went overseas and mothers had to work, and there was no one to care for unattended children.

Children also became available for adoption as "foundlings," who were left on doorsteps, in churches, in hospitals, or in Dumpsters and trash cans, and for whom there was no specific information, date of birth, or name; as a result of chronic illness or mental illness; when a guardian, such as an aging grandparent, could no longer continue to care for them; after the death of one or both parents; following the removal from homes in which neither parent was interested in caretaking; or because of behavioral problems.

At the White House Conference on Child Health and Protection of 1933, the following guidelines for adopting children were drafted:

> For every child a home and that love and security which a home provides and for that child who must receive foster care, the nearest substitute for his own home. For every child the right to grow up in a family with an adequate standard of living and the security of a stable income as the surest safeguard against social handicaps.[25]

This became a guiding light for child placement work and had a profound effect on the creation and formation of adoptive

families. But what was left unspoken in those two simple statements was that the "best" placement option was thought to be
with a family who most closely resembled the child; to protect
all concerned from the many people outside the adoptive family
who viewed adoption as a "second best" way of becoming a family or believed that nonbiological parents were less effective parents than their "natural" counterparts. It was believed to be
important to develop a sense of belonging in an adoptive family,
and one of the first ways for parents to do this was by identifying the ways in which their child was like them. So naturally it
was best to place a blond-haired, blue-eyed baby boy of English
descent in a home with at least one blond-haired, blue-eyed parent—the way adoptive families have been formed in America for
decades.

But in the 1990s this view is no longer the most commonly accepted method of adoption—or the method considered the best.
The veil of secrecy that once traditionally surrounded adoption is
currently being lifted, and along with it has come a more true adherence to the original intent of the children's charter of 1933;
that is, more and more children are being adopted into loving,
secure, financially stable homes where there may be one or two
adoptive parents and where the parent or parents may be a man,
a woman, two women, two men, or of a different race. For
adoptees and adoptive parents, the 1990s is a time of shared parenthood, adoption triangles, single parenting, open adoptions,
transracial adoptions, multicultural adoptions, intercountry
adoptions, step-parent adoptions, donor insemination and in
vitro fertilization with a donor egg or embryo, adoption via sur-
rogacy, and gay and lesbian parenting. What all these changes
have created is families that are as rich with diversity as the fabric
of this country's cultural roots. These families also challenge
today's "traditional family values" rhetoric by expanding the definition of family in ways that place values such as love, commitment, and respect for one's heritage over any particular family
structure.

A History of Gay and Lesbian Families in America

Nonmarital sexual behavior in all its forms became a national obsession after World War II. Many high-level government officials, along with other individuals in influential power positions who advised them, believed there was a correlation between what was called "sexual depravity" and communism. Therefore, "normal" behavior meant a married, heterosexual, monogamous male; a "pervert" was a single male who was obviously immature and irresponsible and who could easily be duped by a female working for the communists. This logic was then used with homosexuals (both men and women), who had become increasingly visible and began to form gay communities after World War II. Those who engaged in same-sex relationships were equated with violent criminals who raped and murdered children; the persecution of gay men and lesbians became vicious and, in some cases, violent. "Gay baiting" was as readily participated in as "red baiting"; careers were destroyed and harassment increased in intensity.

Those who "confessed" were encouraged to name others with whom they associated. The FBI spearheaded the movement by investigating the sexual habits of as many individuals as they could—from those in the military to those in private industry—and assembling files detailing the personal sexual histories of numerous private citizens, including those who were not gay but who chose career or remaining single over marriage and parenthood. As a result, many lesbians and gay men entered into marriage facades that served to protect them as they continued to attempt to exercise their personal freedom; others were so fearful about revealing or acting upon their inclinations that they denied what was in their hearts and did only what was more socially acceptable.

The gay rights movement emerged at the end of the 1960s, but it was met with a great deal of homophobia and widespread myth-making, including false accusations, such as that gay men and lesbians "recruit" children or prefer to engage in sex with children. Beginning in the 1970s, more and more gay parents began to come out publicly; many lost custody and visitation rights solely on the basis of their sexual orientation. In the late 1970s, Anita Bryant launched the Save Our Children campaign in a successful effort to repeal Florida's Dade County gay rights law. A resulting Florida statute prohibited lesbians and gay men from adopting children. At the same time, California Senator John Briggs pushed his initiative to prevent gay men and lesbians from teaching school, which was narrowly defeated. During the 1980s, when more and more gay men and lesbians were becoming parents, Massachusetts and New Hampshire enacted laws to prevent foster care and/or adoption by homosexuals. In his 1992 campaign, President George Bush declared that it was not "normal" for homosexuals to raise children.

But since the 1970s, when the number of custody battles involving gay men and lesbians began to increase, studies have been conducted to determine the impact heterosexual and homosexual parents have had upon children:

> For the most part, these studies compared children of divorced lesbians and children of heterosexual mothers, sometimes also divorced, sometimes not. They asked whether children of homosexuals were more likely to have emotional problems, be confused about gender identity or sex roles, or grow up to be gay. Researchers found no differences with respect to these issues. . . . They dispelled key myths one by one, and allowed many lesbian and gay parents to maintain relationships with their children.[26]

Although much of gay and lesbian family life is in the process of being created, the kinds of families gay men and lesbians create, the way they raise their children, and their contributions to their own community as well as to society as a whole impacts as significantly as any other family that makes up the fabric of family life in America in the 1990s. As will be seen in numerous examples throughout this book, gay and lesbian families have as much to teach—and as much to learn from—all the different families that are part of the American family community. Just how those families came to be families is revealed in the next chapter.

NOTES

1. Benedict, Ruth. "The Family: Genus Americanum," from Anshen, Ruth Nanda. *The Family: Its Function and Destiny*, Harper & Brothers Publishers, New York, 1949, p. 159.
2. Calhoun, Arthur W. *A Social History of the American Family From Colonial Times to Present*. Barnes & Noble, Inc., New York, 1945, pp. 361–362.
3. Leslie, Gerald. *The Family in Social Context*, 4th ed. Oxford University Press, Inc., New York, pp. 148–153.
4. *Ibid.*, pp. 154–158.
5. *Ibid.*, pp. 158–164.
6. *Ibid.*, p. 165.
7. Queen, Stuart and Robert W. Habenstein. *The Family in Various Cultures*, 3rd ed. J. B. Lippincott Company, Philadelphia, 1967, pp. 272, 283, 288.
8. Calhoun, p. 126.
9. Queen, pp. 181–182.
10. *Ibid.*, pp. 182–183.
11. *Ibid.*, p. 181.
12. Leslie, pp. 185–186.
13. Calhoun, p. 141.
14. *Ibid.*, p. 143.
15. *Ibid.*, pp. 360–361.
16. Coontz, Stephanie. *The Way We Never Were: American Families and the Nostalgia Trap*. Basic Books, New York, 1992, p. 24.
17. *Ibid.*, pp. 29–30.
18. *Ibid.*, pp. 32–33.
19. *Ibid.*, pp. 35–37.
20. *Ibid.*, pp. 38–39.
21. Percy, Walker. *Love in the Ruins*. Farrar, Straus, and Giroux, New York, 1971, (page number unknown).
22. Calhoun, p. 251.
23. Leslie, p. 268.
24. Coontz, p. 241.
25. Lockridge, Frances. *Adopting a Child: Where, When and How to Obtain a Healthy, Happy Youngster*. Greenberg: Publisher, New York, 1947, p. 54.
26. Benkov, Laura. *Reinventing the Family: The Emerging Story of Lesbian and Gay Parents*. Crown Publishers, Inc., New York, 1994, p. 9.

CHAPTER 2

❧

Families in Transition

All of the choices regarding family life and how it is to be structured are embedded in a much larger human network, called society, which is characterized by its culture; that is, its shared
values, language, customs, technologies, and so on. So what can
be seen quite clearly from any exploration of family is how the
American family has evolved (and still continues to evolve) in response to changes in society—changes in its economic, political,
educational, religious, and cultural institutions. As a general rule,
hard times make people conservative, while prosperity and war
encourage people to experiment with new possibilities; this rule
certainly applies to the changes in families that were explored in
Chapter 1.

Countless variations on the family theme have developed over
time, based upon the structure and organization of society—
from small independent units that once were set apart and lived
in privacy on large tracts of land, to a sense of family that per-
meated an entire community where all members were kin to
large extended families that today span the country and the
world.

The evolution in America to a more complex society, the creation of stratification through class distinction, the development of cities, technological advances, and many other changes
have created a ripple effect that has been felt within the family.
Thus, some of the major reforms in American family life have

actually been adaptations forced upon family by society as a whole, while others have been based on the founding promise made to every citizen of this country: the freedom of expression. Because of this, new family structures have been created that responded to American society's complexity, diversity, and evolutionary challenges. In addition to the traditional marriage system, for example, or so-called nuclear family, there are now step-parenting and/or coparenting options, as well as nonmarried heterosexual adults raising children. In addition to adoptive families of same-race children, there are now intercountry adoptions, multiracial families, and gay and lesbian adoptions. In addition to multigenerational and extended families, there are now friends-as-family units, kinship families, and nonbiological families.

People are beginning to consciously create new forms of family for a variety of personal, financial, and emotional reasons as well as to diversify, differentiate, experiment, and connect with one another in ways that solidify family structures and empower family values. In reality, no new family structures have been or are being created with the purpose of weakening or undermining the family as the world's oldest, most firmly grounded human institution. Those who adopt children not of their own race are doing so for the same reasons that women are choosing to be single mothers, gay men are raising children, lesbians are seeking to enter legally sanctioned marriage unions, coparenting is becoming a viable alternative to losing contact with one's biological children, and heterosexuals are marrying and raising families. Each new family structure is based on an attempt to *strengthen* the concept of family, not weaken it: to embrace all family members with tolerance and acceptance rather than intolerance and rejection; to connect emotionally, physically, and spiritually with one another in ways that recognize the individuality and strengths of each family member; to be founded upon love rather than arrangement, the need to hide one's sexuality, or the desire to amass wealth and property.

While no one family today is fully representative of what a family is or can be, all of today's families, though different from one another in invisible as well as highly visible ways, share a common thread that draws them together: they are seeking to create an "ideal" family in which each member learns about his or her own potential within a supportive environment. While this may not always be attainable—families are broken apart by preventable conditions (such as substance abuse or illness from lack of health care) as well as unpreventable ones (such as divorce or death)—it is up to society as a whole to accept all types of families in order to safeguard its future as well as to give all of its citizens an equal sense of absolute belonging.

But rather than embrace such changes, today's families—both traditional and nontraditional—are being blamed or made to feel responsible for society's woes. Additionally, they are being made to feel that they are less than whole, less than worthy, or less than wonderful if they do not "fit the image" of what a family should or ought to be. The American family today is in the midst of a despairing society, one that considers the family in general as a failure. Respected professionals in a variety of fields contribute to this outlook by viewing the family only through their own self-serving definitions of what a family is; any deviation from such definitions further degrades the family in their eyes. For example, church leaders may attribute lower and irregular family attendance at services to a decline in the religious beliefs in families rather than to a different spiritual support that may be needed by families today; law enforcement officers may link a rise in criminal activity to a decline in family discipline and moral instruction rather than seeing it as a natural outcome of joblessness, homelessness, drug addiction, or other causes; teachers may blame absenteeism on the unwillingness of parents to support their children's educational goals rather than on the deterioration of the educational system.

Today's families have become scapegoats for a wide variety of social "ills"—from teen pregnancies to drugs to violence to poverty to homelessness. Today's families have become the reasons why young people are abusers, criminals, killers, and addicts.

Today's families have become public fodder whose court battles, struggles, personal lifestyles, traumas, and tragedies feed the media. Today's families have become the focus of political debates and negotiable line items on the country's budget books. Today's parents have become toxic; today's children corrupted, today's families failures.

But it is the integrity of a society that ultimately impacts upon the integrity of a family. Every time a change takes place in society, the effects of the change are felt within the family, and not vice versa. Some changes are big—married men are drafted and sent off to war—while some are small—drive-up windows in fast-food restaurants replace opportunities for sit-down, home-cooked meals. But, big or small, high-impact or low-impact, they are changes nonetheless, and all must be assimilated by families because they are part of the society in which the families live.

In the past, when families lived in their own single courtyards, they were their own societies; so, too, were those families who lived in compounds with two hundred or more other people. Family was community and community was family; thus, society was both community and family. But today things are much different:

> We are experiencing a new family in our midst. Contrary to going back to the good old traditional family structure, we're seeing a new brand of family emerge with a variety of designs. Only 15 percent of our nation's families typify the traditional structure of working father with mother and children at home. . . . Young men are asking questions about their role as husbands and fathers. What is expected of them? Can they learn to be a spouse and to parent in ways different from their own parents so that they can meet the intimacy needs in today's families? . . . Our expectations are higher than ever before. We don't want to live with anyone unless there is love—not some silly idea of romantic love, but the sort of love that nourishes the soul and enables people to grow. [1]

One of the most beneficial outcomes of this evolution of family to its current state, which includes different styles of living, different groupings of people, and different ways of relating the family to society, has been the creation of interest in the family on a national scale. Outside of social work studies, early childhood education, some church study groups, and the creation of Thomas Gordon's Parent Effectiveness Training (P.E.T.) in the 1980s, families have, in the past, garnered little outside attention. What went on behind closed doors was nobody's business; alcoholism, divorce, depression, poverty, illness, suicide, and many other family problems were just that—family problems, to be dealt with solely by the family. A "good family," therefore, was one that was self-sufficient, did not seek help from others, was never tainted by scandal, and starved before it went on welfare or applied for food stamps. Little attention was paid to what actually went on inside the family; the concern was simply whether the family met the more obvious, visible family standards set by society. So if a scandal tainted the family name, society determined that it was best for the family to separate itself from the one who had caused the scandal—the man who had burned his own business for the insurance money, the woman who had had an affair, the child who was messed up on drugs. When a family turned its back on the offending member, they were not considered wrong, cruel, or unloving; rather, they were simply doing what had to be done, for "black sheep" had to be eliminated in order to maintain the image of the family.

It was only when society as a whole began to question just what was meant by a "good family" that the inner workings of a family began to be pondered, examined, explored, analyzed, and debated in open forums. What people then discovered was that families ought not to be considered good simply because they consisted of one working parent and one nonworking parent, were religious, affluent, owned their own home, or were respected in the community. The consensus was that such families were not always nurturing and, in many cases, were fragmented, noncommunicative, lacking in warmth and love, devoid of support; insensitive to each member's needs, incapable of sharing and creating a give-and-take balance, ignorant of how to set aside or spend quality time together, sexually repressed, and discouraging of intimacy. The function of family began to be reexamined; it was discovered that long-recognized family functions had changed over time due to the evolution of society, but new family structures had not been created to accommodate the new social structure. As a result, yesterday's family structures were still trying to meet today's needs, and having little success.

The conclusion that was reached in families themselves was that new solutions had to be developed; merely staying together for the sake of the children or becoming a full-time caretaker was not going to "save" the family. So traditional structures began to be challenged; working together to connect family members—no matter what their race, age, sex, sexuality, or relationship to other members—became more important than trying to fit an image. The new function of families became *relational:* to love and be loved, to join together in the search for intimacy, to share the joys of connecting with posterity, to have children to give and to be given to, and to care and to be cared about. As Abraham Maslow observed, "We are the first generation in the history of peoples sufficiently beyond sustenance to be able to focus on the quality of our relationships."[2]

In order to get a clearer picture of why and how families underwent a transition from traditional structures of the past to their present traditional and nontraditional forms, the evolution of family functions needs to be examined. For how these functions have changed over the years has had a profound impact on families and has ultimately led to the creation of modern American families.

The Evolution of Family Functions

The term "function," as it applies to family, is used to describe what the family has to do or accomplish as a family for its successful growth and survival. Historically the family has had five major functions. The first was to achieve economic survival. Households were once "sole-provider" economic units, which meant that the living was made at home; necessary provisions had to be created, grown, or bartered for. At one time households bustled with activity from a variety of daily economic activities: baking, canning, laundering, candlemaking, gardening, making and repairing clothing, raising livestock, and countless others. Many children were needed to fulfill this function, so the more children a family had the more helping hands were available; the more helping hands there were, the bigger and more profitable a homestead could become.

But industrialization and urbanization eroded the home-based economic unit; economic resources then had to be sought outside the home. That meant that a "father-breadwinner" needed to work at a job away from home to earn money for food, shelter, clothing, and other necessities for his family's survival, while a "mother-breadmaker"needed to stay at home to raise the children and maintain the household. The male was thus considered to be the chief family provider; the female became the chief spender and purchasing agent. Children were economic resources because they could hold jobs at very early ages and then give their wages to their parents.

Gradually, however, men and women found they did not need one another for economic survival. A woman did not have to get married to obtain food, clothing, and shelter; a man did not have to have a wife either to take care of himself or his children. But child labor laws that were enacted to protect children from becoming economic assets turned them into economic liabilities or, in the view of some, costly luxuries. Eventually the cost of providing for children became so astronomical that money from one or both parents was needed to support and care for them.

A second function of the family was to provide protection:

> Family members needed one another as a protection from hostile forces outside the cave, the manor, or the igloo.

They banded together to face the elements, to fight off in-
truders and illness, and to feed and protect their helpless,
who could not protect themselves. . . . They marched together across the prairies to open our country, not because
they couldn't exist without one another emotionally but because they needed the physical presence of one another for
protection.[3]

But industrialization and urbanization affected this family
function. For African-American and immigrant families, this
function evolved into a need for ethnic protection—a need to
band together on a foreign soil in a foreign culture with a foreign
language and foreign customs. For white families, protection was
fulfilled by relocation to suburban developments that provided
them with all they needed in a new, self-contained universe.
There family members began to go their separate ways in pursuit
of recreational activities: fathers spent leisure time at taverns or
the Elks Club, mothers joined bridge clubs or devoted time to
charities, girls belonged to Camp Fire Girls, and boys joined the
Boy Scouts or athletic teams.

As well, police departments, welfare agencies, and other governmental services gradually assumed some of the protective
function of families. During the time of the Depression, President Roosevelt spearheaded reforms that sought to alleviate the
extreme hardships the family was experiencing. From Social Security to numerous public works programs, the New Deal provisions included jobs for unemployed heads of households and
options for federal relief so families would not go hungry or lose
their homes. Today many families are totally dependent upon
government programs to provide them with money, food, clothing, shelter, and health care services; these families willingly hand
over the protective function to government agencies. One example of this is the immunization of children, which, while it has
brought many childhood illnesses under control, came about because school systems were forced to assume this responsibility—
not families.

A third major function of the family was to practice their religion together. Once upon a time families composed family prayers, said grace before meals, and provided religious instruction in the home. Up to the eighteenth century, the family was the primary teller of religious stories, the preacher of religious doctrines, and the instructor in various religious traditions. But just as the government stepped in to assume the protective function of families, churches began to regulate significant family events such as births, marriages, and deaths. Religious stories that had been passed down from generation to generation, which had comforted families and empowered their sense of belonging not only to their immediate family, but also to the spiritual world around them, were replaced with what was taught in Sunday schools, parochial schools, and by Christian educators. Prayer, which was once allowed in the schools, became a volatile political issue. Rules and regulations regarding "family values" began to emanate from churches; church leaders became outspoken advocates on personal and private family issues. Many families chose to follow the teachings of their church; some churches modified their authoritarian role and became more "family friendly" in order to provide religious as well as family guidance; other families left the church or returned the religious function to their homes through spiritual beliefs fostered within their families.

A fourth family function was to educate its children. In the past the boys worked alongside their fathers on the homestead or learned the trade or business of their family's adult males; girls learned homemaking and parenting skills from their mothers. Children who could read, write, and perform basic math skills before the advent of free public schools learned to do so from their parents, using such texts as the Bible and *The Pilgrim's Progress*. As villages and towns were created, schoolteachers became respected citizens and schoolhouses necessary buildings; wealthy families hired private tutors for their children or sent them abroad to study. Over time, the public elementary school was supplemented by kindergarten and nursery schools for the younger children and vocational and academic high schools, colleges, and universities for older children to advance their instruction. Less and less training of children remains in the home today; in fact, any residual parental training that could exist has been further eroded by television, VCRs, computers, and video games.

The fifth and final function of the family was to grant status. The wife took on the husband's family name, a name that symbolized who he was because of who the others were before him who had shared that same name. Sometimes this was beneficial; if the husband's father was a respected member of the community, then the husband (and his family) would often be afforded similar respect. Or it could be detrimental, particularly when the husband's father was a ne'er-do-well, the town drunk, or a criminal. An untarnished family name was the most valuable legacy a man could give to his wife and pass on to his children. Immigrants to this country often changed their family names, however, preferring instead to be unburdened by the discrimination that might result if others assumed their nationality from their name. Others distanced themselves from places where their name and family reputation were known in order to establish a new prestige or image for themselves without carrying the symbolic distinction of their family name.

Today a family name can be significant if it is a famous family name, such as Kennedy, or if it provides a link to a well-known personality. Status in today's society, however, most often comes from family wealth, family profession, and family residence, which command much more status than a last name.

These five family functions were not only used to define a family, but also to determine whether or not a family was "good." A "good" family was one in which the father was the decision-maker, ruler, and sole breadwinner; the mother was the domestic worker as well as the children's caretaker; the children were the workers whose "employer" was the family. A family that met all of its functions was successful; a family that failed to meet one or more of its functions was a failure. When functional roles were not fulfilled—if the husband and father deserted his family, if the mother was negligent in caring for her children, or if the children refused to work—it was therefore acceptable to separate or divorce or even to abandon the children. But what both families and arbiters of social values ignored was what went on *inside* the families. What mattered more was that a family went to church every Sunday and kept its house neat, not whether it was emotionally supportive of its members, communicated openly and honestly, built trust, enhanced self-esteem, and created intimacy in relationships. The belief held that if a family fulfilled all of its functions, it would automatically be close, loving, and problem-free.

Because family functions had to change and thus families themselves had to change, many feared that families were "in jeopardy." In 1934 the Hoover-Ogburn Commission was appointed by the government to study the family; it concluded that because the original functions of families were disappearing, *the family would eventually disappear.* Several decades later, the family still exists, but today it is based upon new functions—functions that are foundational to family life today. These are the functions that will be explored in greater detail in each of the chapters in Part III, but such functions can be summarized as being *relational.* Family functions today are based upon the relationships that are formed within the family and within the extended family, and then outwardly, within society, and within the natural and spiritual world. Families made the transition from being functional units to relational ones in ways that reflected the family breakdowns and ruptures that occurred as family functions began to change.

The Fragmentation of Families: The Issue of Divorce

The only family function to expand and flourish over time has been that of providing affection and intimacy between the parents as well as between parents and children. The relational aspect of family became more evident when the American family was in transition from being a functional institution to one created for companionship, or for "the mutual comforting of each other," as written in colonial times. There were hints about the importance of this function from the time this country was settled, however. In fact, De Tocqueville once remarked that there was "no country in the world where the tie of marriage is so much respected as in America, or where conjugal happiness is more highly or worthily appreciated."[4] Unlike the marriages in other cultures around the world, colonial marriages were based upon choice, not contract. Colonial law did not require parental consent for marriage; most parents consented—or at least acquiesced—to their child's choice. If they did not, it was not unusual for the young couple to run away to a different state to be married. Or, if access to civil officers or clergy to perform a legal wedding ceremony was difficult, couples would live together as husband and wife without any ceremony at all. Such cohabitation was open and visible; friends and relatives considered the couple to be married, and, under varying circumstances, the law deemed them married as well.

The passage of time, constantly changing economic opportunities, new styles of living, greater mobility, and redefinition of family did not alter the desire for couples to unite for the purposes of companionship. Such things did sometimes alter the ability of a man and woman to live together in a harmonious and fulfilling relationship. When relational needs were not being met for either the man or the wife, the search to fulfill such needs often extended outside the family. This search for alternatives to loneliness, alienation, abuse, rejection, desertion, poverty, and other relational-destroyers came in the form of infidelity, separation, divorce, and remarriage. Even though, as in other cultures, American marriages were considered indissoluble, there were separations by mutual consent as well as marriage annulments as early as colonial times. In the beginning, the basis for granting such marriage dissolutions was most often nonrelational:—imbecility or mental alienation, habitual drunkenness, excessive use of opium, or even membership in the Shaker sect—rather than relational—bigamy, adultery, voluntary desertion, and the slighting of conjugal duties. Those grounds came later, but anyone who would cite divorce as a recent phenomenon as well as a prime destroyer of family life and the dissolution of family values would be inaccurate. In 1849 it was concluded that

> There are more divorces in one year in the state of Ohio than there are in ten in the United Kingdom. In the year 1843 there were 447 bills of divorcement sued out in that state, and they were principally at the suit of the women, whose husbands had behaved ill, neglected them or . . . run away.[5]

At the time many people attributed the increase in divorce to the Civil War and assumed that after the war there would be no marked increase. Such predictions proved false, however; in 1889 it was written that "in the old state of Connecticut one marriage is dissolved in every ten, and in the new state of California one in every seven."[6] But whereas in the colonial period and the Revolutionary era marriages were, for the most part, treated as " 'till death do us part" unions—most unattached people at the time were either single or widowed rather than divorced—it was primarily because the functions of the household and society were so substantially interconnected that the couple needed each other and needed to stay together, just as the family and society needed each other in order to operate in sync.

The nineteenth and twentieth centuries, however, became particularly trying times for couples and families. Households shifted from small communities that had fulfilled the emotional, physical, and spiritual needs of all family members to households that had become increasingly more dependent upon society to fulfill some or all of these needs. Families became more isolated and, as such, were viewed as "islands of refuge" whose chief function was to protect their members from society's mounting waves of pressures and stresses. The husband-father became not just the bread-winner for the family, but also its sole representative to the world at large; his success or failure impacted upon the family. The wife-mother experienced a different set of pressures. The conventions of domestic life had thrown up a model of a perfect home that she was to create; the model portrayed a home so tranquil, so cheery, so comforting, so warm, so clean, so organized, and so wonderfully fulfilling to everyone in it that it was almost impossible to attain. Her burden was made even more difficult by a society that needed her to work when the country was at war but then denied her this opportunity when the country returned to times of peace.

Thus, the family changed from "a little church, and a little commonwealth, at least a lively representation thereof. . . . a school wherein the first principles and grounds of government are learned" to a "retreat," "sanctuary," and "refuge" that "many people look to . . . for buffering, or at least for relief, against the demands and pressures of society at large."[7] The family became "inside" and the world became "outside;" the goal was to create a home that was, in effect, "a man's castle," surrounded by a large moat and high walls that could keep the outside from penetrating while fulfilling the needs of all family members. This became impossible to do in a society that encouraged family dependency; thus, the divorce rate soared as husbands and wives tried unsuccessfully to meet their needs. In fact, America was working toward attaining the distinction of having the highest divorce rate in the world.

But as America emerged from the Depression and disbanded the necessary "survival communities" of extended families they had formed during World War II, the divorce rate dropped. Scholars and observers at that time pointed to the trend toward families staying together as a common response to peace and prosperity, but what they neglected to include in their finding was that this had not occurred in any other peacetime. The truth was that the Cold War years inspired high levels of fear, doubt, insecurity, and uncertainty in many Americans. People were prosperous, but they were also panicked; this prompted them to create a family-centered culture that would provide them with physical and psychological protection:

> It [the family-centered culture] took shape amid the legacy of the depression, World War II, and the anxieties surrounding atomic weapons. It reflected the fears as well as the aspirations of the era. Prosperity had returned, but would there be a postwar slump that would lead to another depression, as there had been after World War I? Would the GIs be able to find secure positions in the postwar economy? Women had proved themselves competent during the war in previously all-male blue-collar jobs, but what would happen to their families if they continued to work? Science had discovered atomic energy, but would it ultimately serve humanity or destroy it? The family was at the center of these concerns, and the domestic ideology that was taking shape provided a major response to them.[8]

In creating a domestic version of "containment," the purpose was to keep potentially dangerous forces at bay. Couples stayed together in order to escape the world at large, not to participate in it. In fact, the 1940s and 1950s was not a time of activism or rising social movements that would eventually affect change or growth. Rather, it was a time in which American society stood still, obsessed with security; in which authorities were experts of the time period, and not thinkers for the future; in which people were not challenged to make the world a better place, but to assume that all was well; in which government assumed control of many functions without being challenged; and in which families were the therapeutic treatment that blocked out all the things that were "bad."

Thus, a successful married life became the goal for men and women in the 1940s and 1950s. Men worked hard at jobs not for the satisfaction and fulfillment the job could bring them or to better themselves within their careers, but to achieve promotions and raises in order to provide financial security for their families. A woman's goal was to "find her place in life," which meant finding a man to marry so she could pursue her career as wife and mother. But there were pressures and disappointments felt by both men and women in this arrangement. Men were often bored with their jobs, experienced great financial pressures in the drive to make their homes and lives as self-sufficient as possible, and were subjected to impersonal corporate treatment. For them, work was a source of stress and home a source of serenity.

For women, it was the other way around: they were often bored with full-time homemaking and the constant pressure of raising their families; home was a source of stress, and the only way to find serenity was through therapy or prescriptive numbing. The divorce rate was low in the 1950s not necessarily because husbands and wives were happy and fulfilled in their marriages, but because they were determined to get married and stay married. Men and women psychologically adapted to their marriages, taming feelings of discontent on the inside and managing them on the outside so all appeared to be well.

When the baby boomers from this generation came of age in the 1960s, they challenged their upbringing and the policy of domestic containment. They rejected the rigid institutional boundaries of their elders and carried sex, consumerism, and political activity outside the established institutions. Activism was in vogue, as was liberation and rejection of family security as the only way to live and grow. Marriage rates went down; divorce rates soared. The generation gap widened as different generations each tried to comprehend what the other was doing. Adult children challenged parents who had stayed together despite affairs and unhappiness, by preaching a value system that honored development of healthy relationships within the family, while parents shook their heads at divorces that ignored "the good of the family":

It's difficult for different generations to comprehend these two such different systems. I recall a time when friends of mine, married for twenty years, announced their impending divorce. My mother, who was seventy years old, shook her head and said, "I don't understand why they're divorcing. He's always been a steady worker, and she's such a good mother."

It would have been futile for me to say, "But they haven't grown together" or "They don't share the same values." She wouldn't have understood what I was saying. We were viewing the divorce from two different value systems, hers tied into the old formula for the good family, mine tied into the search for ways and means of developing healthy relationships in the family of today.[9]

But the quest for personal liberation is an old one, one whose seeds were planted shortly after the founding of America, as women began their struggles for personal as well as familial equality. Since women were twice as likely as men to report that they were dissatisfied or regretted their marriages in studies of those who were married in the 1950s, and since the majority of all divorce cases in America have been initiated at the request of women, it is worthwhile to take a look at how the social subordination of American women contributed to family fragmentation.

The Fragmentation of Families: "The Women Issue"

When English law crossed the Atlantic Ocean with the first settlers, women brought with them the constitutional right to vote. New York was the first state to tamper with its charter by adding the "male" qualification in 1778; state after state followed suit. Thus, the male and female pioneers who equally risked their lives and equally braved extremely difficult conditions in founding this country became founding "fathers" and, for no real apparent reason, women lost their right to equal say. Although America prided herself upon being a democracy, such conditions did not include women. In the new world a woman was forced to be dependent and to feel helpless without a man, through economic as well as social restrictions. Even in the mid-1800s women had no recognized individuality in any sphere of life.

At twenty-one a young man was considered "free" (independent) and could earn wages, but a young woman had to continue to work without wages; food, shelter, and clothing were considered adequate reward. Thus, almost every woman *had* to marry. This opened the doors to patriarchal despotism in marriages and tended to make boys overbearing, while the girls and mothers had to submit to a sense of a "woman's place" that prevented the full expansion of their personalities. This meant that married women were reduced to a subordinate and highly cramped position in life in which

> She was expected to embrace her husband's religion, to confine her activities to the home, and to make her husband's pleasure her guiding star. Ignorant of her husband's business, subordinate in the church, barred from politics, and possessing a scanty or silly education. . . . She did not have to think.[10]

Prior to the Civil War, women's education was limited to a few months for needlework, music, dancing, and the cultivation of morals and manners. Acceptable literature for women at the time was *The Good Mother-in-Law, The Good Daughter-in-Law,* and *The Maternal Sister-in-Law.* There was no reason to teach women math or to let them explore the sciences. Geography was forbidden lest women get the urge to travel. The first public examination of a girl in geometry, given in New York in 1829, "raised a cry of disapproval all over the land—the clergy, as usual, prophesying the dissolution of all family bonds."[11] It was feared that education would make women look at domestic life with displeasure and therefore render them unfit for family and social duties (although many women had already come to that conclusion on their own, without the benefit of an education). Thus, the proper education for women had to focus solely on things pertaining to taking care of her husband, the household, and her children.

In 1848 the first woman to try to enter a Harvard medical course was ejected. When the Regents of New York gave a woman's college the right to grant degrees and offer courses similar to those given men, other college presidents were horrified. One president said the whole idea bordered on vulgar; another wrote that the idea of giving women a man's education "is too ridiculous to appear credible." But the organization of Vassar College proceeded nonetheless.[12]

Education was not the only area in which women were subjugated. Their legal status during the first half of the nineteenth century was medieval and riddled with injustice. In every family the husband was the legal head. Any and all of the woman's property and possessions were merged with his. A husband could even sell his wife's property or possessions to pay for his gambling debts or rum bills. The wife had no right to the custody of her children or to their welfare; her children could be apprenticed at an early age or disposed of against her will. If the wife "made trouble" for her husband (a definition that could be loosely interpreted, such as by confronting the husband with proof he had been unfaithful), she could be committed to an insane asylum. The subjugation of women was likened to slavery; in fact, Louisiana was the only state that *did not* allow a husband to beat his wife "to the point of endangering her life without being liable to prosecution."[13]

It may have been because women were able to empathize with the plight of the slaves that the first stirrings of women's unrest and dissatisfaction with their lives began to be felt by American society during the antislavery movement, as women circulated petitions, raised money, attended meetings, and formed societies. But, in reality, in Revolutionary times John Adams's wife had written to him about the status of women in the colonies during his work on establishing an independent democracy. And "the women's movement" could have been said to have officially begun during the opening of the West in America, when pioneer women stood by their husbands and fought side by side for their own lives and the lives of their children.

The first organized body to formulate a declaration of the rights of women was the Women's Rights Convention, held at Seneca Falls, New York, in 1848. Their Declaration of Sentiments contained many points about man's treatment of women, including:

He has made her, if married, in the eye of the law, civilly dead.

He has taken from her all right in property, even to the wages she earns.

He has made her, morally an irresponsible being, as she can commit many crimes with impunity, provided they be done in the presence of her husband. In the covenant of marriage, she is compelled to promise obedience to her husband, he becoming to all intents and purposes her master— the law giving him power to deprive her of her liberty and to administer chastisement.

He has so framed the laws of divorce, as to what shall be the proper causes, and, in case of separation, to whom the guardianship of the children shall be given, as to be wholly regardless of the happiness of woman—the law in all cases going upon a false supposition of the supremacy of man, and giving all power into his hands.[14]

The convention resolved that women should be able to secure their rights. They were met instead by widespread ridicule. It did not help that Amelia Bloomer's creation of a "rational costume to fit [the woman's] new sphere" of working as man's equal created jeering mobs that followed the bloomer-clad women. Conservatives of the day had distinctly uncomplimentary views of the whole movement; they labeled the women of the revolt "Amazons," "unsexed," "disappointed of getting husbands or perhaps of ruling over them," and "a hybrid species . . . belonging to neither sex."[15] Women themselves denounced the movement. In the 1854 Women's Rights Convention held in Philadelphia, an objector in the audience challenged whether women even had souls.

Slowly, however, and by vigorous and relentless efforts on the part of women and men, laws began to change in ways that included or benefited women. Some states eventually allowed women to retain some or all of their property after marriage, granted them the right to will property, rendered women joint guardians of their children, and allowed women to engage in civil or business contracts. As women gained greater economic opportunities outside marriage, they also attained enlightenment and prestige through greater education and work opportunities. These went hand in hand with the growing and continuing democratization of American society.

But the 1950s returned women once again to the home, reestablishing paternal supremacy. No one realized the extent of women's discontent with the postwar domesticity and containment ideals until Betty Friedan published *The Feminine Mystique* in 1963. Also at this time, President Kennedy's Commission on the Status of Women, chaired by Eleanor Roosevelt, led to the Equal Pay Act and Title VII of the Civil Rights Act, which prohibited discrimination on the basis of sex, as well as race, color, religion, and national origin. Consciousness-raising groups formed in the 1970s; at the time, a survey of women entering public universities revealed that they looked forward to their future role as " 'married career woman with children'—a vast change from the 1950s, when most women of all classes saw their future career as homemaker."[16]

But despite the advances made by women throughout the years, a young woman today faces enormous obstacles to her future family life no matter what choices she is free to make. If she chooses to be married and a full-time mother, then her husband needs to be able to support her and their children on his earnings. If her husband should die, then she needs to be able to step into a career in which she can earn comparable pay, which will be impossible to do if she has not had the proper training or ongoing experience. If a woman chooses to combine a career with marriage—or to be a single parent—then she faces day-care problems, parental leave difficulties, and the burdens of housework, in addition to pay inequities and career advancement that still trails the opportunities afforded to men. When both parents are working, she may also face extremely harsh societal judgment if she holds a job outside the home.

Then, if she and her husband divorce, she may be confronted by a decline in her standard of living. Since she will most likely gain custody of the children (in the nineteenth century fathers were favored in almost all custody cases as chiefs of their families and because children were their namesakes; in the early twentieth century, courts began asserting the importance of a loving mother) but receive less-than-adequate child support. She and her children may run the risk of falling into poverty, having the quality of their health care compromised, or losing a variety of other options that might have been available with a higher standard of living.

If custody is contested, fathers today often have an edge, as witnessed in the 1994 case of Sharon Prost, counsel to Utah Senator Orrin G. Hatch. A Washington, DC, judge awarded custody of her two sons to her ex-husband, stating that "she was more devoted to and absorbed by her work and her career than anything else in her life, including her health, her children and her family"[17]—a sentiment which, if it had been used to describe her husband's focus, would have been deemed a compliment rather than a condemnation. Single divorced women also face discrimination if they choose to further their education so they can get a better-paying job to take better care of their children, as evidenced in the 1994 case of Jennifer Ireland. The University of Michigan student lost custody of her daughter to the baby's father because, the judge said, "she put her education first by placing her daughter in day care while she was in class." It did not matter, however, that the father was in class too, and so needed to leave his daughter in his own mother's care.[18]

But often women have no choice but to take the risk of divorce and then suffer the consequences which, in many cases, are often better than the oppressive, brutal, violent, abusive, and troubled marriages and home life both they and the children have faced.

The Fragmentation of Families: Battered Children, Battered Wives

The American home has been and continues to be a source of love and security, but for far too many of its members, it has also been, and continues to be, the center of violence, abuse, drug and alcohol addiction, incest, and a wide variety of other problems that result in pain and misery. Centuries ago, when home discipline was relentless and the phrase "Spare the rod and spoil the child" was an oft-invoked adage, stern and arbitrary punishments were delivered by fathers to compel obedience and foster submissive behavior in children. Children could be put to death for cursing, hitting their mother or father, or disobeying them. Women, as has been cited previously, could be beaten frequently and quite severely. Such maltreatment of women and children has been justified for many centuries because it was based on the belief that severe physical punishment was necessary to maintain discipline, to transmit educational ideas, to force compliance, and to dictate direction. Such violent behavior was an accepted way of life, just as buying and selling children for slave labor was a common practice for the times. Thus, family behavior that is termed abusive today and evokes feelings of horror, shame, fascination, anger, and disgust has, in reality, always been present. But in the past there was no such thing as a battered child or a battered woman, just as there were no drug addicts (snuff, cocaine, and opium were both popular and legal) and no alcoholics (just "town drunks").

When historical research began to broach the subject of family life in general and childhood in particular, what was discovered in regards to the treatment of children was eye-opening. While little documentation exists for examples of child battering, the cases that do exist are stomach-churning. From the following chilling description from Governor John Winthrop's journal, from another century, an analogy to Susan Smith's 1994 murder of her own children can certainly be drawn:

> A cooper's wife of Hingham, having been long in a sad, melancholy distemper near to frenzy, and having formerly attempted to drown her child, but prevented by God's gracious providence, did now again take an opportunity, being alone, to carry her child, aged three years, to a creek near her house, and stripping it of the clothes, threw it in the water and mud. But the tide being low, the little child scrambled out, and taking up its clothes, came to its mother who was set down not far off. She carried the child again, and threw it in so far as it could not get out; but then it pleased God that a young man coming that way saved it. She would give no other reason for it, but that she did it to save it from misery.[19]

The earliest recorded instance of actual child abuse was a New York girl named Mary Ellen, who was savagely beaten by her adoptive parents in 1874. Mary Ellen was removed from her home following a lawsuit instituted by the American Society for the Prevention of Cruelty to Animals, the only protective society at the time that could stand up for her rights. Years later the Society for the Prevention of Cruelty to Children was founded, but little was done to effect change in this area. Children remained at risk throughout the Industrial Revolution, when they were relegated to overwork and abuse in factories, and abandoned by the thousands during the Depression, either finding their way into orphanages or living on the streets as this nation's first homeless population.

Many years later, the prestigious *Journal of the American Medical Association* first brought child abuse to light in an article titled "The Battered Child Syndrome," authored by five highly respected physicians. But the authors expressed the feeling that physicians themselves experienced "great difficulty . . . in believing that parents could have attacked their children and often attempted to obliterate such suspicions from their minds, even in the face of obvious circumstantial evidence such as broken bones that showed up on X rays."[20] From the pages of professional journals, however, discussion of child abuse spread from the news media to charitable organizations and various levels of government. Research money began to pour in to study the issue; resulting reports were widely publicized. Elected officials rushed to create legislation that would strengthen protective services for children: in 1973, the Child Abuse Prevention and Treatment Act was passed.

Today, however, certain questions remain unresolved on the issue of child abuse—questions that revolve around the cultural and historical context of child abuse and family issues:

> Is there something inevitable and irreducible about all this, regardless of particular social settings? Must we assume a certain *residuum* of abusive impulse—and behavior—in any given human population? Does the incidence of such behavior vary significantly when measured across a range of human cultures? And, within the history of our own culture, do we find child abuse as a continuous presence or a variable one (depending, in short, on time and place)?[21]

There are many today who believe that harsh and strict discipline of children should resurface in families as well as in schools; that it is the lack of such physical pain and humiliation that creates an atmosphere of permissiveness for children and restricts the control parents once were able to exert over them. There are others who feel that children can be brought up with the appropriate values and moral behavior without needing to inflict bodily harm or damage to children's psyches.

This discussion of child abuse does not even touch upon the issue of incest, although incest cases were commonly noted in the records of caseworkers from 1880 to 1960. The problem was increasingly defined as a component of "female delinquency," however. By 1960, despite overwhelming evidence, experts described incest as a "one-in-a-million occurrence." Not until the 1970s, with the support of the women's movement, were women first able to speak out about the sexual abuse they had suffered as children.[22] They also began to talk about physical abuse, even though wife battering was not even considered a real crime for centuries. Psychiatrists in the 1950s, for instance, "regarded the battered woman as a masochist who provoked her husband into beating her."[23] The subject began to receive some public attention with the upward surge in assault and murder in America following the Vietnam War; the attention increased as women's issues came more and more into the spotlight.

But it was not until the 1980s that laws began to be written to protect women from spousal battering and prevention and treatment programs were initiated to assist women. Up until this point in time, there were many who did not take the wife-battering problem as a "serious issue." The idea that the marriage license was also a hitting license was reflected in the media—for example, on "The Honeymooners" TV show, Ralph Kramden would often shake his fist in front of his wife's face and scream, "One of these days, Alice . . . Pow! . . . To the moon!"—in experiments conducted in 1976, which showed that people will often not respond to a woman's cries for help if they think that the man attacking her is her husband; and in national studies such as one conducted by the U.S. Violence Commission in the 1970s, which revealed that nearly 28 percent of husbands rated a couple slapping each other as "normal," and 24 percent of the wives agreed.[24] So the belief held for many years (and by some men and women today) was that a certain amount of violence in the family was "normal violence;" in fact

> Most of the violent acts which occur in the family are so much a part of the way family members relate to each other that they are not even thought of as violence. At what point

does one exceed the bounds of "normal" family violence? When does it become wife-beating? [25]

Such questions are still being deliberated or, in some cases, ignored. Reducing violence in the home toward women, children, and even men who have been verbally and physically battered by their wives needs to be a goal set by families—and by this country's government—to break the cycle of cultural norms and values that tolerate, legitimize, and glorify violence in ways that contribute to the violent nature of the family.

The Fragmentation of Families: The "Blame Game"

In tracing the history of families in America, it can be seen that they have always experienced fragmentation. There have always been separation and divorce, death and disease, orphans and infant mortality, war and poverty, stresses and pressures. The difference between family fragmentation in the past and in the present is that the causes in the past were directly linked with the five acknowledged functions of the family, and therefore could be readily dealt with. When one of the functions broke down, it was simply a matter of other families, the community, or society stepping in to help rebuild the family. For example, children who became orphans were taken in by other family members or nonbiological families, or were cared for through social programs. The defenseless were defended, the ignorant were educated, and the godless were given religion. As long as the five functions were met, then the family was not a fragmented family; it was a "good," "solid," and "healthy" family.

But when, in the course of history, the functions began to go by the wayside, then families no longer had the external protective walls of the family functions. The internal workings of the families were revealed; such revelations were often shocking. For, in reality, many families were miserable, confused, chaotic, dysfunctional, scared, addicted, struggling, alienated, anxious, expectant, noncommunicative, stressed, and hopeless. Families were then told that they were decaying; they were on the verge of collapse; they were damaging the country; they were failing. They were told they needed to return to the days of yore—to the good old family functions—but even though many tried, most found this to be impossible. One paycheck could not take care of an entire family. Child care had become more complicated, with expensive and restrictive insurance policies and skyrocketing medical costs. School systems mainstreamed children who could not keep up with the speed and complexity of learning; overworked teachers could no longer give each student the necessary attention he or she deserved. Churches focused more on policies than on prayers. Laws were enacted that overtaxed the working class while the rich got richer and the poor grew poorer.

People began to question the policies of their government toward family issues, but were snowed under piles of paperwork or were never given the courtesy of a personal reply. People watched helplessly as elected officials gave their support to programs that would ensure reelection or voted contrary to the desires of their constituents. Whereas once society had strolled hand-in-hand with families because they needed each other to work together to build the nation, now society was racing ahead at its own pace and leaving families behind. Society did not need the family, so society abandoned the family.

Once they had been abandoned, people felt the trust they had had in the partnership of the country and the families become corroded and corrupted. People became filled with anger and despair, guilt and anxiety. They grew more and more defensive at each new charge that was leveled at them and their families as the cause of so many of the nation's cancers. So the people started to play the same blame game, pointing fingers around them just as society was pointing the finger at them. The country had become a "whinefest," and now families were going to pipe up and have their say. They offered up a multitude of excuses for the so-called demise of the family: "Drink, drugs, depression, my mother/my father, post-traumatic stress disorder, steroids, pornography, the full moon are all to blame."[26] "Not us," they were saying. "It's not just the family."

Today there are countless reasons why the family is supposedly on the brink of collapse. To discover some of them, simply ask your peers as well as your parents, your boss as well as your coworkers, your partner as well as strangers, your relatives as well as your neighbors, your gay friends as well as your heterosexual friends, single people as well as married couples, those who are raising biological children as well as adoptive parents, grandparents as well as grandchildren. The answers you get may range from television to movies, from talk shows to political debates, from women working outside the home to men not working inside the home, from sex at an early age to not enough sex, from homosexuals to African-Americans to Mexican-Americans to any other American minority group, from single parents to parents who stay together for the sake of the kids, from the National Rifle Association to the People for the Ethical Treatment of Animals, from Prozac to alcohol to cocaine, from government to the church to the schools, from a litigious society to divorce lawyers, from white males to white females, from violence to New Age philosophies, from video and arcade games to sports to any form of competition, from teenage mothers to abortion to artificial insemination, and so on.

What you will find is that your answers and the answers of others, as well as the answers provided by society as a whole, are emotionally charged. Those who are on opposite sides—grandparents and grandchildren, for example, or those who are gay and those who are straight—will answer from their heart, based upon their own value systems. And that is exactly what is happening in society today. Society is coming from its own value system; families are coming from their own value systems. The views have become almost destructive in the sense that they have become divisive; therefore, neither side is likely to seek or find any common solutions.

But this can be a good thing. Leo Tolstoy once said, "All happy families resemble one another; each unhappy family is unhappy in its own fashion." Both families and society can no longer blame one another for the evolution, transitions, functional changes, and fragmentations that have occurred in families. Nostalgia for the "good old days" of family life and "traditional" family values has exacted its price. Urie Bronfenbrenner, professor of psychology, human development, and family studies at Cornell University once remarked that he wished

> we could discuss the family without nostalgia because only then can we learn something about its terrible weaknesses and great strengths. When we suffer from nostalgia, we fall into the danger of selective memory. All of the families of the past were not good families, and all of the families of the present are not hurting families. Each is a family in its own time with its own needs and strengths.[27]

As a nation, we have put far too much focus on what is wrong with families, rather than on what is right. And there *is* much that is right about today's families. Family members are trying to improve their communication with one another in a computerized, television-addicted world. They are seeking to relieve the trapped feelings experienced by single parents as well as those who are full-time house managers. Parents are attempting to forge healthy sexuality and sexual exploration in their children while the world around them abounds with print and video pornography. Fathers and mothers are striving to be positive role models for their children, while children hero-worship annoying, sexist, racist, and idiotic personalities. The face of fatherhood is changing; men are expressing the desire to participate in and become greater contributors in their children's upbringing, while corporate leave policies continue to favor mothers.

Single parents and working couples are teaching children to become more self-sufficient and responsible in household chores and sibling caretaking, but are being condemned for raising latchkey kids. Families are instilling profound spiritual and relational values in their members as well as teaching tolerance and acceptance, while sometimes facing, on a daily basis, relentless discrimination because of their color, ethnicity, or sexual preference. And, as in the past, families are reaching out to other family members, to friends, to neighbors, to coworkers, and to a multitude of others and forming close-knit, nonjudgmental, and supportive communities—contrary to the call to return to the traditional, nuclear families of the 1950s.

No one family today can be representative of or speak for all families. Each family today has its own voice; each needs to be able to speak, and each needs to be heard. What families are seeking now is to create, cultivate, and nurture *their own experience of family* in ways that can help them to develop a family soul—a connection with themselves, with one another, and with society as whole. What this means is that despite evolutions, transitions, fragmentations, and changes, the family today is safe. *The family is safe,* although times have certainly changed for families:

> The transition from log house, fireplace, hand churn, washing kettle in the back yard, wool from the sheep's back to the children's back, and home-produced foods—from all these marks of pioneer life—to steam-heated apartment, electric lights, vacuum cleaner, garbage disposal, packaged foods from delicatessen and supermarket, ready-made clothes, automobile, radio, and TV—this transition has been accompanied by great changes in use of time, changed roles of all ages and both sexes, changed structure and function of the family. [28]

Families have survived changes that took them from across the seas to a new land, from the country into city tenements, from times of peace and plenty to times of war and poverty. Through it all, the family has survived and continues to survive. The majority of families today are doing wonderful things; the majority of families today are not in trouble. Rather, it is society itself that is in trouble—*in deep trouble*—when it can only condemn such a striking and strong diversity of families, who only ask that society "set aside its differences and work together towards helping today's families rather than simply judging them and finding them worthy or unworthy of support."[29]

Until society can do this, families will continue to do what they have always done—to care for themselves and their souls—so they can strive to find solutions to the problems they face, to develop a sense of optimism in a difficult world, and to be more willing to listen, communicate, support, share, and affirm one another.

NOTES

1. Curran, Dolores. *Traits of a Healthy Family.* HarperSanFrancisco, 1983, pp. 14–15.
2. *Ibid.,* p. 10.
3. *Ibid.,* p. 4.
4. Calhoun, Arthur. *A Social History of the American Family From Colonial Times to Present.* Barnes & Noble, Inc., New York, 1945, p. 255.
5. *Ibid.,* p. 45.
6. *Ibid.,* p. 260.
7. Demos, John. *Past, Present, and Personal: The Family and the Life Course in American History.* Oxford University Press, New York, pp. 27–35.
8. May, Elaine Tyler. *Homeward Bound: American Families in the Cold War Era,* Basic Books, Inc., New York, 1988, p. 11.
9. Curran, p. 11.
10. Calhoun, p. 81.
11. *Ibid.,* p. 89.
12. *Ibid.,* p. 90.
13. *Ibid.,* pp.94–96.
14. *Ibid.,* p. 119.
15. *Ibid.,* p. 124.
16. May, p. 220.
17. McNamara, Eileen. "Working moms: guilty," *Boston Globe,* March 4, 1995.
18. *Ibid.*
19. Demos, pp. 78–79.
20. *Ibid.,* p. 70.
21. *Ibid.*
22. Coontz, Stephanie. *The Way We Never Were: American Families and the Nostalgia Trap.* Basic Books, New York, 1992, p. 35.
23. *Ibid.,* p. 35.
24. Straus, Murray A., Gelles, Richard J., and Steinmetz, Suzanne K. *Behind Closed Doors: Violence in the American Family.* Anchor Press/Doubleday, New York, 1980, p. 39.
25. *Ibid.,* p. 47.
26. English, Bella. "Blame game hits new low," *Boston Globe,* April 5, 1995.
27. Curran, p. 12.
28. Queen, Stuart, and Habenstein, Robert W. *The Family in Various Cultures,* 3rd ed. J.B. Lipincott Company, Philadelphia, 1967. p. 302.
29. Curran, p. 12.

PART II

❦

Farming the Family Soul

"The aim of soul work, therefore, is not adjustment to accepted norms or to an image of the statistically healthy individual. Rather, the goal is a richly elaborate life, connected to society and nature, woven into the culture of family, nation, and globe. The idea is not to be superficially adjusted, but to be profoundly connected in the heart to ancestors and to living brothers and sisters in all the communities that claim our hearts. . . ."
—Thomas Moore

CHAPTER 3

❦

Soul and the Family Soul

Throughout the ages spiritual teachers, mystics, philosophers, doctors, psychologists, musicians, astronomers, activists, writers, artists, and countless others from a variety of cultures and time periods have tried to explain what soul is. But soul, like love, eludes definition, and yet, at the same time, begs explanation. Soul is considered as ethereal as a ghost that leaves the body after death, as essential as the need to breathe and sleep; as contradictory as the self and the nonself.

For some soul relates to the physical aspect of life—an integral component of the human body just as the heart, lungs, and brain are integral components, and without which the body ceases to be alive. For others soul relates to the emotional aspect of human interactions—a basic element that raises sensitivity and increases the ability to give and receive affection, warmth, care, love, and understanding to oneself as well as to others. For still others, soul relates to the spiritual aspect of living—a sustaining force that fosters the development of principles and values as well as beliefs and concerns about "a world beyond" the tangible world. Soul can relate to all three aspects of life—the physical, emotional, and spiritual—or to none of them at all, depending on personal interpretation.

Soul is a term rarely used with precise definition in any field of study—science and psychology, psychic research and parapsychology, Western philosophy and religion, transmigration and reincarnation, or Eastern philosophy and religion. Conceptions of soul vary from culture to culture, philosopher to philosopher, spiritualist to spiritualist. The idea of soul can change shape and meaning even in everyday life. Certain words seem to be naturally attached to soul, words such as connection, depth, meaning, spirit, value, passion, and mystery, but they do not adequately or succinctly define what soul is. Words have been created that connect soul with a variety of emotions, thoughts, behaviors, and actions, such as soulful, soulmaking, soul music, soulwork, soul wisdom, soul food, soul mates, and soul hunger; such connections may help to make the concept of soul more understandable, but they still neglect to impart a concrete meaning to the word.

While the indefinable aspect of soul can make it an unsolvable mystery, it can also make it profoundly rich, deeply meaningful, luxuriously pliable, and intensely personal. Soul can become a word with many associations and, because of this, can be viewed from many different and evolving perspectives. The notion of soul can become a link to one's self, as a symbol of self-consciousness and self-awareness, as well as a connection to the world, as a measurement of the spiritual dimensions of one's existence.

Primitive religions associated soul with the vital force in humans and identified it with particular parts or functions of the body (the heart or kidneys, the breath, or the pulse). The Greeks and followers of Plato, however, viewed soul as a separate entity from the body, existing apart from it and therefore capable of surviving the death of the body. North American Indians believed in the duality of souls; the thought was that one soul goes out in dreams while the other stays behind, just as at death one soul remains behind while the other proceeds to the land of the dead. The early Christian church lived under the influence of Greek ideas about the body and soul, although biblical teachings about the resurrection were imposed upon them. Modern psychology added a further dimension to the concept of soul by focusing on unconscious faculties, mechanisms, and experiences and their role in influencing soul. Philosophers speculated about the existence and nature of soul and its relationship to the body. And in the twentieth century, many philosophers argued that the concept of the soul was neither verifiable nor necessary to an understanding of human existence.

In moving toward the twenty-first century, there are many who would agree with Thomas Moore, author of *Care of the Soul* and *Soul Mates,* when he writes that

> we've lost an appreciation for the mysterious factors that bring people together and force them apart. . . . When our focus is on the surfaces of life, we seek out mechanical causes and solutions to problems, but if our attention were on the soul, we would explore instead its dreams and fantasies, its own unpredictable intentions.[1]

Yet similar sentiments were felt over a century ago by Henry David Thoreau. As a nation, the United States had begun to focus on external forces through the swift industrial development of the Northeast, the creation of urban civilizations, an increased influx of immigrants, a rapidly expanding network of free-working capitalists, and accelerated mechanization that strived to prove that force and might could prevail over nature and soul. In responding to such changes, Thoreau held that it was best to be "uncontrolled by social obligation;" he believed that "the young man or young woman should give up tending the machine of civilization and instead farm the soul" and that "the soul truth assures the young man or woman that despite the Industrial Revolution certain things are as they have always been, and that in human growth the road of development goes through nature, not around it."[2]

But the call for "farming of the soul" was felt even further back, at a time in the nation's history when black Americans were held captive by white masters. Even in the most desolate and hopeless of circumstances, black slaves used resourcefulness, wisdom, strength, and creativity to rise above their deplorable conditions. They emotionally and spiritually escaped the physical dominance of their white slave owners and at the same time strengthened their own community. They created a legacy of Southern cuisine from food rations that were doled out once a week, on Saturday nights. Using their imagination and skill, they created hearty and spicy dishes that would make them sing and dance and give thanks for what little they had and what little they could share with one another—a cooking style that came to be known as soul food, with its "legacy clearly steeped in tradition; a way of life . . . handed down from generation to generation, from one black family to another."[3] The next day, Sunday, was a day of worship, and the slaves once again had their own way of lifting up their souls. They would sing songs that would offer hope to ward off the despair of their lives and salvation to lift the weight off their troubled souls. Such music formed the basis of almost all the music of the time and even music that was to be created in the future; both the blues and gospel were influenced by it, and they in turn influenced the emergence of what was called soul music.

In the 1960s, when an entire generation of young white people was challenging its consciousness and black people were empowering themselves as a culture through the preaching of powerful leaders like Martin Luther King, Jr., soul music hit its peak. It played at black activist centers and white fraternity house parties. It went to Vietnam. It flooded the airwaves. It preached its message for the black community (and challenged and enlightened the white community) with songs like James Brown's "Say It Loud, I'm Black and I'm Proud." It launched the careers of the "King of Soul" James Brown and "Lady Soul" Aretha Franklin. It became "music with a philosophy" and was "bullish on hope."[4] It captured the tangled racial history of the nation and brought more clearly into focus the message of the black people: the bond between technique and feeling, music and the church, self-restraint and unbridled freedom, and hybridization and self-invention.

Soul music emerged when America was entering an era characterized by a new style of life, art, and identity—a postmodern era.

While the modern world had been shaped by the Industrial Revolution and mass production, the postmodern era was and continues to be "shaped by the information revolution, the ethic of consumption, fast-changing styles, and lack of commitment to any single perspective."[5] The upside of the postmodern era is that people are less willing to be consistent or homogeneous, preferring instead to mix moods, attitudes, styles, and behaviors as it pleases them. The downside is that people are less willing to go below the surface, to search for depth or meaning in their lives. Instead, they keep themselves amused with malls, videos, computers, and other playthings; they sample spiritualist and New Age philosophies when they feel they have become temporarily lost or out of touch with themselves or life; they prefer fleeting romances or short-term commitments rather than relationships with substance; they base their choices in life upon taste rather than right or wrong, upon aesthetics rather than morals. In sum:

> Postmodern man . . . is no longer trying to improve his soul, develop his willpower, or save himself for some future heaven. . . . You could call him disillusioned except that he has never dared care about anything passionately enough to have developed hope or illusion.[6]

What soul music, soul food, and the various interpretations of soul share in common is that they all suggest that soul, in whatever form it takes—whether mortal or immortal, conscious or unconscious, inwardly focused or outwardly connected—adds animation, power, and emotion to a person's physical existence. Soul not only highlights a person's image of himself or herself, but also helps to form that person's image as a member of a clan, tribe, family, religious congregation, or an even larger community. Gospel music, for example, was an expression of the ultimate joy that could be elicited from uniting the souls of a people whose lives had known precious little happiness. And, years after soul music had come and gone, sociologists concluded that black men and women had strengthened their individual souls as well as drastically changed their social position in America through their music.

Clearly, then, soul needs to be viewed as it is connected not only to an individual, but also to the individuals with whom that person interacts. Soul is as much derived from the human experience as it is an extension of the human experience; it is self-relational as well as socially relational because it confirms social solidarity, group consciousness, and a sense of connection to a community. As Thomas Moore writes:

> The soul needs a felt experience of family. . . . "Family" is no mere metaphor, but a particular way of relating that can take many different forms . . . a special grounded way of relating that offers deep, unconditional, and lasting security. . . . The family the soul wants is a felt network of relationship, an evocation of a certain kind of interconnection that grounds, roots, and nestles.[7]

The family soul, then, is as much a part of an individual's soul as the individual's soul is a part of his or her family's—a family that can be structured in a variety of ways and can include biological, adoptive, and stepparenting/coparenting constructs, as well as friends and people with whom the family shares projects or goals. To think otherwise—that an individual does not need any experience of family in order to shape his or her soul—is to hold with the philosophy that each individual ends at his or her own skin; that even though the world is made up of billions of individuals, life energy only happens within each individual and not around him or her. This is a philosophy one might ascribe to if living a hermit's existence. But the moment the wind blows, a bird sings, a ripe blueberry is savored, lilacs release their scent, or the full moon casts its pale shadow, the hermit knows that his or her philosophy of myself/my world/my soul ceases to exist.

Individuals exist because they are alive in a world that is also alive; they are active because the world around them is also active; they are animated because the world around them is also animated. Individuals bring their lives into the world; the world brings life into individuals. Thus, even though soul is unmistakably an energy that develops within each person, it is also an energy that is conceived, created, cultivated, and nurtured outside each person, through an intermingling that links each individual with the natural and social world in which he or she lives. Whether this contact with the outside world comes from a swell of humanity surging toward a crowded car on the morning commuter train or the swell of sparkling blue waves surging toward a sun-baked shore does not matter, just as it does not matter whether the experience of the family that helps to develop this soul is of a man, woman, and child living in a home in the suburbs or a single woman and her three children living in an apartment in the heart of a city. What matters most is that there is a connection—a connection that "grounds, roots, and nestles"— and which assists the physical, emotional, and spiritual maturation processes in ways that facilitate the formation of the soul.

Families Without Soul: Understanding Soul Loss in Families

When such a meaningful connection does not take place between you and your family (or within the family as a unit), what results is a soul loss. With soul loss, you lose special parts of yourself that provide you with the life, growth, and vitality you need to develop your soul. Some of these special parts can be lost through some sort of trauma—the death of a loved one, for instance, which may impart the feeling of being dead inside, or the experience of being locked into an abusive relationship that erodes inner strength and personal happiness.

But people within a family can become soulfully disconnected from one another in a variety of other ways. Those who are adopted may lose a meaningful connection with their biological parents as well as be denied honest and open discussion with their adoptive parents about the circumstances of their adoption; the soul does not grow in those who feel abandoned or unwanted.

Those who grow up in dysfunctional family homes may be denied a meaningful connection with a parent or parents whose focus is outside the family; the soul does not flourish in those who are ignored or who do not feel loved. Those who are raised in homes in which financial matters or material goods are of utmost importance may lose the opportunity for a meaningful connection; the soul is not nurtured by money and material possessions. Those who separate or divorce may lose that meaningful connection with an intimate partner; the soul leaves those who feel fragmented and unhappy. Those who are laid off or who retire may lose that meaningful connection with their "work family;" the soul does not materialize in those who lose hope and interest in life. Those who relocate may lose that meaningful connection with their "neighborhood family;" the soul does not thrive when it is depressed and lonely.

Yet, on the other hand, those who are adopted may be blessed with many meaningful connections—with their adoptive parents as well as with their biological mother and/or father—and may also be supported in their desire to understand why they were adopted. Those who grow up in dysfunctional family homes or homes where financial matters or material goods were of utmost importance may create a meaningful connection with siblings, relatives, or friends of the family who can give them time and attention rather than neglect or abuse. Those who separate or divorce may reconnect in a more satisfying way with another intimate partner. Those who are laid off or who retire may discover new meaningful connections in a different job or profession or while pursuing a new pastime, or may deepen the bonds with their former "work families" by sharing activities and interests outside of the work atmosphere. Those who relocate to new neighborhoods may form new "neighborhood families" that help them to feel safe and secure.

Yet soul loss within a family does not always have such obvious causes. Those who grow up in seemingly "good" homes or who have happy marriages may still experience a sense of soul loss; they may feel as if they are missing part of themselves or find they are more deeply traumatized by life's ups and downs than others. Happy childhoods and good marriages do not guarantee the creation of family soul. In fact, most people experience some degree of soul loss as it relates to family, often because they are conflicted between what they think a family should or ought to be and what their family really is. Those who were raised in families that fell short of their image of family may spend most of their adulthood striving to create or find the mythical image of family that they feel their soul craves. This soul-searching process is evident in those who complain about the loss of traditional values and the "current state of family" and who then drift about aimlessly in their lives, blaming any number of personal problems or discontents on the loss of those mythical "family values."

What these people fail to recognize is that "a particular family doesn't need to reproduce the ideal family in order to give the soul what it needs."[8] Their image of family is in conflict with what their soul needs; because of this, until they are able to fashion the family of their dreams (or until they are able to let go of their family fantasy and allow their family to take on a form and life of its own), they will not be able to find their family soul.

The first step in retrieving the loss of the family soul, then, involves identifying the desired image of family and then determining how that image relates (or does not relate) to the actual family in which one grew up and/or which one is striving to create. For example, while some may desire a warm and wonderful stay-at-home mother and a father who has a neat job and time to spend at home, odds are that such a desire will not be attained. There are fathers who abandon their families and mothers who have drinking problems; there are economic pressures that force both parents to work; there are terrific parents who divorce; there are wonderful parents who get sick and die.

There are countless other images of family life that may be unrealistic: living in a house large enough so all family members can have their own rooms, for example, or being geographically close to all family generations. It is fine that a longed-for image of family resides in the heart and in the imagination, but it is foolish to literalize such a family image. A family soul cannot be created until the imagined structure of a family unit is replaced by the actual experience of a family, no matter what its structure. This means coming to terms with the fact that *no* family will ever be a perfect model; it also means accepting that *any* family can develop a healthy family soul—if it has the appropriate qualities.

What the soul needs is a family in which vitality, security, harmony, peace, trust, intimacy, growth, and respect can be created or restored; what the soul craves is a family that is physically, emotionally, and spiritually well; what the soul desires is a family that can provide valuable raw materials for shaping individual lives within that family; what the soul seeks is a profound connection with a family unit that has a heritage as well as goals for the future.

Families with Soul: Soul Making in Families

In many ways, society still acknowledges the five basic functions of a family. A family needs to offer its members the comforts of home or, at the very least, shelter from the elements, whether that shelter is provided by a palatial mansion, a single-family dwelling, an apartment, a mobile home, or the back of a station wagon. A family needs to protect its members from pain, illness, injury, or death. A family needs to guide and educate its members. A family needs to provide physical and emotional security. And a family needs to give love.

But what society does not emphasize is that the family needs to cultivate the formation (or nurture the restoration) of the family soul—the part of human nature where feelings, ideas, ideals, and morals are centered. This "encompasses integrity, honesty, loyalty, virtue, conscientiousness, ethics, values, usefulness, self-esteem, and significance."[9] Some families consider that this comes from the religious development of the family—from faith in God, prayer, and/or membership in an organized religious body such as a church or temple. Other families feel this manifests itself by a sense of spiritual wellness—through a faith in humanity, ethical behavior, unity with all living things, concern for others, involvement in worthy causes, or living by a strong moral code. But no matter where the soul comes from, families tend to the needs of the souls of their members by planting the seeds of the family soul. This then cultivates a caring center within the family that promotes sharing, love, and compassion for each member; in such a nurturing atmosphere, the seedlings of soul begin to sprout. These seedlings of soul then grow strong and flourish as family members learn and accept that they are multifaceted creatures—physical beings with emotional and social sides as well as creatures of intellect and spirit—and trust that the family supports and nurtures these aspects physically, emotionally, and spiritually.

How does a family do this? Roman writer Apuleius has said, "Everyone should know that you can't live in any other way than by cultivating the soul."[10] So, just as farmers cultivate their fields, families need to cultivate their souls. What families do with the "soul gardens" they plant, tend, and harvest—and how diligent and dedicated they are in ensuring that each living entity in the family plot receives proper nourishment and care—will determine the strength of the family's soul. Part III will explore, in greater detail, six significant family "soul gardens." Proper "preparation" of these gardens includes the following necessary "soul-growing" starters.

- **Provide a place family members can call "home."**

Isabelle Eberhardt, a French-Moroccan adventurer, wrote in her diary on Wednesday, June 27, 1900:

> I would like to go to Ouargla, settle there and *make a home, something I miss more and more.* A little mud house close to some date palms, a place to cultivate the odd vegetable in the oasis, a servant and companion, a few small animals to warm my lonely heart, a horse perhaps, and books as well.[11]

The Greek phrase *oikeios topos,* or "favorable place," was used centuries ago to characterize the harmonious relationship between a living creature and its healthy environment, such as a fish in an unpolluted stream, a tree in a thriving forest, a cactus in a desert. Every living thing needs a favorable place in which all the energies and conditions are suitable to its flourishing. So too do family members need a favorable space in which to live and grow.

For a long time in the history of America, a house meant little more than four walls and a roof, with no subdivision into rooms, and the total living space of an average-sized living room—approximately twenty-four by fifteen feet. When rooms were built, they did not have designated functions as they do today (the breakfast nook, the library/den, the study, the bedroom, the kitchen, and so on); rather, they served a multitude of purposes, from eating and sleeping to cooking and storage. Even the idyllic hearth, which today is viewed as a symbol of a spiritually and emotionally bonded household, was often a source of great discomfort. Smoke was a constant annoyance, dirt and soot inescapable, and fire an ever-present danger; children were often burned, clothes became ignited from sparks, and entire houses burned to the ground. Yet the family soul was still cultivated. But later on, when attention was given to space management in homes, which created family living and play space as well as space for the privacy needs of individual family members, the family soul was sometimes not cultivated.

Home, therefore, was and still is not so much a place in which there is material or physical comfort but a space that provides emotional and spiritual comfort—a place that does not change even when the person, or the world around the person, changes. For some, this can be an address; for others, a rocking chair and grandmother's quilt; for still others, a sensory button which, when pushed, releases a flood of soul-evoking images. "Bring it on home," the classic line from a soulful blues song, meant that anything that served as well as preserved an imaginative link with the family was home. Thus, what fosters a family spirit more is not an actual living space or its contents, but the space in which each family member can merge heart and mind, and fashion his or her soul by rooting it in a personally soul-stimulating retreat.

• **Encourage love and intimacy.**

Years after Victor Frankl, German psychiatrist and author, survived the German concentration camps during World War II, he sought to explain why some prisoners of a less hardy makeup seemed to survive camp life better than those of a robust nature. To do so, he relied upon his memory of a personal experience:

> We stumbled on in the darkness. . . . The accompanying guards kept shouting at us and driving us with the butts of their rifles. . . . Hiding his mouth behind his upturned collar, the man marching next to me whispered suddenly: "If our wives could see us now! I do hope they are better off in their camps and don't know what is happening to us."
>
> That brought thoughts of my own wife to mind. And as we stumbled on for miles, slipping on icy spots, supporting each other time and again, dragging one another up and onward, nothing was said, but we both knew: Each of us was thinking of his wife. . . .
>
> Then I grasped the meaning of the greatest secret that human poetry and human thought and belief have to impart: *The salvation of man is through love and in love.* I understood how a man who has nothing left in the world still may know bliss, be it only for a brief moment, in the contemplation of his beloved.[12]

It has been said that "A world without soul offers no intimacy."[13] It can also be said that a family without love offers no soul. At a time when more than half of all marriages end in divorce and there is a decline in the desire to commit to long-term relationships, couples who have stayed together for decades speak of feelings for each other that are based on love.

"Young people today are so impatient," said a woman who married her husband fifty-one years ago. "The first quarrel, they want to separate. That's not love."[14] Longtime couples explain that their unions have survived because they have focused much less on the material things and career goals that people want nowadays and instead on how to treat their partners with respect and love. As well, family love needs to include physical expression—passion and satisfying sexual relations, as well as physical connection with one another through touches, caresses, embraces, and kisses.

In order to create soulful family love, emotional and spiritual expression of such love needs to be developed so it can be given and received among family members. This includes helping family members recognize and develop their sensitivity to one another's needs; encouraging family members to give affection, warmth, care, love, and understanding to one another; and supporting family members as they give and receive love and affection with relatives, friends, or others outside the immediate family circle. As Alan Jones, American author and dean of Grace Cathedral in San Francisco has written, "To be a soul (to be fully mature and alive as a person) is to struggle in hope with love, because we know that at our deepest we are loved."[15]

• Pull together.

Members of a family with soul unite to face the challenges they must confront, whether such challenges be in the form of a trauma or crisis (such as the illness of a family member or a natural disaster that destroys the family home) or a change that affects the family (a job loss, the birth of a child, or the need to relocate). A family develops this cooperative soul when it encourages participation as a team, sees itself as a group of individuals who need to assist one another in order to live and grow effectively as a unit, and honors commitments made to family members in ways that create a balanced give and take.

This pulling-together spirit welcomes the family's ability to help itself as well as supports any decision to seek and accept help outside the family when needed, such as from agencies, self-help groups, and/or professional sources. As a result, the family is able to meet its crises or traumatic experiences creatively and constructively in order to develop family strength, solidify family unity, and cultivate a family soul.

In addition, fostering a belief that life has meaning and purpose even though the family may be dealt a serious blow helps family members to maintain their perspective and weather more successfully life's ups and downs. The loss of a family member's job, for instance, which may lead to a financial crisis, can result in a united and supportive effort that can bring everyone closer together in understanding and affection. As one husband and father said after the loss of his wife and his children's mother: "Life and death are such integral parts of the human condition that we can hardly feel we were unfairly chosen for tragedy. In our twelve years of marriage, we had many good things. . . . I guess to love is the highest purpose, and if we do that, we can get through anything."[16]

• **Communicate openly and honestly with all members.**

Many years ago, adoptees were kept in the dark about their adoption or were not told about their adoption until they stumbled upon the fact themselves. Later, parents were advised to tell their children that they were adopted, but not to tell them much beyond what they asked. An adopted child who asked no questions about his or her biological history was thought to be well adjusted; the inquiring child was thought to have problems. Parents of foreign-born children or children who were racially different from them had little choice but to tell their children as soon as possible that they were adopted, but many wondered just when the "right" time was to reveal the truth. Trying to "blend" an adopted child with his or her adoptive family, to deny an adoption, or to obsess about the "right" age to tell a child about his or her adoption, however, should never be as important as creating an ongoing, open, honest dialogue between parents, child, and other family members.

In a family without soul, sensitive areas are rarely discussed. Instead, they are dealt with in one of three ways: they are denied, they are lied about, or they are hidden away as secrets. There are many sensitive areas that may be difficult for a family to discuss with its members: money, unemployment, dreams and desires, past criminal records, sexual orientation, chronic illness, death, or handicaps. But a family with soul discusses these issues with all family members, even though the truth, and the acceptance of it, may be difficult. The father who discusses the fact that the mother is going to die and openly and honestly explains her illness to their children helps to prepare the children for the reality of the situation. When such a basis of communication is established, verbal expression as well as sensitive listening are encouraged between family members. This fosters an openness that grants equally the freedom for all family members to share and talk about any and all matters of concern to them—from expressing a wide range of emotions and feelings to sharing ideas, concepts, beliefs, and values.

Without such genuine listening and sharing within a family, family members cannot know one another; when family members do not know one another, they often do not care about one another, becoming instead "a household of roommates who react rather than respond to one another's needs."[17] Tune in to interviews and news reports in which the parents or relatives of troubled youths or adults speak, and what is often heard is "I didn't really know him/her very well, but he/she seemed like a nice person." One of the dilemmas in today's society is that when people get into trouble, it is often too late to build communication within the family. As a result, a wealth of voluntary, support-based organizations have been created to address this breakdown of communication within the family; while many provide alternative places where individuals can go to talk, to be heard, to air feelings, and to receive responses, they still do not replace the need for such communication to take place in the home.

Because the primary family function is relational and communication is basic to creating loving relationships, a family that acknowledges, accepts, and shows feelings, as well as shares openly and honestly with each of its members, not only creates a healthy, soulful family, but also healthy, soulful individuals who can effectively communicate with others. As Virginia Satir says:

> I see communication as a huge umbrella that covers and affects all that goes on between human beings. Once a human being has arrived on this earth, communication is the largest single factor determining what kinds of relationships he makes with others and what happens to him in the world about him.[18]

Thus, open and honest communication is integral to the creation of a family's soul.

• **Create and honor family rituals and traditions.**

The family soul is nourished by rituals and celebrations that are important to the family. Families that treasure their rituals and traditions seem automatically to have a sense of family:

> A family's clanship embraces its legends, its characters, its history, its focal places and persons, its hospitality, its network, its deceased, its elderly, its babies, its traditions, and its rituals. The family who owns a rich sense of kinship is able to withstand stresses and disappointments that destroy other families. It's able to do so because its members have the support that comes from knowing they are not alone, either in the neighborhood or in history. It is in this kind of family that individuals are loved not for what they have or do but for who they are—members of the family.[19]

Family rituals and traditions are often links to the past as well as bridges to the future, both for the family as a unit and for each family member. "Anyone who looks deeply into the life of the soul," explains German anthroposophist Rudolf Steiner, "will see that these two streams, one from the past and one from the future, are continually meeting there. . . . Closer observation shows that the impressions left on us by past experiences, and [the ways] in which we have dealt with them, have made the soul what it is."[20] The family legacy of what it has done, felt, and thought in the past—its traditions and rituals—plays an active part in making the family what it is today; similarly, the family rituals and traditions give the individual family members the sense of security they need when facing an unknown future.

A ritual can be as simple as letting the youngest child get the first piece of cake or as traditional as an annual family outing. Such long-standing activities provide stability and security in an otherwise unstable world as well as give the family hope and courage to face each day and look ahead to the future.

- **Encourage independence.**

The family soul strengthens itself through the unique development and growth of each family member. While it is important that the family members cooperate with one another as a unit, it is also important that the family as a whole recognizes that the unit is made up of individuals. Providing room for such individual growth and nurturing involves encouraging personal risks, travel or time spent time away from the family, personal renewal, and the development of a spirit of adventure that can stretch the individual soul into new and exciting dimensions.

While a family needs to give each family member a sense of belonging for their souls to thrive, the family also needs to provide a structure in which each individual feels safe to risk growth and secure to know he or she is accepted as an individual:

> Good identity is always rooted in belonging. . . . Such a person is able to relate to his family system in meaningful ways without being fused or joined to them. This means that one is emotionally free and can choose to move near without anger or absorption and move away without guilt.[21]

As the individual souls within the family take on their own unique growth, so too does the family grow along with them, participating by offering advice, support, love, and encouragement. The family, then, becomes a place where "individuation and differentiation" take place—a stable and secure place that provides the opportunity for all members to get their needs met through the attainment of self-esteem, self-worth, self-acceptance, and self-love because of the freedom they have been given to pursue their individual differences.

Souls are not self-made; rather, they are formed as a result of relationships with others—the family being the primary soul provider. So when each family member is given a feeling of security, has a sense that the family is behind him or her with moral and other support, and has been provided with encouragement and ego support in his or her various endeavors, the formation of soul can take place within each individual.

• **Establish community relationships.**

One of the ways to create a strong family soul is to seek out opportunities that create a rich individual life that is linked not only to a family, but also to a community outside that family—"to be profoundly connected . . . to living brothers and sisters in all the many communities that claim our hearts."[22] The ability of family members to relate to one another as well as to other people outside the nuclear and extended family circles fosters ongoing growth and maturation. Implicit in this is the concept that interpersonal relationships are the major facilitators of personality growth as well as a primary source of stimulation. Individual family members, as well as the family as a whole, need to maintain and build friendships and relationships in the neighborhood, school environment, or vocational setting; parents and children need to have an established base of friends and to continue to make new friends and acquaintances.

In addition, family members benefit from participating in local school, social, religious, cultural, and political organizations and activities; from keeping up-to-date on vital developments on a local, state, national, and international level; and from sharing opinions, beliefs, and concerns on a variety of issues. When support is given, both from the family as a unit and from individual members within the family, to worthy causes or others during times of illness and loss, as well as during times of joy and celebration, the heart of the soul of the family beats stronger.

- **Maintain flexible family functions and roles.**

A boy whose primary caregiver was a work-at-home sales-rep father told his full-time attorney mother one night when she came home from work that he had seen a daddy bunny with its babies. The child's statement provides a valuable lesson for American life today and current economics; both demand greater flexibility in "established" as well as stereotypical family functions and roles. Man can no longer be the sole provider and woman the sole nurturer. Research suggests that those families that are not locked into traditional gender roles survive better in the world and in their relationships; in fact, the more androgynous each partner is, the healthier, more adaptable, and more resilient their relationship is. So whether the family is a two-parent, heterosexual family; a single-parent family; or a two-parent gay or lesbian family does not matter as much as whether the parent or parents possess attributes commonly linked to both genders: "Women need to be able to mete out discipline, fix a bike, and become knowledgeable about things they might historically not be interested in, like sports and computer games. Men should be able to manage a household, listen to and talk about feelings, or braid a daughter's hair."[23]

When family members can fill in for one another and assume different functions as needed within the family—with the father assuming aspects of the mother's role or functions and vice versa, as well as children exercising parental functions—the entire family benefits. In this type of atmosphere, family members learn to recognize, respect, and treat one another as individuals, rather than as stereotypes or categories, which encourages tolerance both within the family and without. In addition, when family members are treated without the constraints of traditional gender norms, they are more likely to cooperate with one another, work together for the good of the family, and contribute equally. When the quality of family relationships transcends gender, everyone is recognized as an individual and a person in his or her own right, which helps to build character, enhance self-esteem, and foster independence and self-reliance.

- **Attain spiritual wellness.**

A family soul benefits when each member is allowed to get in touch with the resources of wisdom and peace that lie within him or her. Sometimes these resources are hard to find—the family may not have a rich spiritual or religious heritage on which to rely for support and guidance, the family may not participate in religious traditions or rituals such as church worship or saying grace before a meal, the family may not be committed to a spiritual lifestyle the moral values of which the members live by on a daily basis, or the family environment may not be conducive to the peace and quiet needed for prayer and meditation.

Spiritual wellness is a very personal matter for each family member, but the impact it has upon the family as a whole—and upon the family soul—is of utmost importance. Because of this, the primary expression of spirituality needs to be included in everyday life—not simply on Sunday mornings, at Passover meals, or when someone is ill:

> Our family has certain values: honesty, responsibility, and tolerance, to name a few. But we have to practice those in everyday life. I can't talk about honesty and cheat on my income tax return. I can't yell responsibility and turn my back on a neighbor who needs help. I'd know I was a hypocrite, and so would the kids and everyone else.[24]

The challenges and trials of life become more bearable and difficulties easier to overcome because of the spiritual resources that are developed within the family and within each family member. Without such a spiritual dimension, the family lacks purpose and direction and suffers from alienation and depression. Being spiritual helps families to feel that they are a part of something bigger than they are, which in turn gives them perspective, hope, optimism, and confidence. Such a positive outlook encourages family members to be kind and supportive of one another as well as more open, accepting, forgiving, and loving, of one another and of themselves.

Thus, the family not only has a shaping influence on each of its individual members—in physical, emotional, and spiritual development—but also upon the souls of its members—in the formation of a healthy relational network that connects each individual with his or her own inner self as well as with the community in which that self and soul is created, cultivated, and nurtured. One of the major components in caring for the soul of the family is the strengthening of the family's soul-growing capabilities, which will be explored in greater detail in Part III. Another is the strengthening of the family through its experience of family as a small community unto itself, as well as within the larger cultural and social community in which it survives and thrives.

NOTES

1. Moore, Thomas. *Soul Mates: Honoring the Mysteries of Love and Relationship.* Harper Perennial, New York, 1994, p. xiii.
2. Cousineau, Phil, ed. *SOUL An Archaeology: Readings from Socrates to Ray Charles.* HarperSanFrancisco, 1994, pp. 130 and 132.
3. *Ibid.,* p. 176.
4. Hirshey, Gerri. *Nowhere to Run: The Story of Soul Music.* Times Books, New York, 1984, p. 315.
5. Cousineau, p. 114.
6. *Ibid.,* pp. 114–115.
7. Moore, pp. 71–72.
8. *Ibid.,* p. 73.
9. Stinnett, Nick and DeFrain, John. *Secrets of Strong Families.* Little Brown and Company, Boston, 1985, p. 101.
10. Cousineau, p. 140.
11. *Ibid.,* p. 127.
12. *Ibid.,* pp. 75–76.
13. *Ibid.,* p. 168.
14. Grunwald, Michael. "Longtime couples toast to golden opportunities," *Boston Globe,* April 24, 1995.
15. Cousineau, p. 143.
16. Stinnett, pp. 103–104.
17. Curran, Dolores. *Traits of a Healthy Family.* HarperSanFrancisco, San Francisco, 1983, p. 35.
18. *Ibid.,* p. 31.
19. *Ibid.,* p. 199.
20. Cousineau, p. 202.
21. Bradshaw, John. *Bradshaw On: The Family—A Revolutionary Way of Self-Discovery.* Health Communications, Inc., Deerfield Beach, FL, 1993, p. 42.
22. Cousineau, p. 140.
23. Blau, Melinda. *Families Apart: Ten Keys to Successful CoParenting.* The Berkley Publishing Group, New York, 1993, p. 236.
24. Stinnett and DeFrain, p. 119.

CHAPTER 4

❦

The Soul of the Family's Community

The integrity of a society rests upon how well its families integrate with their own communities as well as with society as a whole. This does not mean that a heterosexual couple, their biological children, and the second and third generations with whom they share holidays and family celebrations provide the only basis of this integrity. Nor does it mean that a lesbian couple that adopts multicultural children and participates with other gay and lesbian couples as a large, extended family in such events as Gay Pride parades and political marches on Washington hampers the formation of this integrity. Rather, first and foremost, each family, in its own way, creates its own integrity. The integrity of any family rests upon its ability to help each family member learn about him or herself as well as learn how to relate to others: to work and play together, to make friends, to love others in an intimate way, to choose a life-long partner, and with that partner, to choose whether or not to raise children. In effect, the integrity of each and every family rests upon its ability to create its own family community.

But what exactly constitutes this family community can be open to a wide range of interpretation. Chapters 1 and 2 hinted at the fluidity and flexibility in the definition of family, through descriptions of how human beings have constructed different styles of family living and different ways of relating the family to the larger community in response to evolving family functions, family structures, and societal impacts. From the sixteenth century to the middle of the eighteenth century in this country, for example, servants were considered part of the family, as valued and contributing members of the production-and-consumption unit, thereby cementing the already commonly accepted notion in the Western world that household and family tended to overlap. (In fact "family" came from *famulus,* the Latin word for servant; the first definition of family in Samuel Johnson's dictionary of 1755 stated that family was a "synonym for household.") Family originally had nothing to do with being related by blood or marriage but rather referred to the live-in staff of a domestic establishment; thus, "co-residence was considered more important in defining a family than a blood relationship."[1]

Although industrialization and the Emancipation Proclamation effectively eliminated the widespread use of household servants in America, other nonrelatives entered into the family structure: single people who shared apartments, lodgers who helped with the rent, neighbors who assisted in the care of orphans and widows, friends who pitched in during times of stress and strife, and many others who enlarged the family circle and satisfied the definition of family as a cohabiting household that might or might not include blood relatives.

But this open-ended view of family has narrowed through the use of such terms as "nuclear family," which today is synonymous with "traditional family," and "extended family," now the most common family structure (and also the most maligned). Both terms entered into the language at a time when it was deemed necessary to provide an appropriate definition for an institution that had survived for centuries without set guidelines and structure. "Nuclear family" came to mean a mother and father and their children; "extended family" meant all the other relatives, which often included affinal relatives (those related by marriage) rather than blood relatives.

In exploring the evolution of families throughout the world— even before America was discovered—complexities to both definitions had already complicated the meaning of family. Such complexities were based on personal choice, on societal constructs at the time, or on unforeseen circumstances, such as the death of a spouse. Sometimes two or more nuclear families—married couples with or without children—lived together. Sometimes generational extensions of the nuclear family were created, commonly called stem families, where sons and daughters who reached adulthood continued to live with their parents and contribute to the household; they might then marry and bear children, and choose to remain in the same household, thereby creating a household that consisted of three generations—grandparents, parents, and young children. Stem families, however, most often ended upon the marriage of a son or daughter, who would then seek separate housing; this differed from the joint family, or multiple-family household, where the sons and/or daughters married and did not move out.

Some people set up family communities not based on biological kin, in order to care for a sizable piece of property owned by one; for example, two nonblood relatives might live together, with their wives and children, and have a contractual agreement. Many others lived together in joint-family households composed of fragments of nuclear families—for example, a "complete" nuclear family as well as the child of a deceased brother or sister, the widow of an uncle or brother, an orphaned cousin, and so on.

In reality, then, there has really never been a period in American history—or, for that matter, in the history of the world—in which there have been a plethora of models of the "perfect" nuclear family or examples of the "perfect" extended family. In reality too the shape of the households of the past, even of the past five centuries, was not radically different from the shape of households today. There are, however, two main differences between the past and the present in regard to composition of the family. The first is that the elderly of the past rarely lived anywhere but in households; there were no retirement communities (although monasteries and convents sometimes served that function), no nursing homes, and no round-the-clock health care providers. The myth was that "old people always lived with their children, were cared for by them, and shared in household activities—the extended family at its nicest."[2] But often elderly family members created tense and ambiguous feelings in the family, had their authoritarian powers usurped, were relegated to a status no higher than a servant, and were cared for by children who were supposed to be responsible for "every poor old, blind, lame and impotent person."[3]

A second difference was that membership in households of the past was quite impermanent and transient. Death constantly eroded stable family foundations, as did the presence of nonrelated members who came and went depending on the needs and capacities of the house. Who the members were became insignificant; rather, the purpose they were fulfilling was what granted them membership in the family. Once their purpose was satisfied, then there was no need for their continued inclusion in the family.

In 1790, when the first United States census was taken, the median-sized household was 5.7; in 1965 it was 3.7.[4] Such a difference is significant because it reflects the sharp decline in domestic servants and dependent elders living at home (and a lower birthrate). It also shows that lodgers, "hired hands," and other nonrelated family members had been eliminated from the household. A census taken today might reveal a similarly lower figure when compared to the first census and, while it would provide a truthful "head count," it would not accurately reflect the ties of kinship that bind families together outside the household—kinship that includes blood relatives, affinal relatives, friends, expartners, stepchildren, biological and adopted children, coworkers, neighbors, and others who are considered not so much a part of an extended family as important extensions of the nuclear family: integral spokes that hold the circle of family together. A family that has actively extended its family to include others can be said to have added soul to its family community, for the extensions it has made to others have been made not out of necessity or obligation but out of desire to connect, out of a depth of heartfelt feeling, and out of love. Such freedom to actively "broaden out" family interactions beyond the nuclear structure is essential not only to the formation of the soul of the family, but also to the creation of the soul of society:

> Tightly drawn family groups become deeply involved in their own internal loves and hates. For a society to survive, there must be a broadening out of human relationships. Children must have opportunities to meet and play with other children. . . . They must learn to know and trust others beyond the narrow family fold and beyond the small communities within which everyone is related through the marriage of cousins. . . . Indeed, it may be said that civilization rests on the ability to make and keep friends outside the kin group and the group of those related through marriage.[5]

Yet society as a whole has not encouraged the formation of networks extending outward from families, with interdependent family connections. The message given to families has been and continues to be that the less help a small, nuclear family takes from its relatives, neighbors, and friends, as well as from public authorities and government, the more successful it is. There are some places where this family structure can work. In a very simple society, where all the houses are pretty much alike, all the same traditions and rituals practiced throughout, all the possessions about the same, and all the activities performed similarly, members of different families learn that where they live, what they do, what they eat, and the knowledge they have acquired resembles the life of all other families. Thus, they do not need to extend their families outward, because what goes on in their family is customary to all families. But even among the simplest food gatherers, there has always been the desire to extend outward from the family unit and to seek out others—other families, other playmates and companions, trusted confidants and friends.

In today's complex society, where there is a great diversity in the ways of different families, families who do not "broaden out" suffer. They do not learn about variation and contrast, similarities and differences, privileges and deprivations, agonies and ecstasies, wealth and ill-fortune, lack and plenty, and a multitude of other alternatives that will invariably confront them when they need to leave the protective structure of their small familial retreats. Rather than learn how to accept and embrace societal as well as familial diversity, individuals from such families instead become adept at recognizing and then gravitating toward the houses that are most like their own, the people who are most like them, and the activities most familiar to them, becoming wary and watchful in situations that are contrary to their own. In today's already stratified society, this does not build integrity, either within the family or within society. Rather, this only serves to further stratify individuals who have been raised or who lived in small, "closed-network" households; it teaches them to view themselves (and others) solely by class, race, and ethnicity.

Family members who grow up in small, closed households receive only a fragmentary representation of the wide range of possibilities that exists in the world for them and are deprived of their individual sense of place in the larger whole. But family members who are raised in households that extend outward "will be prepared to work in and for a world in which there is equal opportunity in a sense that can never come about through the family alone, or a society that is modeled mainly on the family."[6] As the family "broadens out," their world too broadens out; the family then includes "greater differences within its symmetry, differences of education, nationality, race, and sex, and boys and girls and men and women can find in each other both likenesses and contrast."[7]

Creating such an enriching family community, however, is not always easy. It does not simply mean opening the doors of the family household to anyone, just so the family can say it has extended itself. It does not mean seeking out diversity simply for exposing and teaching differences to family members. It does not mean purposely reaching out to others who belong to different groups, who look different, or who arrange their lives in different ways in order to inspire tolerance. Creating a family as well as a family community in America's open, rapidly changing culture can be exciting but also challenging, particularly when striving to create a workable family community and then to effectively integrate this community with society.

The best way any family can accomplish this is for the family to extend itself naturally to others in ways that are founded on a community of interest. This interest can be created in the present, forged on looking ahead to the future, or sometimes molded by shared experiences in the past. Yet no matter what the basis of interest is in "broadening out" a family, it should be done effortlessly and in ways that are right for that particular family.

"Forced" Family Soul: Experiments in the Creation of Family Communities

Are the evils of today's society the result of flaws in the traditional family system, or is the family system the victim of society's failure to give it the support and help it needs in order to deal with today's enormous and rapid social, economic, political, and cultural changes? This is a question that has often been posed throughout the history of family at times when it was felt that the "contemporary" culture suffered from grave deficiencies and family life was deemed to be in serious trouble. But even though many in the past willingly accepted the view that families were to blame and returned to the traditional family system in droves, the evils of society did not go away. Visit this country a little over a century ago, and there is little difference between what was going on in society then and what is going on in society now. The 1850s saw this country violently divided by a bloody civil war that had, as its central issue, basic human rights; America still struggles with nativist bigotries against all races and ethnicities of American citizenry. In 1854 the New York *Atlas* reported: "Horrible murders, stabbings, and shootings, are now looked for, in the morning papers, with as much regularity as we look for our breakfast. . . . Scarcely a day passes that we do not hear of the most outrageous assault with a deadly weapon."[8]

Today, while people are sometimes killed by more sophisticated weaponry, their deaths are still as shockingly violent as those that occurred over a century ago. In 1856 the San Francisco city government became so corrupt that a citizens' vigilance committee violently overthrew the elected and appointed officials; recent local, state, and national elections have ousted incumbents and redistributed party control. During the birth of American organized labor in 1886, riots, a bomb, and seven police officers killed in the line of duty were the outcome of the Haymarket Square demonstration; today, terrorist acts against government agencies, corporations, and abortion clinics, as well as inner-city rioting, are not uncommon. Thus, when one reads D. H. Lawrence's remark over a century ago that "the essential American soul is hard, isolate, stoic, and a killer,"[9] it may give pause to wonder if the same statement could be applied to today's "essential American soul."

As society has strayed further and further from its goal of providing a stable society for its citizens, the traditional families the people once struggled to create and maintain—and which were once recognized as an evolutionary advance over the nonstructured and diverse family structures of the past—have come under closer scrutiny. What was formerly viewed as America's savior—the traditional marriage system—has come under fire by many who believe that it has failed to provide a secure base for a civilized society; thus, the search for something better has begun.

Experiments in many styles of nontraditional living—which often took the form in the 1960s of cohabitation, multiple sex partners, open marriage, and communal living—were considered the products of the rebellious minds of a youthful counterculture that was railing against modern American society. Yet, in reality, the purported "new" styles of family forms were quite old and had played an integral part in the evolution to modern family structures:

Julius Caesar reported that the early Britons practiced group marriage, and anthropologists have found it in South India and elsewhere. Polygamy is still widely practiced in Africa and on a diminishing scale in Asia. Cohabitation is simply a modern form of the "clandestine marriage" of medieval Europe and the common-law marriage of more recent times. Extramarital sex has always been with us, openly practiced in the later years of the declining Roman Empire, among the French aristocracy during the Renaissance, and in avant-garde communities on a wide scale. Experiments in communal living have occurred from time to time in most societies, a number of them in earlier years in the United States. One-parent families have been imposed . . . on widowed or deserted mothers everywhere; they have been part of the cultural heritage of black communities here and in the Caribbean, and they are widespread among South American Indians.[10]

In the early 1800s, the first of a long series of group living experiments—so-called utopian communes—sprang up in the United States, and they prospered during the years before and after the Civil War. In 1846, a former lawyer who gave up law following a religious conversion at a revival meeting entered the seminary and began to preach the doctrine of perfectionism. John Humphrey Noyes gathered a loyal group of followers and formed the Putney Community in Putney, Vermont. Their community was based on the shared belief in perfectionism, the desire for shared wealth and property, and the principle of complex marriages, which allowed for shared sexual privileges between consenting adult men and adult women. Two years later, when Noyes and his group were driven out of Putney, the group reestablished itself in central New York State, on the Oneida Creek. There the commune of about three hundred people existed for nearly thirty years, prospering financially not from the more commonly accepted communal business of farming but by creating a silverware business that was profitable and continued after the breakup of the community.

In the early 1930s the Bohemian style of communal living emerged. Centered in New York City, this highly transient group's community of interest came from shared artistic and liberal beliefs. After World War II and until the 1960s, there were few developments in communal living, but the decade of the 1960s witnessed the rebirth of communal living. The first of these communes was established in the Haight-Ashbury section of San Francisco in 1964. Hippie "crash pads" sprang up all over the country, and bizarre communal settlements clustered both in the cities and in isolated rural areas. Even though on the surface such rebellion appeared to be against established family structures and an attempt by the young counterculture to investigate the effectiveness of discarded family forms in a contemporary culture, there were many other factors that drove American youth of the 1960s to reject traditional ways of living and to find new and better ways.

First, the overly large bulge in the teenage segment of the population, due to high post–World War II birthrates, created a huge group of notably rebellious teens, who railed against parental and societal authority. Second, the 1960s brought living conditions that alienated young people from the values of the larger society. Postindustrialism shrunk the potential job market for this enormous number of young adults; colleges and universities became "holding cells" for directionless and jobless young people, many of whom opted to prolong their stays at higher institutions by dropping in and out for periods of time. Such conditions effectively imprisoned a large percentage of the population, holding them at a financially dependent stage and slamming shut the doors of opportunity that could have afforded them ways to channel their learning and physical stamina. Such frustrating conditions set the stage for articulate and idealistic youths who had time on their hands to focus on making moral, social, and political changes.

No one knows exactly how many communes sprang up in the United States during the late 1960s and early 1970s; a *New York Times* survey in 1971 accounted for approximately two thousand communes in thirty-four states, while an estimate from the National Institute of Mental Health placed the number at approximately three thousand.[11] But no matter what the number, from group to group the goals for creating nonconventional family living and an idealistic family community were nearly the same: "to provide a total way of life, minimizing contacts with the surrounding community [and to] strive for economic self-sufficiency . . . the complete sharing of relationships and possessions, personal growth and development, and freedom from the 'hang-ups' of conventional society."[12]

But communes were unstable, the ideal of economic self-sufficiency was often not achieved, highly valued sexual freedom and group sharing of all people and possessions created problems, few communes stayed together long enough to participate in the care of babies and small children, and most communes did not learn how to deal with generational issues, for there was no place for grandparents and other elders in communal family living. By the mid-1970s, the number of communes had shrunk drastically; those that remained focused on the realistic advantages of the cost-sharing arrangements they had created rather than the idealistic goals they had been striving to achieve.

The exploration of alternative lifestyles (such as group marriage, wife swapping, swinging, and so on) and utopian experiments (such as communal living) were attempts at finding better ways of living together as family communities within the larger social context. Such searches, however, focused on creating "ideal worlds"—forced spaces in which everyone was thought to be able to live happily ever after by simply following the objectives of the group. Because such divergent communities did not evolve naturally and because oftentimes their focus was less on what they could create for themselves as individuals and as a family community than on what moral, social, economic, and political statements they could make by what they had designed, their family communities were unable to create, cultivate, and nurture a soul. Without such an integral basis for a soul, they lost a deep and meaningful connecting force. And, because of this, they failed.

"Natural" Family Soul: A Diversity of Rewarding Family Experiences

What happens when individuals, on their own, strive to create a group of like-minded, determined people, both within their families of origin and outside of those families, who are willing to work together to improve the overall emotional, physical, and spiritual well-being of the individuals as well as of the group as a whole? What is then created is a new kind of family—one in which an emotional commitment is made to one another that can have deeply satisfying results both inside and outside the constraints of a traditional family structure.

Choosing and creating one's own experience of family means that "We can create our own bondings, choose them as they meet our needs; we can define, with others we have chosen and who have chosen us, what the nature of our bondings will be."[13] Such a broadening out, which can start from a nuclear family as well as from a nontraditional family base, opens the doors to new possibilities for love, commitment, and continuity. When a diverse, blood- and non-blood-related group of people become a family—when married couples form close relationships with other couples, when single men and women forge friendships that are as intimate as the relationship between brothers and sisters, when college and military buddies continue to share their holidays and birthdays together and include their own families in these celebrations, when neighbors share in raising children, when AIDS buddies become integral to the lives of people who are HIV-positive and/or have full-blown AIDS, and when ex-lovers end their intimate relationship but continue successfully to coparent their children—what is being created is a new dimension in biological and nonbiological family structure that gives the family a community and the family soul new possibilities. These possibilities emerge from the concept of choice as well as from the human need for communication, for sharing, and for love.

Any shared experience can make available the option to broaden a family. Those with whom there is a common history, a shared present, or a mutual future goal invite strong bonds of love and affection. People who have shared history—for example, army buddies who have survived battle—have lived through a major part of each other's lives together; their experience is just as crucial as that of a biological family that lives through major parts of one another's lives together. Those who share a common present—coworkers, friends, housemates, and neighbors—often live together or interact on a daily basis just as family members living in the same household would. Those who anticipate working on future goals together—members of a support group, for instance, or those involved in a community project—create, both consciously and unconsciously, bonds that are oftentimes equal in strength to those in their families. Thus,

> A big-city publishing office, an army camp, or a suburban home . . . can create a family in its midst. When people spend daily time together, sharing a common chore, and when that time expands to months or even years, bondings can take place that are deep and loving. They can be as nourishing and enriching as any biological bonding.[14]

Nonbiological families have, for centuries, coexisted with biological families, although they have rarely been so identified. The nuclear family has always been actively infused with relatives, friends, and a variety of "kin;" as well, it has been sustained emotionally, physically, and spiritually by neighbors, extended family, village, and tribe. When Africans were kidnapped, separated from their families, and thrown onto slave ships, children began calling their adult shipmates "aunt" and "uncle;" the adults considered all the children on the ship as their own. This "suggests that the real need is less for bonds of blood and marriage than for bonds *themselves*. When the form of bonding that people are accustomed to is taken away, people create other bonds."[15] Yet nonbiological families can be formed without such a basis of need. The mill houses, or boardinghouses, set up in industrial communities such as Lowell, Massachusetts, provided safe and supervised households where families could send their daughters to live while they earned money in the factories to send home. The same was true in coal-mining towns, where the men formed close, connected relationships with their fellow miners. Certainly the primary reason for such bonding was survival, in order to face their daily dangers together, but the miners would often "stick together . . . for years on end, sometimes for a score of years and even a working lifetime."[16] Other nonbiological families simply grew out of individual lives and needs, where family circles included many others.

As the functions of family shifted to being more and more relationally based, rather than economically driven, the need as well as the desire to belong to a larger family group became more significant. The emotional isolation imposed upon families during the late 1940s and the decade of the 1950s created a craving for close, meaningful relationships, particularly by those young adults in the 1960s who felt that they had grown up in emotionally isolated childhoods. Their wistful attempt to obtain love and security in the kinship environments of communes reflected a desire to recapture the loving, accepting family relationships that were either lost to them or had never existed for them at all:

> Our main objective was to get together a group of people who wanted to establish very emotionally close relationships with each other. We wanted to be part of a family where members really had time for each other and really cared for each other. Most of the people here did not have that type of experience while growing up.[17]

In addition, many of those who joined communes in the 1960s did so not because they needed to be part of a homogeneous group with common goals and ideals but because they needed to be heard, accepted, advised, criticized, and guided as individuals within that group (just as individual family members desire to have similar needs fulfilled within their families). That the communes modeled themselves after extended families was evident in the names they adopted—"The Lynch Family," "The Chosen Family," "A Family of Peace," and simply "The Family"—as well as in their expressed ideals of creating close, meaningful human interactions; facilitating the personal growth of each member; seeking spiritual growth and guidance; supporting the value of each members' contributions by deemphasizing competition; and creating ideal living environments that would benefit the group as a whole.

Indeed today the idea of family is being similarly challenged, modified, and redefined in the thoughts and experiences of society as a whole. Only 11 percent of American families are made up of two parents functioning in the father-breadwinner and mother-breadmaker models. The proportion of adults choosing to remain single has nearly tripled over the past three decades, and a large proportion of the population now shares housing, both out of economic need and the desire to create a community.[18] Designing nontraditional ways to seek and/or maintain warmth and intimacy with others, attempting to understand one another better as well as to learn and grow with one another, sharing in spiritually rewarding activities and philosophies, and assuming greater responsibility for one another are just some of the ways that today's families are creating more open borders. But, unlike the communes of the 1960s, which instantaneously tried to create such "families"—and then readily "disowned" them when conflicts could not be resolved—today's families are realizing that creating the right foundation of significant others does not just happen. Today's families know that establishing such deep, meaningful, and lasting connections with others takes time, and that even with time the results are not always guaranteed to be consistently "right." Trying to successfully blend a multitude of needs, varying schedules, diverse lifestyles, divergent opinions, and differing standards can be hard work.

There are many ways of extending a family so it creates a family community. As Carolyn Shaffer and Kristin Anundsen write in *Creating Community Anywhere*, "You don't have to uproot yourself or your family or move to the country to experience the kind of mutual support and connection people often associate with small-town life. . . . You can begin to create satisfying community wherever you live and work."[19] This means looking to churches, schools, neighborhoods, child-care and day-care centers, support groups, and the workplace as potential sources in which to create a family community. There are options to stretch in many directions, some of which may make perfect sense and others that may seem to be "bizarre." For example, maintaining previously established family ties even when those ties have been broken may seem to others (or even to yourself at times) to be strange; not only may children from a previous marriage be included in family get-togethers, but also ex-lovers and their relatives. Extensions that include former family ties along with new ones can continue to enrich family life and provide assurance that families are more than just single households.

Creating family extensions that are different from the "norm" can provide challenging ways to extend a family, to celebrate its diversity, and to cultivate its soul—the commitment, connection, and love family members have for one another. In her book *Families: A Celebration of Diversity, Commitment, and Love,* author Aylette Jenness writes about seventeen children who discuss their own diverse and loving families and family communities—including Ananda's family of her parents and the other members of her religious community, the Happy, Healthy, Holy Organization; Nhor, a boy whose parents died in Cambodia and who lived for three years in a camp in Thailand, until a new home was found for him in the United States with his single adoptive father David; Jennifer, her single mother, and her sister Merryn, who invite others to share their household and become members of their family in a communal style of living; and Elliott, whose family consists of two fathers.[20]

The creation of such nontraditional families and their oftentimes unique family communities are not knee-jerk reactions to bad childhood experiences. Nontraditional families are usually not founded on what people feel they did not experience in the past with their families or what they feel they are not getting from their families in the present, although this is sometimes the case. For the most part, people do not turn to friends, neighbors, coworkers, or others simply because their biological family has not "done the job" or because they do not have families of their "own."

Rather, most people who choose to include others within their family circle want to broaden the positive effects a family can have by either continuing to expand upon an already strong family concept or by creating a chosen family based on a family/community network they have previously experienced at a different time or on a different scale. They do this with people who have been and will continue to be accessible in times of emergencies, with those who have a shared history of being involved in important parts of one another's lives, and with those who, no matter the spans of time or geographical distance between them, continue to provide continuity and a sense of stability in the midst of ever-changing lives.

Love, commitment, and continuity can create deep and stable bonds within a family and its community—bonds that exist no matter what the family structure is or who the people are that are considered to be integral parts of that structure. Such bonds can provide an emotional involvement that oftentimes is more powerful and life-enhancing than any genetic involvement.

What this means, then, is that the traditional nuclear family structure is not the *only* family structure that can provide such things; rather, it is merely one type of family. Some families are exact replicas of the stereotypical nuclear family. Some adhere to the principles of the nuclear family, although the "parents" may be grandparents, an aunt and uncle, cohabitating adults, gay men or lesbians. Some families are nonbiological nuclear families. And others—many others—are non-nuclear, nontraditional families comprised of people who focus less on creating an "acceptable" structure and more on caring about one another.

People have created and are continuing to create diverse families and family communities within a culture that has told them and continues to tell them that such families are not "good," "right," or even "a true family." What this seems to indicate is that the "human capacity to love, to nurture and seek nurturance, to create the conditions under which that love and nurturance can best express itself is large and beautiful, and utterly inspiring."[21] So, if people created so many variations of the traditional, nuclear family unit centuries ago and continue to do so today, what does that mean for the future of American society? The ongoing creation of nontraditional, non-nuclear families during a time that so idealizes and promotes traditional nuclear families communicates a clear message: people are doing what they need to do in order to preserve the integrity of their families. They are not "setting out to destroy a myth, or to break down the nuclear family, or even to create alternatives. They've simply done what they needed to do, even while believing at times in the sanctity of 'the family.'" [22]

The reality is that nontraditional, non-nuclear families can work as well as, if not better than, traditional nuclear families as long as their souls are cared for—as long as their weaknesses and problems receive far less attention than their strengths and the progress they can make, as individuals, as a family, and as part of a family community. To create such a transformation in focus requires a desire on the part of the family to identify and then work hard at developing positive and enduring family "soul traits," or the characteristics, desires, goals, and qualities that the family needs to enrich the ongoing creation, cultivation, and nurturing of its soul.

Identifying Family Soul Traits

If the quality of a family's life is not good, if that family's teachings about family values have grown ever more silent, and if the family is no longer viewed as important to its members, is all hope lost for that family? It is if all that family hears, time and again, is that they are responsible for creating most social ills and that they can only get better as a family if they restructure their unit in ways that are not right or workable for them. It is if that family continues to mislead and corrode some of the very institutions that were created to protect its well-being and dignity at times when it needs temporary help. It is if mental health professionals, law enforcement officials, psychologists, sociologists, and others in positions of authority continue to focus on the family's ills and suggest that the family's quality of life is declining and will continue to get worse. And it is if that family is only given the tools to fix itself financially and is not provided with blueprints for its physical, emotional, and spiritual rebuilding.

But it is the good in families, rather than the bad, that ought to be well understood and garner the most attention. Across the nation and around the world are millions of good, strong families—families that bring out the best in their members and the communities they create. But when was the last time a newspaper printed a positive story about such a family or a newscast focused on the contributions this family has made to its community? Instead, journalists race to write stories that address the negative things that happen in some families—suicides, drug abuse, and violence—and the shocking events that occur in a handful of families—polygamy, child abuse, and murder. Researchers choose to focus on family pathologies and problems rather than study family strengths and families that are happy, joyful, and fulfilled.

Without question, weakened families abound in America; without question, weakened families do not help America as a society. But also without question, strong families will not be created unless a sense of what makes a family strong and healthy can be recognized. This means that for those families who have become weakened by their problems and lackluster in their desire to reconnect as a family, what has been lost to them must be articulated and then restored so that they can begin to pull together and establish (or reestablish) a sense of commitment to one another.

But knowing exactly what a family needs to make it strong is not always easy. Much more is known about what makes families fail than what makes them succeed. To begin such a search means first recognizing that the bottom line in life ought not to be money, career, fame, a fine house, land, or material possessions but "the people in our lives who love and care for us. People in our lives who are committed to us and on whom we can count for support and help are what really matter."[23]

Efforts must be made not to distinguish between the qualities that comprise a strong family and the ones that are part of a weak one, for discovering what works for one family may not always uncover answers about what is missing in, or what will work for, another. Thinking that functioning as a strong, healthy family means being without problems must also be avoided, for strong families often have troubled lives too. Sometimes asking the question "What's right with this family?" rather than "What's wrong?" can help to focus on the things a particular family can do rather than what it ought not to continue doing; this can help start the shift to a more positive family focus. But essentially what makes a family healthy and strong is the presence in that particular family of important guidelines that enable the members to work together to improve the overall emotional, physical, and spiritual well-being of the individuals in the family as well as of the family as a whole, so that, as individuals, as a family, and as a family community, the family learns how to deal capably with all of life's inevitable challenges when they arise. These important guidelines for living can be thought of as family soul traits.

Family soul traits vary from family to family because each family is unique in its composition, how it is defined by its members, what its goals are, what its members require, and what its members are willing to give to it. While families often share common soul traits—such as respecting the privacy of one another or developing a sense of trust—some will place a higher priority on things that do not matter to other families—such as metropolitan mores or a high income. Because of the diversity of today's families, some will value traits that play no part or have no meaning in other families. For example, gay and lesbian families may value active political involvement to promote and protect gay and lesbian rights; single parents may place much more emphasis on each family member taking responsibility for others. And yet, even though some of today's families may be quite different from one another, they will often find that they share soul traits. For example, adoptive families may emphasize the telling of their children's "birth" (adoption) story as much as biological families may emphasize their own children's birth stories; ethnic families may value family celebrations just as much as other families, even though their holidays may be different.

Soul traits, then, are the actions, behaviors, thoughts, feelings, and values the family as a whole considers to be integral in helping it to create healthy individuals, a healthy family, and a healthy family community. Soul traits can be as all-encompassing as "The family needs to communicate and listen to one another" and as specific as "The family needs to pray together once a week." Identifying the soul traits that are personally important to a family means that the family feels they are important, and thus it encourages that these traits are not only understood, valued, and respected by all family members, but also that each family member takes responsibility in making sure that they are followed.

In her book *Families Apart: Ten Keys to Successful Co-Parenting,* author Melinda Blau identifies ten "keys" that can be considered as essential soul traits for divorced couples and their families, including "Divide parenting time—somehow, in some way, so that the children feel they still have two parents" and "Know that co-parenting is forever; be prepared to handle holidays, birthdays, graduations, and other milestones in your children's lives with a minimum of stress and encourage your respective extended families to do the same."[24] Such co-parenting soul traits suggest an important consideration in developing individual family soul traits, and that is that family soul traits will not always stay the same. Personal problems, stresses, illnesses, deaths, separations, divorce, relocation, and many other changes are inevitable and will thus require that new soul traits be formulated from time to time to address such changes.

But no matter what soul traits are identified as necessary to work on by a family or how such traits fluctuate or change over time, a family's soul traits can become the "glue" that binds its members together in a meaningful way, keeps them together through thick and thin, forms enduring relationships that nourish the soul and enable each family member to grow, and creates an island of stability in an ever-changing society. Family soul traits that are flexible and fluid as well as personally stimulating and life-enhancing for each individual enable family members to be dedicated to actively promoting the trait within the family and to be appreciative of the benefits the trait can provide. This helps to create a family that is internally healthy, right to the "heart" of its soul.

Part III of this book is divided into six chapters, each of which can be seen as a broad soul trait "umbrella" that covers a wide range of smaller soul traits. The six chapters are intended as guidelines in helping families to search for and develop their strengths. Some families may find that they benefit from putting into action the suggestions for developing all of the soul traits; others may find that certain soul traits do not apply to their family. But by merely becoming aware of these traits and studying their hallmarks, a family is taking its first step in its journey to rebuild.

Strong families are not born; they are made, step by step, by constantly and consistently working on what makes them strong. Thus, by working to incorporate personally challenging soul traits into your family and into your family's community, a path can be forged that can guide your family in the present and in the future toward ongoing care, concern, and commitment for its soul—a soul that includes everyone who loves and cares for you and all those whom you love and care for in return.

NOTES

1. Gottlieb, Beatrice. *The Family in the Western World: From the Black Death to the Industrial Age.* Oxford University Press, New York, 1993, p. 7.
2. *Ibid.,* p. 18.
3. *Ibid.,* p. 20.
4. Queen, Stuart and Habenstein, Robert W. *The Family in Various Cultures,* 3rd ed. J.B. Lippincott Company, Philadelphia, 1967, pp. 302–303.
5. Mead, Margaret and Heyman, Ken. *Family.* Macmillan, New York, 1965, pp. 165–166.
6. *Ibid.,* p. 168.
7. *Ibid.*
8. Morrow, Lance. "The Bad Old Days," *Time,* May 8, 1995, p. 73.
9. *Ibid.*
10. Stinnett, Nick and Birdsong, Craig Wayne. *The Family and Alternate Life Styles.* Nelson-Hall Inc., Chicago, 1978, p. viii.
11. Leslie, Gerald. *The Family in Social Context,* 4th ed. Oxford University Press, Inc., New York, 1979, pp. 138.
12. *Ibid.*
13. Lindsey, Karen. *Friends as Family: New Kinds of Families and What They Could Mean for You.* Beacon Press, Boston, 1981, p. 10.
14. *Ibid.* p. 105.
15. *Ibid.* p. 35.
16. *Ibid.* p. 99.
17. Stinnett and Birdsong, p. 110.
18. Alexander, Shoshana. *In Praise of Single Parents: Mothers and Fathers Embracing the Challenge.* Houghton Mifflin, Boston, 1994, p. 319.
19. *Ibid.* p. 355.
20. Jenness, Aylette. *Families: A Celebration of Diversity, Commitment, and Love.* Houghton Mifflin Company, Boston, 1990, pp. 30–31.
21. *Ibid.,* p. 271.
22. *Ibid.*
23. Stinnett, Nick and DeFrain, John. *Secrets of Strong Families.* Little, Brown and Company, Boston, 1985, p. 4.
24. Blau, Melinda. *Families Apart: Ten Keys to Successful Co-Parenting.* The Berkley Publishing Group, New York, 1993, pp. 32–33.

PART III

Growing a Family's Soul

"The family is our refuge and springboard; nourished on it, we can advance to new horizons. In every conceivable manner, the family is link to our past, bridge to our future."
—Alex Haley

CHAPTER 5

෮∾ఌ

Becoming Sensitively Attuned

Throughout the history of families in America, there has never been a time when becoming sensitively attuned to other family members has ranked high on the scale of qualities important to developing the integrity of the family. Predominantly patriarchal family structures of the past rarely focused on the needs, thoughts, desires, feelings, or opinions of the women or the children, and since a family was for so long an economic unit, the emphasis was placed on actions that would ensure the family's survival rather than on paying attention to, listening to, and communicating with other family members. While the Industrial Revolution and urbanization were catalysts for creating more relational family functioning, the continued oppression of women and children allowed few opportunities for an equal exchange of caring and sharing among family members.

Particularly trying periods in American history—the hard economic times of the 1930s and the upheavals experienced during World War I and World War II—did bring families closer in more empathetic ways, but such connections were not based on the choice of getting to know one another better but were done out of necessity, to cope with the tragedies and sacrifices of those particular circumstances. In the 1950s, family members appeared to be more in tune with one another, but such appearances were quite deceiving; husbands, wives, and children were often unhappy and felt as if no one understood them—or even wanted to.

It was only natural, then, that the attitude of the 1960s and 1970s became less homeward bound (family-focused) and more "inward bound" (me-focused) as people chose to get in touch with their individual selves rather than on the collective selves of their families. The backlash from all the changes that had occurred within families in previous decades was felt in the 1980s, and the outcry that followed called for a return to traditional family structures and values, which many believed would somehow lead family members to become more sensitively attuned to one another in ways that had not happened before.

But now, in the 1990s, the question families need to ask themselves is not "Is my family structure or are my family values wrong or deficient?" but "What are the people in my family really like, and how can I convey who I am to them?" The family today is considered a system, not a structure. A family structure shows a delineation of well-established roles and how to fulfill such roles—mother, father, child, grandparent, and so on—while a family system shows how each family member fits into the entire system, no matter what role he or she fulfills. Because a family system considers each family member, it allows everyone in the family to see and understand how all members are the same as well as how they are different. Thus, a family system allows for individuality and, because of this, requires that each family member become more sensitively attuned to the others in order to integrate all members into the "whole" of the family. As John Bradshaw describes this:

> To study the family as a system, one must see the various connections between the individualized persons and how they interact. Each person in the system relates to every other one in a similar fashion. Each is partly a whole and wholly a part. Each person within the system has his own unique systemic individuality as well as carrying an imprint of the whole family system.[1]

A generation ago such sensitive attunement was not even considered important to the family. Yet without becoming more sensitively attuned to all of its members, today's families are doomed; because the major function of family is now relational and the members' needs primarily emotional, attunement provides the intimacy basic to forming lasting and loving relationships.

Sensitive attunement is more than just listening to and communicating with other family members. It means paying attention to the things that are said as well as the things that are not said. It means responding to family members in ways that acknowledge their value and worth. It means noticing how family members behave, what their interests are, and the dreams to which they aspire. It means being able to close your eyes and know what each family member looks like, how that person dresses, and how he or she acts. Sensitive attunement is the energy that fuels the caring, giving, and sharing that are essential to creating a family's soul; without it, family members become isolated and estranged from one another—mere strangers on a train speeding along the tracks of life.

Being a member in an unattuned family—a family of strangers —is not only damaging to the individual, but also to the family as a whole. Without sensitive attunement, "you don't know one another, you don't care about one another, and that's what the family ballgame is all about."[2] Communication is key; naming, owning, and expressing feelings is critical; dealing openly and honestly with the needs of one another is central. Family members need to know that they are valued beyond the paycheck they contribute, the chores they perform, or the good grades they receive. They need to know that they are appreciated, that their feelings are valid, and that they are valued.

Yet one of the most common complaints wives have about their husbands is "He won't talk to me" or "He doesn't listen to me;" one of the most common complaints husbands have about their wives is "She never hears me." In an effort to determine the amount of time the average couple spends in conversation with each other each week, portable microphones were wired to a number of couples to record their every word. The study revealed that out of a possible 10,080 minutes in a week couples spoke an average of *seventeen minutes*![3] More recent studies have revealed that working mothers communicate with their children eleven minutes a day—or less; mothers who stay at home spend fewer than thirty minutes a day talking with their children; and fathers interact with their children about eight minutes a day during the week and fourteen minutes a day on weekends![4]

Such minuscule couple communication makes it easy to understand why, in 1993, 2.3 million couples got married and, in the same year, 1.2 million agreed that their marriages could not be saved. Despite optimism about recent falling divorce rates and the fact that 4.6 million couples a year now visit some fifty thousand licensed family therapists—up from 1.2 million in 1980—couples have not gotten much better at becoming or even staying attuned to each other.[5]

Most people in families tend to react to one another rather than to respond, thereby cutting off communication. For example, the teenager who confides to a parent "I don't think I can handle college" and is told "Nonsense, of course you can" is denied his or her feelings and is effectively stymied in any further conversation. Couples who talk at each other rather than take time to listen to what each is saying, to offer feedback, and to truly connect with the other person's message cannot make contact or create intimate and lasting interactions. Families that accept yes or no responses, that fail to recognize nonverbal expressions, or that use silence in destructive ways cut off channels of communication. And families that tune in to television or computer games rather than to one another learn how to pursue solo pastimes rather than appreciate mutually enjoyable activities.

Families that are sensitively attuned to their members talk a lot about small, trivial topics as well as the profound, deep issues of life. They want full contact among the entire family. They feel that it is important to know about one another, so they take time to "get into" each other's world by asking questions, listening to answers, and discussing issues; in so doing, they learn to see things from that person's point of view. They create an atmos-

phere in which there is "caring sharing"—one that avoids prejudice, mockery, insult, and ridicule and instead validates, advises,
and comforts. They communicate openly and honestly about the
other parent or parents in a child's life—a biological parent, a
birth parent, a former partner, or an unknown sperm donor—
whether or not this person is actively involved in that child's day-
to-day activities. They limit noninteractive activities and
encourage both times of solitude and times of socializing. They
focus communication around individual awareness and differentiation, thereby taking into account who each family member is,
what his or her perceptions, interpretations, projections, feelings,
and desires are. And, finally, they develop a pattern of reconciliation that allows for venting "occasional discord, unhappy feelings, anger, sadness, disappointment, and frustration" but also
encourages resolution of conflict through rituals or responses
that signal when "it's time to end the fighting and to pull together again as family."[6]

Such sensitive attunement can rarely be taught; rather, it is
something that becomes more gradually fine-tuned over time.
Much information about effective and ineffective styles of communicating can be gleaned from printed materials on the subject
as well as from putting into practice the advice of professionals
such as family therapists and individual counselors. Understanding what can impede good, effective communication and sensitive attunement can help identify areas in which families can
begin to make changes.

Information Anxiety

As this country was settled, most everyone had the same
knowledge base or at least access to this base. For hundreds of
years that followed, information in this country was produced at
a gradual rate, allowing for incremental assimilation. But then in
the 1950s the advent of computer technology made possible low-
cost data production and processing, and the rate of information

produced began to soar. With the explosion of new information came a new focus: learning new concepts and new vocabularies as well as trying to assimilate a body of knowledge that was expanding by the minute.

It's shocking to realize now that more new information has been produced in the world in the past thirty years than in the previous *five thousand*. Add to this the fact that nearly ten thousand different periodicals are published in the United States each year, almost one thousand books are published internationally every day, and the total of all printed knowledge doubles every eight years, and the result is conclusive: information has become the driving force in people's lives.[7] The sheer volume of printed information alone—not that disseminated by radio, in classrooms, or during TV news broadcasts—creates an ever-increasing quantity of materials that demand attention and make it nearly impossible for people to find time to separate the significant from the irrelevant or to put into use the knowledge gleaned from such information. Simply "keeping up" takes a couple of hours every night or entire weekend afternoons; bit by bit, consuming and gathering information becomes a major life activity.

Almost everyone suffers from information anxiety to some degree, which is produced by the "ever-widening gap between what we understand and what we think we should understand. . . . Information anxiety makes people . . . read without comprehending, see without perceiving, hear without listening"[8] as well as creates a dependency upon those who produce the information—newspapers, TV and radio broadcasters, publishers, and so on. From computer E-mail to cable television to cocktail party conversation, communication has become information.

Information anxiety impacts on American families—from couples trying to maintain intimate relationships with each other to parents trying to connect with their children. Today's computer networks are inhibiting human interaction by convincing people that it is far more exciting to "talk" computer-to-computer than to communicate person-to-person. With so much information and not enough intellectual, emotional, and spiritual substance in their lives, millions of people are participating in one-sided, worthless computer "conversation."

Most people would agree that although technology serves a useful purpose, it cannot replace human interaction. Rather than develop a relationship to information, then, families need to develop experiences they can share together—experiences in which individuals have the freedom to express thoughts, feelings, and opinions. Rather than try to create "computer families," family members need to turn off their computers for good or set aside computer-free time on weeknights or during weekends. They need to limit the number of newspapers and periodicals delivered to their homes. They need to curtail chronically complaining about not being able to keep up with the sheer volume of data. They need to be less frenzied about acquiring information, as if it had some sort of monetary value. And they need to start communicating person-to-person with one another.

One way to practice communication with other family members is by discussing current events around the dinner table (or other communal meal) or before bed. In this way, rather than spend time away from one another accumulating news and information, families can spend quality time together and learn much more about what the news and information means to them, by offering individual thoughts and opinions about certain events, striving to see patterns and relationships between these events, and placing such events in a historical context. In doing this, families not only keep abreast of information they learn in a less anxiety-producing way, but they also receive the additional benefit of getting to know other family members through listening to their viewpoints.

Fragile Silence

It was once remarked that the creak of a wagon on a distant road was "sometimes noise enough to interrupt Thoreau's reverie":

Thoreau was perceptive enough to know that the whistle of the Fitchburg Railroad (whose track lay close by Walden Pond) heralded something more than the arrival of the train, but he could hardly have imagined the efficiency with which technology has intruded upon our world of natural science. Thoreau rejoiced in owls; their hoot, he said, was a sound well suited to swamps and twilight woods. The interval between the hoots was a deepened silence suggesting, said Thoreau, "a vast and undeveloped nature which men have not recognized." Thoreau rejoiced in that silent interval.[9]

"Silence," writes Max Picard, "is the source from which language springs, and to silence language must constantly return to be re-created. Only in relation to silence does sound have significance."[10] The careful listening to others that is afforded through silence, for example, helps the listener learn why the speaker is acting, thinking, feeling, or speaking in particular ways. Such an understanding improves communication, for the listener thus gains entrance into the speaker's world. The wisdom gained from this new understanding can then help frame an appropriate response that will serve as an extension of the speaker and the way he or she perceives the world. When understanding and wisdom combine from such "listening from the heart," they can create a communication experience in which two people are making contact with each other in ways that make a significant and lasting impression, such as the one experienced by a teenager named John:

The best time I have had with my dad was when burglars broke into our summer cottage at the lake. The police said we should come up to see what was missing. Well, our whole family's made the trip dozens of times, but this time there were just the two of us. It's a six-hour drive. I've never spent six hours alone with him in my whole life. Six hours up, six hours back. No car radio. We really talked. It's like we discovered each other. There's more to him than I thought. It made us friends.[11]

As well, the careful listening to oneself that is afforded by taking advantage of moments of silence is valuable in "giving voice" to innermost thoughts and feelings that may rarely be heard. Such inward awareness aids communication; the clearer the inner feelings, the easier it can be to translate such feelings into words. The ability to translate feelings clearly into words—feelings that come directly from the heart— shows "ownership" of feelings, perceptions, interpretations, and desires in ways that help both listener and speaker get below the normal surface level of communication, so that the communication can become more significant to both parties.

In the earlier example of the teenager who confided to a parent, "I don't think I can handle college," the parent who truly listens to such a statement and perhaps even observes the child's facial expression—who thus uses the silence effectively—would be able to hear as well as see that the child was anxious and afraid; then the parent could try to discover the source or sources of the child's fears and alleviate them. The parent might recall a past experience in which he or she felt similar feelings and then translate the feelings of this past experience into words that would provide validation and support in the present; for example, "You know, before I went to college I was scared because I thought everyone would be smarter than me." Such a response gives the child room in which to continue to process his or her feelings with the parent. Taking time to appreciate the fragile silence that is part of the natural process of communication not only gives time in which to think about and provide beneficial feedback, but also serves to connect the parent and the child to each other by allowing them the space in which to speak openly and honestly.

Learning to listen with one's whole self is what can come out of silence. But silence requires limited distractions; it is hard to experience silence while keeping busy or when there is a lot of background noise. When someone in the family wants uninter-rupted time in which to share problems or feelings or a quiet space in which to think before speaking, he or she may find this need competing with "the modern family hearth"—the most "maligned, praised, damned, cherished, and thrown out"[12] mem-ber of the family: the television.

Television: The Family Silencer

Conversation and silence in the home have stiff competition not only from increased family time spent watching television, but also from increased time spent watching television alone. Ever since television became an American living room fixture in the 1950s, the way family members communicate with one an-other has changed. It used to be that evenings found the entire family (and, oftentimes, entire neighborhoods) gathered in front of the only television set a family owned, to watch Uncle Miltie, Sid Caesar, Jackie Gleason, Eve Arden, Lucille Ball, and many others. But the family affair once afforded by television— where families could crowd together in one room, snuggle to-gether on the couch, group-process what everyone watched, and converse during commercials—has become a thing of the past. The days in which television was more than background noise—the days in which it was a conversation-starter that sparked dialogue and interaction among family members—have long since gone:

> Remember Sunday evenings when Ed Sullivan and family viewing were synonymous? Those days are largely gone. In-stead, Dad is more likely to stretch out on his recliner in the living room to watch basketball; Mom's in the kitchen or bedroom tuned into her favorite sitcom; Johnny is in his room watching "Rescue 911;" Susie is supine on her bed en-grossed in "Melrose Place;" and Timmy is almost comatose in the family room playing Nintendo.[13]

Television watching has evolved over the past few decades from a family affair that elicited discussion and debate into a solitary experience that not only discourages communication but also even eliminates the potential of physical proximity to other family members. Once considered a luxury, television sets are now treated as necessities. As compared to the past, most sets today are relatively inexpensive, affordable even to teenagers with after-school jobs; in fact, a survey of ten- to sixteen-year-olds revealed that 66 percent have three or more television sets in their homes, with half reporting they have televisions in their bedrooms. With the majority of parents working outside the home, children have taken charge of their television viewing, watching on average over two hours a day (the average American watches more than four hours of television each day).[14] And with the advent of cable television and programming that includes some sixty channels, family members choose more often to watch their favorite television shows alone rather than to negotiate with others on programming, or if the family is watching together, they "channel surf" during the "free talk" times once afforded by commercials.

What this means to family communication, according to Steve Bennett, author of *Kick the TV Habit*, is that "with family members rushing off to their own sets, there's no communicating and negotiating between kids and parents over what is to be watched. And this is a loss for everyone, especially children."[15] But parents today would much rather encourage their latchkey kids to come home from school, lock the door to their homes, and watch television until their parent(s) get home from work, rather than have them out on the streets. Television, therefore, has become the family baby-sitter as well as a survival tool, but unlike both, it provides little support, guidance, or valuable life instruction for children. Television does not help children learn how to build relationships with others. Television creates a life for children that is based on unreal experiences rather than real-life experiences. And because children's television watching now goes on without parental input or discussion, children often run the risk of losing their perspective on reality; with no adults to interpret what is being watched, children can receive a distorted view of society (one that might include "witnessing" up to twenty thousand "murders" before the child turns eighteen, for example), which is an important influence on their views and judgments. Because television watching is no longer a family affair, children are also losing the opportunity in making viewing choices to learn the skills of negotiation and compromise, which will prove valuable later on in life.

Such concerns about the impact of television viewing on families has provided the impetus to form the organization TV-Free America. Its goal is to support an annual national television turn-off week each spring so families can reacquaint themselves with a more interactive family life and experience a myriad of satisfying ways to spend time together as a family. Maine Governor Angus King was the first governor to endorse the national "TV turn-off" campaign; to kick off his state's "TV Turn-off Week" in 1995, he offered a list of ten alternative activities for young people who wished to stop watching television for a week:

1. Read a book.
2. Visit the library and find a magazine you never knew existed.
3. Visit a nursing home and ask people older than 80 what they did before TV was invented.
4. Call your grandparents and other relatives and draw up a family tree.
5. On Sunday, review next week's TV listings with your parents and agree on four hours of programs that you will watch together and discuss afterward.
6. Go to a lake and skip rocks across the water.
7. Form a club at school and hold at least one meeting.
8. Shoot basketball hoops with a friend.
9. Take your mother and father out for pizza.
10. Walk around your town and make a list of buildings built before 1850.[16]

All this does not mean that television watching is bad or that family members will never be able to communicate with one another until all their televisions have been unplugged. What is most important is to recognize how television watching impacts your family. When someone in the family wants time to converse or share a problem and is told, "Shhh, I'm watching TV," then that provides a strong clue that the family television is far too important. As well, if television watching provides the only way to relax or "wind down," then other forms of relaxation are being ignored. If the hobbies, passions, interests, or dreams of other family members are unknown, then far too much time is being spent looking at television rather than looking at one another. And if the television set is the only way to soothe friction in day-to-day interactions, rather than talking conflicts through to resolution, then television watching has become a pacifier and not a pleasant pastime.

On the other hand, television can, in fact, bring a family closer together, open up channels of communication, and even play a major role in children's learning. Television can help to initiate discussion on subjects that are not likely to come up at other times, such as corporate ethics, sportsmanship, marital fidelity, sexuality, and so on. Even totally unrealistic programs can elicit conversation that begins with open-ended questions such as "Is that possible?" "Could that ever happen?" or "Has anything like that ever happened before?"

Educational television can introduce and reinforce positive values and cultural diversity, touch upon subjects ranging from science to history, and motivate young people to read books on subjects they view programs about. Discussing a program after it has been seen or following a television show with a family activity that ties in to it (such as playing baseball in the backyard after watching a baseball game) can create better a television-watching experience and improve family relationships. As long as television viewing is not used in place of family communication and is balanced with interactive activities among family members, it need not be perceived as a culprit in problematic family life.

But one of the places where the greatest impact of television has been felt is at the dinner table, where conversation could naturally take place. Work schedules, organized activities, and numerous other individual commitments can limit the amount of family dinner table time, but the biggest detractor is often television. A family that wants to improve the communication and sensitivity among its members "should look closely at its attitudes toward the family table":

> Is family table time and conversation important? Is it optional? Is it open and friendly or warlike and sullen? Is it conducive to sharing more than food—does it encourage the sharing of ideas, feelings, and family intimacies? Is it a battleground between cook and eaters?[17]

But, more importantly, does table time exist *at all?*

Table Talk Time

Traditionally the family dinner table was not just a symbol of socialization, but also the location in the home where socialization most often took place. It was the place at which to process the day's events and where each family member could listen to and learn about the others. But with the onset of industrialization, the creation of home conveniences, the increased pace and stress of living, the need for two-paycheck families, the proliferation of fast-food restaurants, and the need to dine with the television, the trend has moved away from families having conversational table time together. More and more, meals are unplanned; frantic work schedules have led to more meals eaten on the run and consumed out of the home. Those meals that do occur at home usually take place in front of the television set. Where people once used to tune in to one another, talking and listening at mealtime, they now tune in to the television. Even if table time cannot occur on a daily basis, the dinner table can still be a gathering place for families. Together the family can find overlapping times in their schedules in which a conversational, sit-down meal can be planned. Perhaps such dinners could happen once or twice a week; maybe only on Sunday evenings. But the quantity of dinner table meals is not as important as the quality of the few that may be available; in fact, the busier the family is and the more infrequent such table times are, the more valuable such mealtimes can become for the family members.

Today dinner table talk can be about dreams, about the day, about frustrations, about future plans—about anything. But the most important guideline to follow is that the television ought to be prohibited from the family table.

Acknowledging Differences

When sitting at the dinner table one evening, Curtis, the three-and-a-half-year-old child of Teri, his white adoptive mother, told his mother, "When I get older, my skin will be your color." But Curtis is Cape Verdean, with skin a beautiful shade of brown; he is also at that age when children begin to notice differences between themselves and others. Dealing with such a special situation requires that parents be particularly sensitively attuned not only to their children and how they feel about themselves, but also to how the children are viewed and treated by others outside the family.

Because that child is yours, it is often easy to forget that he or she looks or acts "different;" you love the child no matter how he or she appears to others. But it is a great mistake not to acknowledge such differences and help your children learn to deal with the potentially painful, hurtful, and vicious situations they may experience outside the home—from unintentionally hurtful comments to intentionally demeaning slurs and insults. Adults as well as children are not separable from the society they inhabit, no matter how safe, secure, and supportive the family is that they create. Unfortunately, despite political and legal gains and protections for minority populations, in many ways society has not emotionally and spiritually embraced all colors, nationalities, and lifestyles.

Intolerance for such things as heritage, culture, color, sex, single parenting, adoption, and lifestyle can complicate life for adults and their children. Such intolerance is not always based on obvious issues, such as race, but exists also "because being different within a family can affect everything from self-esteem to parent-child-sibling relationships. . . . As a result . . . parents need to equip themselves and even their youngest children with some unique coping skills."[18] The built-in visibility of transracial adoptions, as well as many other visible as well as invisible differences in traditional and nontraditional families today, have made issues such as racism, sexism, and homophobia important topics that need to be discussed openly, honestly, and with understanding in families. How such topics are approached is critical, for the parent's or parents' point of view will send messages to the children that will either result in children who develop high levels of self-esteem and are capable of tolerantly embracing all people, or children who are insecure, angry, ignorant, and incapable of recognizing the value of all people.

While most white parents and nonadoptive parents might be at a loss with how best to respond to Curtis's observation, his mother was happy. She explains, "It let me know what's on his mind. Dealing with our skin color openly is a lot better than having him imagine all sorts of things."[19] One way the parent or parents of transracially adopted children can help to minimize the confusion of differences is to give belonging messages to their children. For example, "We don't look alike, but we have so many things in common: reading, skiing. . . ." Parents can provide honest answers to questions such as "How come my eyes (or skin or hair) are different?"—"Because you were born in your birth mommy's tummy, and your eyes are just like hers."

As well, parents can become familiar with their children's culture of origin and learn such things as the idiosyncratic ways to care for the hair and skin of those from specific ethnic groups. White parents of transracial children can take special care with situations in which white strangers ask, "Where did you get that child?" or "Is he/she really yours?" in the presence of the child. Angry responses or choosing to ignore such remarks can make the child feel insecure, as though he or she had something to hide. Ruth McRoy, a professor of Social Work at the University of Texas who specializes in transracial adoption, suggests being matter-of-fact in your response, by saying something like "'This is my child.' That reaffirms to your child that he belongs to the family."[20]

Lesbian and gay parents need to be concerned about the attitudes toward homosexuality and their nontraditional family system that their children will be exposed to. One of the first things lesbian and gay parents often choose to do to help their children cope with homophobia is to establish a sense of community that fosters an experience of belonging. Providing opportunities for their children to socialize with the children of other gay and lesbian couples helps the children feel that they are not the only ones living in their nontraditional family structures, or the only children who have to deal with the issues that result from being a child with gay or lesbian parents. As Marcy, the mother of two boys, explains:

> It's one thing to say to our children that there are different ways to have a family—that some families have a mommy and a daddy and some families have two mommies—but if all they ever see are families with a mommy and a daddy, it's going to be hard to get across the idea that this is just another way to be.[21]

When a society fails to acknowledge and appreciate the lives of all its citizens and does not lead everyone to embrace differences with compassion, respect, and understanding, then families that follow suit fail to stop the process of fear and hatred that perpetuate the "isms" and the phobias. How do couples help themselves as well as their children not only to thrive in such a society, but also to develop the strength to respond to bigotry, insult, and discrimination? When should couples be advocates for each other and their children, and when do they need to stand back and let others find their own way of dealing with hurt? Telling children not to spray-paint a swastika on a subway wall without also teaching them what meaning the swastika has to Jewish people and their culture does not foster tolerance. Telling children they cannot play with another child because of his or her appearance or who the child's parents are provides no understanding of differences and inhibits receiving a multicultural, diverse experience. Recounting ethnic jokes or ridiculing a minority population promotes cultural opposition rather than inclusion.

Instead, families need to approach the issue of differences both inside and outside the family by providing family role models—adults who show that they are proud of who they are and comfortable with their appearance, culture, beliefs, or lifestyle. Such role models are fostered by parents who may or may not be different from each other, but who are committed to working together to raise such future role models in their children; by constant recognition given to what is good about the family's makeup by emphasizing its advantages and strengths; and by creating an accepting environment that is rich in diversity.

But perhaps the best way to develop sensitive attunement for the differences among family members is to recognize that each member is ultimately together and connected with the others because of love and the desire to live harmoniously as a family.

Promoting Family Harmony

Everybody in a family fights. Couples fight with each other, relatives fight with one another, and children fight among themselves. To say "Good families don't fight" is to propagate a myth; all families fight, and such discord is often necessary for developing good health in the family. Fighting helps get things out in the open, affords chances for emotional expression, develops empathy, provides circumstances in which to learn and apply creative problem-solving, allows family members to recognize their differences, and offers practice in negotiation, compromise, and reconciliation. As long as each fighting episode is eventually resolved and peace and harmony are restored on that particular issue, a family can consider itself a healthy, sensitively attuned communication center. But when family fights go on and on or the home is filled with an emotionally charged, tense atmosphere, the family needs to work on learning how to pull itself back together and to restore a balance of conflict and resolution.

Good patterns of reconciliation are often passed from generation to generation; for example, newlyweds may be told by their in-laws never to go to bed angry or not to bring up a sensitive subject in public. Most often, however, couples and parents and their children develop their own patterns of reconciliation over time. While some families like to control situations in which members are in conflict (or may be in potential conflict) by scheduling family meetings as appropriate times in which to vent emotions before they reach a more volatile stage, today's time pressures on both couples and children can make such family meeting times luxuries. Even trying to abide by the rule not to bring up potentially explosive situations before leaving for work, before company arrives, or before going to bed can be difficult to follow when no time seems to be "the right time" in which to discuss an issue heatedly, rationally, and completely—and then to resolve it effectively.

More often than not, family conflicts occur as sudden brushfires that need to be extinguished before they do more harm than good. This means couples as well as parents need to be capable of determining when it is appropriate to call a timeout and separate from one another or to pull children apart from one another—particularly when a fight has progressed so far that one or more of the participants is extremely angry or unable to calm down—and when it is appropriate to try to work on solutions.

Working out family conflicts can be an exciting as well as an infuriating process, but it is also a necessary exercise, integral to ensuring that a family can remain full of love and hope for one another and can be a place where each member is valued and respected for himself or herself. Some techniques families can use to restore couple and family harmony during times of discord include the following:

• **Have realistic expectations.**

Partners will not always be best friends, nor will children always get along wonderfully. It is more realistic to think that partners as well as siblings will get along well and love one another part of the time as well as have negative feelings toward one another another part of the time.

• **Look at the bigger picture.**

It can be much easier to focus on seeking temporary, short-term solutions that will soothe anger, ease pain, or dry tears than to step back from the emotions and take time to objectively look at a situation in order to find a permanent, long-term resolution. For example, coparents who live in different locations and argue over which high school to send their child to would do better to resolve the situation by recognizing that the most important thing is to give their child the *best* education, no matter which school provides that.

• **Listen to all sides of an argument.**

Until the family members who are in conflict can listen to all opinions, they will be incapable of considering options, other than their own, that might help to resolve their conflict. One way to help particularly vocal, self-focused members to consider other viewpoints is to suggest that they reverse roles with those who have opposing views and take that person's side in the argument. In so doing, they learn to listen to and consider where other people are coming from in the conflict, thereby raising an awareness that can result in a more compromising point of view.

- **Express feelings fairly and with respect.**

One party will never be able to reach resolution with another as long as verbal punches are still being thrown through aggression, "scorekeeping" (bringing up other times in the past when the person was "in the wrong"), lecturing, blaming, and being judgmental. Compromise and reconnection can only take place when unfair fighting has stopped.

- **Fight about one issue at a time.**

Conflicts that begin on one topic and rapidly move to others are "avalanche arguments": what starts out as a small, single snowball rolls down a hill, accumulating more and more snow and growing larger and larger until it "buries" the family underneath an enormous load of conflicts. Families can only work on resolving one issue at a time, so they must strive to keep the focus in the present, on what is bothersome in the here and now.

- **If necessary, obtain objective input.**

Sometimes resolution cannot be achieved by family members. When this happens, the same conflict gets revisited time and again. In such instances, the advice of an objective party (or parties) who is (are) free of an emotional connection to the situation can provide the necessary logical, rational, and acceptable solution.

- **Know that whatever resolution is reached, it can always be modified.**

Over time, some solutions to conflicts do not work out. This may mean the solution was not the most ideal, that the feelings that led to the solution have changed, or that the circumstances between the partners or within the family have been altered in ways that necessitate searching again for possible solutions. End solutions ought not to be cast in stone; rather, in most cases they can work much better when they are tried out for a predetermined amount of time and then reviewed at the end of that time period in order to create the greatest, and most long-lasting, harmony.

When problems are acknowledged and resolved between family members and within families as a whole, all members learn not only that they can express their thoughts, feelings, desires, fantasies, and perceptions, but also that such things will be heard. This gives family members the courage to be different from one another as well as delivers the message that all members are equally valued as people. As a result, family members learn that the family exists for the individuals, that the individuals exist for one another, and that the family exists as a whole because it is sensitively attuned to each of its members.

NOTES

1. Bradshaw, John. *Bradshaw On: The Family—A Revolutionary Way of Self-Discovery.* Health Communications, Inc., Deerfield Beach, Fl., 1988, p. 28.
2. Curran, Dolores. *Traits of a Healthy Family.* HarperSanFrancisco, New York, 1983, p. 31.
3. Stinnett, Nick and DeFrain, John. *Secrets of Strong Families.* Little, Brown and Company, Boston, 1985, p. 58.
4. Schwartz, Pepper. "The Silent Family: Together, but Apart," *New York Times,* February 16, 1995.
5. Gleick, Elizabeth. "Should This Marriage Be Saved?, *Time,* February 27, 1995.
6. Curran, pp. 53–55.
7. Wurman, Richard Saul. *Information Anxiety.* Doubleday, New York, 1989, pages unnumbered.
8. *Ibid.,* pages unnumbered.
9. Cousineau, Phil, ed., *SOUL An Archaeology: Readings from Socrates to Ray Charles.* HarperSanFrancisco, 1994, p. 159.
10. *Ibid.,* p. 160.
11. Curran, p. 42.
12. *Ibid.,* p. 36.
13. Doten, Patti. "Tuning In & Tuning Out," *Boston Globe,* April 6, 1995.
14. *Ibid.*
15. *Ibid.*
16. Associated Press. "Maine entices youngsters to watch less television," *Boston Globe,* April 19, 1995.
17. Curran, p. 58.
18. Meltz, Barbara F. "The Transracial Adoption," *Boston Globe,* February 2, 1995.
19. *Ibid.*
20. *Ibid.*
21. Benkov, Laura. *Revinventing the Family: The Emerging Story of Lesbian and Gay Parents.* Crown Publishers, Inc., New York, 1994, p. 190.

⹁

CHAPTER 6

Affirming and Supporting Self-Expression

The original functions of families in America, as well as the pressures and stresses brought about by settling the new land, necessitated that families focus on survival. This meant that they had to be more concerned for the "greater good" of the family than for the "greater good" that could be developed in individual family members. Family members knew that family economics came first or the family would not survive; thus, children and spouses learned to accept that they often had to sacrifice their own personal ambitions and interests, give up consideration of an avocation different from the family business, or put off schooling to support the family homestead.

But even as family functions became less radically focused on survival and more strongly geared toward the creation of a relational foundation, the family's purpose most often revolved around the father's "greater good" and furthering his political, executive, or military ambitions. Other individuals' interests and goals were often subordinated to that parent's career goals and, during leisure time, to ensuring his enjoyment of recreational activities.

Today, to care for the creation, cultivation, and nurturing of the sense of individuality in each family's member—an integral part of the family's soul—the family needs to do two things. First, it needs to affirm and support self-expression in all of its members. This means affirming and supporting the individual for who he or she is, not for the role he or she fulfills within the family. Allowing for self-expression requires a family atmosphere in which everyone is expected to affirm and support one another equally, without a greater value being placed on certain individuals (such as focusing on the "star" athlete while ignoring the passions or interests that are important to other siblings, or assuming that one partner will readily give up jobs and friends so the other partner can maintain career success through job transfers).

Second, the family needs to convey its respect for the privacy of each individual so individuals can learn how to be alone, how to be different, how to change and mature, and how to become more independent. Families that take the time to ensure that the family has these two key elements will be rewarded by adults and children who can be independent and strong within a community, who can develop a high level of self-expression and their own forms of creative expression, and who can challenge traditional gender roles in ways that make a positive impact on themselves and on the family as a whole. Therefore, knowing how to create the atmosphere within the family in which individuals can flourish in such ways is essential.

Family Affirmation and Support

Family members need to support one another, for better or worse, in their similarities as well as their differences:

> . . . Although we may not understand or agree with a particular stand taken by one of our children or siblings, we'll defend that person's right to take that stand. . . . Although we may not want Mom to go back to school or work, we celebrate her A's and we fold the laundry without being asked. . . . . Even though we may be disappointed when Dad's work takes him out of town and away from us, we pretend it's okay so he won't feel guilty.
> . . . It means that the squeaky concert presented by the

third graders playing recorders is as important as the semi-professional jazz concert of the high-school senior, that the girl who is fat feels lovable in spite of it, and that when an election is lost or a prized spot on the team isn't won, the family doesn't value the loser less.[1]

In creating families in which the members affirm and support one another, what is most needed is a strong foundational base where family members like and love one another—and keep telling one another and showing one another these feelings. This visible and verbalized caring imparts value to each individual and helps to develop self-worth. To be liked, to be loved, and to be able to share these feelings within a family gives each family member a valuable sense of personal worth that matters more than acceptance of sexuality, ethnicity, handicap, and a variety of subtle differences that distinguishes family members from one another.

In most families, however, this emotional affirmation and support still comes from the mother as she fulfills her expected and traditional role of family nurturer. The "duties" of the father in the home have long been established as disciplinarian and related to the family's financial support system rather than to the family's emotional support system. In most families too children rarely show much interest in or support of one another's activities, most often going their separate ways. This creates an atmosphere in which one person—the mother—is required to emotionally affirm and support all family members, which in turn creates individuals within the family who expect that, as they mature, someone will always be there to affirm and support them. As a result, family members do not learn to affirm and support themselves or others.

But interest can generate support. Family members need to create a more balanced support system for one another in order to create more self-expressive family members. Both parents and children can serve as support systems for one another, with neither adults nor children doing all the giving or all the receiving. One way this can happen is to create conversations with all family members that show interest in what each member is doing—not just the usual "How was your day?" which requires a short answer such as "Fine," "Okay," or "Not bad." Such a standard question-and-answer dialogue, whether conducted between couples, between parent and child, or between children, can become as uncomfortable as a session at the dentist, with one member tensely reciting the "required" question and the other member mumbling a yes or no in response, with no elaboration. This type of nonconversational communication often becomes quite evident as children start to grow older; many withdraw from their parents and show resentment at any question directed at eliciting information about them and their lives. But asking questions about specific projects or issues can generate discussion and show a genuine interest in learning more about what is going on in individual's lives.

Another way for family members to support and affirm one another is to remove any form of pressure from the desire for the happiness and success of others. The emphasis in this country on "Winning isn't everything—it's the only thing" can create a fine line between healthy competition and high goals as effective motivational tools for individual achievement, and unhealthy competition, where winning becomes the only acceptable outcome. School athletics used to be for exercise and socializing; today they are considered stepping-stones to scholarships and future professional contracts. Recreational summer camps, which once balanced learning with the creation of good friendships and fun-filled memories, have evolved into specialty camps that offer accelerated and intensive programs in such areas as athletic training, computer programming, and stock market selection. Getting an education is no longer as important as getting into the "right" schools; where once attending Harvard University was the goal, today "there are preschools in the United States that allow parents to put their children's name on the waiting lists as soon as the pregnancy is confirmed."[2]

Children as well as adults respond to such pressure by either overachieving (with such expected "fallouts" as high anxiety, suicidal tendencies, chemical dependency, and burnout) or by simply losing interest in even trying because they fear falling short of the only goal that has been conveyed to them as acceptable. The problem is, in a family's desire to want the best for each member and to hope that each achieves happiness, "happiness" often translates into "success," and success more often than not means being "the best" and "coming in first." This neither affirms nor supports the capabilities or the desires of individuals, who may not want what others want or may be satisfied by what others view as "not enough."

But not everyone can be the best in every situation, nor can personal pride and satisfaction come from participating in an activity where even the best efforts cannot achieve the desired "successful" outcome. Therefore, competition needs to be kept in balance, with individuals pursuing what interests them in ways that make them feel competent and successful by their own standards. This means motivating family members to do their best at what they choose to do and encouraging that they be committed to doing what they want for as long as they learn from and enjoy the experience. There are a number of specific ways that this can happen within a family. Children can try out many activities as they grow up so they can benefit from having a variety of experiences. They ought to be allowed to grow and mature both intellectually and emotionally at their own pace, without comparison to others their age. And parents can oversee coaches and activity leaders to ensure that a healthy level of competition is maintained.

A final suggestion for creating a family atmosphere that affirms and supports each member is to pull together as a team—to rally around those family members that need encouragement during times of difficulty or stress. Every family is beset by problems, ranging from such highly stressful circumstances as the loss of a job, a major health problem, or an accident, and annoying and problematic setbacks such as flunking an important test, spraining an ankle before a game, or not being accepted into a first-choice school. Yet when a family conveys that it is there for each family member, the basic attitude that is relayed is that all personally challenging circumstances matter.

In sum, family affirmation and support should not be considered luxuries that are to be provided only when something marvelous or something terrible has happened to a family member, but necessities that are part of the family's everyday life—from physically supportive and affirming hugs to emotionally supportive words of encouragement, praise, and love.

Family Respect for the Privacy of Individuals

There is a big difference between respecting the privacy of an individual and withdrawing from that individual. For example, when parents allow their teenaged children to physically and emotionally retreat from them, as teenagers will often do, these children report that they feel they are being abandoned, even though their parents are giving them exactly what they demanded—to be left alone. Teenagers still rely upon their parents for advice and guidance, as well as for an exchange of confidences, feelings, worries, mistakes, opinions, hopes, and dreams— all of which are necessary to help them gain perspective on who they are. How to create the balance of being there and yet not being there for a child as well as for a partner can be difficult. As one fifteen-year-old girl who has a good relationship with her biological mother suggested: "It helps when you talk like girlfriends. When it's like parent and daughter, it doesn't work as well."[3] And as Dr. Jerry M. Lewis further explains, "The family has two main tasks: to preserve the sanity of the parents (or to help each parent's personality grow and mature) and to produce kids who can emotionally leave home, kids who can come to love someone else more than they love their parents."[4]

There is also a big difference between being a disciplined family, with established rules of morality and behavior, and being a permissive family, with an indulgent attitude that allows individuals to find out who they really are. The effective family is one

that is disciplined as well as permissive—capable of providing individuals with important "life guidelines" and teaching them to
become more responsible, and also willing to create opportunities that will enable individuals to relate to themselves, to one another, and to people outside the family. This fosters a willingness
in the parents to be able to let go and stand back, thus giving
each child the opportunity to solve his or her own problems and
to make his or her own decisions about fads, friends, fashions,
music, and so on. This same transitional formula can be also be
applied to partners as they affirm and support each other's need
to take responsibility for their own problem-solving and personal
development.

There is also a big difference between parents helping children
and each other in healthy ways and assisting in ways that perpetuate unhealthy situations detrimental to the development of the
individual. For example, the increasingly common phenomenon
of young adult children coming back to live with their parent or
parents can create an unhealthy situation that ignores the privacy
of all parties. As well, the parent or parents may find that their
identity is so tied in to fulfilling the role of parent that they do
not want their children to leave and to have to face the resulting
emptiness and ultimately the privacy that will give them space to
discover who they are.

To begin addressing this concern while children are still young,
parents need to encourage independence through the maturing
process. To deal with young adults who have not been given that
opportunity for independence while growing up, parents must
"serve notice that the young adult's home living can't go on forever. You must reassure the child that you are not rejecting him
but are helping to launch him."[5] In either scenario, the goal is not
to create a sudden emotional cutoff point but to gradually affirm
and support independence.

It is also important to give family members privacy so they can
feel a sense of confidentiality about issues that are important,
sensitive, or potentially embarrassing to them. Privacy invasions
can be as blatant as looking through a partner's desk drawers or

reading through a child's diary, and as subtle as sharing the confidences of one family member with others or joking about a family member's private issue. When these happen, the boundary line that shows respect for the individual is crossed, trust is impacted, and the ability of that person to resolve for himself or herself the private matter that was shared or discovered can be seriously hindered. Respecting privacy means not prying into the lives of other family members or their personal possessions unless there is an exceptionally good cause, such as strongly suspecting drug use, the need to investigate possible involvement in a criminal activity, or having to find a friend's telephone number in an emergency.

Finally, there is also a big difference between too much time spent apart from family members and time allowed for the solitude of each family member. Just because work, school, or other obligations have given family members a geographical distance from one another or, in some cases, a great deal of time spent out of one another's presence, it does not necessarily follow that family members have been given the space in which to enjoy solitude in the family home. Just as family members need personal space in which to put and keep things that are special to them, so too do family members need to be able to find space within the living environment in which to "get away" from everyone else for a short time.

While many family members do not have the luxury of having their own rooms, communal spaces such as dens, kitchens, or living rooms can be shared in ways that give necessary time to each individual, so he or she can read, listen to music, write letters, work on a puzzle, or simply do nothing. Such time alone gives family members the chance to resolve personal issues, rejuvenate themselves, and to restore a more positive outlook.

But it is not just children who need time for solitude. Adults as well—especially single parents who must spend large amounts of unrelieved time with their children—need "me time" because parents who cannot nurture themselves are certainly not going to be able to nurture a child effectively, nor will they be appropriate

role models for teaching their children about the balance between giving to others and taking for oneself.

Thus, respecting the privacy of individual family members
means allowing each person within the family time and space to
be a private person, which, in turn, nurtures individuality in ways
that allow each person to mature and grow in a fashion unique to
him or her.

Promoting Initiative and Independence

One of the most fascinating stories about children who were
raised to be independent self-starters is that of Bill and Julie
Brice, two seemingly ordinary kids who were raised by parents
who taught them early on that they could do anything they set
their minds to:

> When Bill was 19 and Julie 18, their father told them
> about an opportunity to gain some business experience by
> managing a yogurt shop near the college they were attend-
> ing . . . they sold some stock . . . and invested $10,000 to-
> ward purchasing the fledgling operation. Today "I Can't
> Believe It's Yogurt" includes more than 1000 franchises
> worldwide. Last year, total sales reached $85 million.[6]

Yet the story of how Bill and Julie got to where they are today
is not so unusual, nor is it too difficult for other families to replicate. Very simply, promoting initiative and independence in family members begins with one or two parents who have a good
level of self-esteem or who are working hard at feeling better
about themselves. It does not matter at what age the parents seek
to strengthen or develop this confidence in their own self-worth,
learn how to appreciate their own goodness, become capable of
recognizing their problems and do something about them, and
realize that their shortcomings are far outweighed by their positive qualities. What is most important is that the attitude of con-

fidence, security, and the ability to like oneself develops and becomes apparent to all family members.

The most familiar scenario in the past few decades that displays this drive for enhancing self-esteem has been the wife-mother who has for years sacrificed for the good of everyone else in her family and feels undervalued at home and who, when her children reach college age, decides to go back to school. Family members need to give one another such opportunities to help each of them develop skills such as decision-making and self-reliance, which can assist all members in meeting the challenges they face both inside and outside the home. These skills usually cannot be developed by watching hours of television, by never reading a book, or by seldom participating in outside activities. Such passive inactivity breeds short attention spans, little initiative, and dependence; for example, it becomes much easier for family members who are bored to play a computer game, mindlessly flip through television channels, or rent a movie rather than create excitement through participation in enjoyable activities or by using their own imaginations.

Everyone has a special interest, but finding that interest can be difficult when family members are not exposed to the many wonders and choices in the world or are not encouraged to broaden their horizons. As with self-esteem, adult family members can be role models who can show younger family members that while they may not enjoy everything, they will never discover what they do enjoy unless they try many things.

Practice in making decisions that can help to build self-reliance and foster personal decision-making can spring from simple options presented to family members such as "What would you like for breakfast?" or "Which coat would you like to wear?" and then can gradually evolve into the consideration of more complex choices, such as which after-school activities to become involved in or what job offer to accept. Such simple-to-complex decision-making can help to promote confidence in children as well as in adult family members, particularly those who prefer to put off decision-making or who allow others to make choices for them.

Initiative and independence are also promoted in families that encourage everyone to express his or her views. It is not necessary that all family members agree with one another; on the contrary, it is best that they learn to listen to and share divergent opinions in order to prepare for the diversity of the world outside the confines of the home. To this end, having more conversations with family members and truly listening to them, as discussed in the previous chapter, gives value to the family members. "Once a child believes his opinion has value," comments Dr. Lillian McLean Beard, a pediatrician and associate clinical professor at George Washington University School of Medicine, "he has a ticket to go further than one who feels it makes no difference what he thinks."[7]

Finally, family members become independent initiators not by always being handed things—even for their best efforts—but by learning how to work for what they want. The "ancient" quality of industriousness in children, once revered in families, has long since been replaced by generations of parents who want their children to have more than they did when they were growing up. So while parents who have worked hard to achieve the goal to make life better for their own children are certainly giving their children more than they ever had—money, cars, credit cards, clothes, and so on—what they are creating are children without ambition, who are not learning the value of achievement through hard work.

This does not necessarily mean that all family members ought to be put to work either outside or inside the home; the industriousness once revered in the past was, for the most part, forced upon children and enforced with inhumane practices. But when family members desire something, they need to learn its financial value (how much it costs and how it will affect the family budget or future allowances), the time commitment required (how many afternoons and nights during the week will be taken up), and the impact this may have on other family members (for example, a promise that was made to another family member may need to be broken, or a household responsibility may end up being neglected).

The Boy Scouts merit badge program has for years helped youngsters learn how to work, compete, and achieve in a unique initiative-independent reward system; to earn badges, the Scouts first explore different subjects, initiate a project based on a subject that interests them, and then follow this project through to completion with the guidance of their Scoutmaster. The sole material reward for all of their efforts is merely a patch of embroidered cloth, yet what they gain emotionally is a positive feeling about the efforts they have made in achieving their goal. A similar reward system can be created within families, with family members being given opportunities to earn such things as a chance to choose what to have for dinner or to use the bathroom first.

Ultimately, the goal in promoting initiative and independence in family members is to create active, motivated, self-confident self-starters. This initially happens through the affirmation and support of family members; it continues to happen outside the family through involvement in affirming, supportive communities created by individual family members.

Creating Individual Communities

Amanda Bearse, an actress on the prime-time television show "Married . . . With Children" who is also a lesbian and the mother of an adopted baby girl, once said that "If a child is born and raised in a home that is loving and nurturing, where there is complete truth about who we are, you can't give a child any greater place from which to fly."[8] But unless a child also has someone with whom to fly—unless that child has the opportunity to share important things about him or herself with others outside the family—such flying can become solo, isolating, and damaging to the development of self-expression.

Journeying alone in the world outside a family can hinder the development of self-expression because even though it is within a family that members often establish their own identity, it is outside that unit that people truly show themselves off as individu-als, who may be, in many ways, different from the rest of their family. In addition, a positive identity, or self-concept, evolves best with interactions with people outside the family—people with whom family members can identify and from whom they can differentiate themselves. This is particularly noticeable in chil-dren's development in adolescence, when adolescents naturally need to move away from their parents and become more depen-dent upon relationships with others, to see who they are and where they "fit in." They oftentimes feel more comfortable ex-ploring who they are with the help of nonrelated adults—teach-ers, group leaders, coaches, neighbors, and friends of the family—as well as with their friends. Peer identity is an important phase on the road to adulthood which, if denied to children, can take away valuable opportunities for socializing, experimentation, decision-making, and other growth-enhancing activities, thus making it harder for those individuals in adulthood to function well on their own and in group settings.

While some of the people who are included in the community a family member forms for himself or herself can seem to be "wrong" to other family members because they are from a dif-ferent class or ethnic group or dress and act differently or are "bad" influences (for example, having values contrary to the fam-ily's value system, such as the lack of a curfew on school nights), an important part of self-expression includes sometimes being drawn to others who are quite different from the family. Any per-son chosen to be part of a family member's community may be there for any number of reasons, but the most important is what can be learned from and through that person—a new form of music, a new way of communicating, a unique cultural form, a different taste in clothes, and so on.

As long as the results of any interactions with those outside the family are not destructive to the family members themselves, then the inclusion of those people in each family member's community should be encouraged. In fact, families that refrain from passing judgments about "outsiders" and seek instead to create a supportive, positive atmosphere that welcomes all of the friends of family members can promote the selection of people chosen not because they are symbols of rebellion against overly intrusive parents, but because they give family members positive support and guidance for who they are and who they may be becoming.

Because building a community outside the family is an essential step toward easing the sense of isolation each individual family member naturally experiences on his or her journey toward self-expression, such communities become particularly important to nontraditional, minority families whose members may or may not be like one another.

In the case of children with gay and lesbian parents, for example, homosexuality carries a stigma that can lower children's self-esteem, particularly when their sense of isolation is made more profound by the feeling that they are the only ones who have gay parents. Studies conducted on gay parents who are "out" and who provide their children with interactions with other gay and lesbian families report that the children experience a greater overall sense of well-being than those children of gay and lesbian parents who are "closeted" or who are "out" but maintain contacts solely with gays and lesbians who are not parents. As well, those children of gay and lesbian parents who join groups, camps, synagogues, or Sunday schools where there are other gay families establish their own identity as individuals in a supportive and affirming community much faster than those who do not.

In any household structure that differs from the "norm" or the "accepted" structure, it often becomes harder for family members to focus on a natural development of their self-expression. More often, the family members function as "advocates" for their particular lifestyle, spending a great deal of their time constantly dealing with the backlash toward their nontraditional family and having to explain and describe themselves to others. In the case of those who are adopted, being unable to answer their friends' questions about their family background or being forced in classroom assignments to trace family trees or the genetic origins of such things as their hair color can hinder self-expression because they learn that being so radically different can be a painful, humiliating, and difficult experience—one that can make them refrain from wanting to be different at all.

But family members who know they are "different" need to be taught to embrace their differences rather than feel they are stigmatized. So being able to grow within a culture—whether or not this is a culture shared with the parent or parents—deemphasizes the constant need to reexplain and reaffirm so self-expression can be given room in which to thrive. As well, exposure to such a community serves to show value in family members' "differences" in self-affirming, positive ways so that family members are more willing to be unique human beings.

To help to develop a sense of heritage, culture, or lifestyle in family members in ways that embrace their differences from others outside the family, contact with other people who share the same race, ethnic group, or lifestyle is important. As well, exposure to information through books, television, films, toys such as dolls, books, and museum exhibits is valuable. Assimilation of aspects of this information can be included in the family home—for example, in the language spoken, in traditions followed, or in the foods that are prepared. Finally, it is vital to ensure that there is always room for open and honest discussion in the home, for the goal is to make each family member proud of his or her background, heritage, or parental lifestyle so self-expression in its many forms can be heard.

Fostering Creative Self-Expression

"Creativity is a lot like being a clown," says Arina Isaacson, founder of the Clown School of San Francisco. "Both rely on being willing to unmask the truth and follow the thread of the moment." If you develop these skills, Isaacson promises, "you will be creative in whatever you do—whether it be making cookies, painting, or doing office work."[9] But too often families today have very little time to devote to being so creatively expressive—

to laugh and joke with one another, to play cards and board games at the kitchen table, to fly a kite or go on a picnic, to be spontaneous and noncompetitive, to pursue hobbies and favorite activities, to experience the joy in simply being alive, to be amused and entertained by the company of others, and so on.

When America was an agrarian society, there was a much slower pace to family life that allowed for time in which to have fun. Families sat on their front porches and conversed with others; children from different families made ice cream together; neighbors walked into town on summer evenings to enjoy band concerts. Up until the 1930s, Americans could usually find or create a balance between livelihood and leisure; when they worked, they worked hard, but when they played, they played hard. But the Depression forced families to concentrate once again on survival, the 1940s sent men off to war and women out of the homes to keep the country running, and the 1950s stressed material possessions and the passive creativity that could be experienced through watching television. The ensuing evolution into the computer revolution defeated any hopes of ever returning to a slower-paced, family-fun-based society and instead increased the pace of living and the pressure to succeed.

Adult family members today often experience a sense of urgency and hurry that seems to have no letup and allows very little time to simply sit back and relax. The resulting tension can create a supercharged atmosphere of stress in the home that makes having relaxed conversations impossible and transforms simple exchanges into verbal sparring matches that compound the level of stress. With the constant feeling of frustration that evolves from having too much to do in too little time and stressed-out families in which couples are constantly bickering or children are incessantly fighting, more often than not family members choose to retreat to the privacy of their own rooms or a space in the house or to retreat emotionally from others by passively sitting in front of the television—rather than seek creative and fun ways to ease frustrations.

It is not only adult family members who experience this overwhelming stress. Some children too have lost their ability to be joyful, playful, and spontaneous. They have lost the neighborhoods where they could once play stickball in the streets under the watchful eyes of adult family members and neighbors. They have been deprived of the joy of getting together with friends after school because they need transportation to and from the homes of their friends. Places where they could once safely hang out and laugh and joke together have been taken over by drug dealers or are part of gang turf. So play for children of the 1990s is far different from play for the children of the past:

> Our children, when they go out to recess, they don't know to play with each other. We have to teach them to throw a ball, play with other kids. Their neighborhoods are dangerous and their parents are afraid, so the minute they get in the house, they're in. [10]

Creative expression is the play and humor that family members need to experience on their own and with one another on a daily basis so they can divorce themselves from their work, school obligations, and other responsibilities in order to have the time and space in which to develop, through self-expression as well as interaction with others, their capacity for joy and happiness and their ability to use their imaginations. Some suggestions for doing this include:

- **Play at work rather than work at play.**

Because there is often very little free time in which families can be creatively spontaneous together or in which individuals can sit back and relax, to allow room for creative expression, too often families work too hard at satisfying the need to have fun rather than the desire to have fun. When time is set aside from the busy schedule to participate in a fun activity, more often than not a last-minute hitch—an unexpected visitor, for instance—or an unanticipated obligation—such as a relative's birthday or a work problem that needs to be solved—takes priority over honoring the promise made to have fun. What family members learn from such overscheduling or nonpriority scheduling is that, in either case, responsibility and work are sacred, and pleasure is expendable.

To get around this, it is important to use words like planning, executing, canceling, rescheduling, and postponing only for work-related situations—not for play activities. It is also a good idea to cut back on scheduled activities by attending one less meeting a week, signing up for one less lesson, and joining one less group.

Then allow something enjoyable to happen every couple of weeks or so by setting aside two days out of every fourteen—one for your personal time and one for a family outing. Encourage your family to join or form an informal group with other couples and/or their families that share similar interests, such as mountain climbing, train lore, sailing, and so on, so each family can take turns planning fun times in which to get together. Such things can make play more fun—and a lot less work!

- **Be a role model.**

When you are able to keep work and play in perspective, you as well as your family will learn to devote time to creating and pursuing joy, spontaneity, laughter, song, dance—anything and everything it takes to experience creative expression. Rather than "medicate our creative urges with passive entertainment—watching someone else do things on television instead of doing them ourselves; voraciously reading everything we can get our hands on rather than writing our own work,"[11] we should be role models who can show family members an adventurous spirit and a motivated, creative self.

People become better parents not just by watching television, but by being more creative in their own lives. One way to start being such a role model is to make a list of at least a dozen things you would like to do but that you have not allowed yourself to do—and then do each of them. Go for a walk on a new path around the neighborhood or eat at an ethnic restaurant you have never been to before. Take up a musical instrument. Sign up for a college course. Go to the movies alone. By fostering your own creative expression, you let all family members see that they too can foster their own.

• **Become creative as a family.**

Would you describe your family as more work-obsessed or play-crazy? If your family is more work-obsessed, then the message given to each family member is that it is far more important to be *doing* something than it is to be *enjoying* something.

Think back to the last time your family did something together. Most likely it was to satisfy an obligation (such as attending the wedding of another family member) or to perform a task (such as cleaning out the basement) rather than to satisfy a desire (such as going to the beach). Whether or not you have children, you and your partner can satisfy obligations in fun-filled ways (such as by creating a "secret" code word that only your family members know and that you can use with them to make being at the obligation more fun). You can also make necessary group work fun,

> whether the job is an annual cleanup or a painting or gardening spree. Members work as a unit, laughing and playing as they work—the same method used in the barn raisings or quilting bees of old.[12]

Too, your family can plan fun times together in ways that do not require a great deal of scheduling, effort, or expense. "We don't have the money to have fun" is a much-overused refrain that is really an excuse employed by family members so they do not have to use their imagination and come up with nonexpensive pastimes the family can enjoy together:

> Picnics, ball games, pot lucks, hikes, a day in the mountains or at the beach—all of these are inexpensive, often requiring only transportation. . . . Some families are beginning

to cluster together for such simple pleasures as sing-alongs, caroling, square dancing, play readings, volleyball, crafts and cooking projects, and the like.[13]

When a family collectively gives itself the opportunity to share creative expression through any number of activities, both planned and spontaneous, it allows family members to expect play times, to look forward to them, and to enjoy them.

- **Allow space and time to wonder.**

For the most part, education imparts knowledge, but it neglects to teach the wonder of such knowledge. The irony of this statement is that everyone begins life as a natural scientist, eager to investigate the world and to explore all possibilities, yet education stresses that answers are only right or wrong; there are no maybes or what-ifs or why-nots. Sadly, most "I don't know" responses are not followed by "But let's find out together."

Creative expression is not so much about finding answers to questions as it is about simply posing the questions—or, in the case of younger family members, allowing them the space and time in which to think about and frame their questions. Mary Budd Rowe, a professor of science education at Stanford University and a science advisor for two PBS children's programs, suggests several ways of encouraging rather than suppressing a child's need for creative expression. Listen to a child's questions about the world around him or her, from "What makes tears?" to "Where do little spiders get the stuff to make their webs?" Resist the impulse to respond quickly if you know the answer, so that your knowledge does not stifle a potentially interesting discussion. Give the child time to think in order to encourage independent and creative thinking; sometimes remaining silent for a few seconds will reveal some fascinating and exciting stream-of-consciousness thinking on the part of the child.

Show a child a fact rather than tell the fact; for example, ask children to look at their fingertips through a magnifying glass so they'll understand why you want them to wash before dinner.

And use everyday activities to provide fascinating answers to questions: build a go-cart to demonstrate how design affects speed, or plant flowers to witness the effect of water and sunlight. Creative expression can be profoundly and positively influenced by such things.[14]

Caring to spend enjoyable and fun time with yourself, with your family members, and with the freedom to question and explore the world around you gives everyone the opportunity to embrace all possibilities and to chase his or her dreams—dreams that family members are equally entitled to realize, no matter what their gender.

Challenging Traditional Gender Roles

In America's earliest days, when family functions were centered around economics and survival, it was not unusual for males and females to share equally in all of the household chores. But as men gained more political, economic, and social power, women and girls were relegated to what is now known as their "traditional" gender roles: wives, mothers, nurses, teachers, nurturers, cooks, cleaners, and household managers. Years ago, such traditional gender roles severely restricted women outside the home but, as well, restricted the roles men could have inside the home, particularly in raising their children.

While in many ways women have challenged their traditional gender roles, in many ways they are still viewed as the primary caretakers of both their partners and their children, even though they have, out of choice as well as out of necessity, become economic providers. On average, for example, "the working mother spends 44 hours at work *and* 31 hours on family responsibilities per week—in effect holding almost two full-time jobs. . . . The average working father spends 47 hours at the office—and only 15 hours on family matters."[15] What this fact reveals is that men have much more free time in which to creatively express themselves than women do, which deprives children of two effective role models they can observe and learn from as they develop their own creative expression.

The desire to challenge traditional gender roles and the flexibility required to change such roles mean that all family members should be able to see themselves and other family members less as masculine or feminine and more as *both* masculine *and* feminine. Even though society still is not embracing the concept of stay-at-home daddies and career-building mommies, allowing for the evolution of roles within a family encourages all family members to become more creatively expressive as human beings as they challenge their own concepts of who they are, as defined (as well as not defined) by their gender. Thus, adults as well as children can learn that they can be "assertive, ambitious, and self-confident—traditionally masculine qualities—*and* . . . emotionally attuned, interested in interpersonal relationships, and sensitive to other people's rights and needs—traditionally feminine qualities."[16]

When family members are allowed to express themselves in ways that come from desire rather than definition, they can discover much more about themselves. Decisions become much more personal and purposeful—the father cooks as the son learns ballet; the mother cleans gutters, and the daughter takes up wrestling—rather than directed by societal constraints or "girls don't/boys don't" judgments that suppress individual taste and selection.

And too the more proud parents can become with their own growth and accomplishments in so-called nontraditional spheres, the happier they can become as individuals and the more they can discover about themselves. One father notes, "My cooking isn't bad, I'm a great emoter, encourager, and cheerleader. And my daughter comes to me for advice and support about sex, romance, and even gynecological matters."[17] This does not mean that all mothers now need to take their sons fishing every weekend, and all fathers have to go out and buy their daughters tampons. But what it does mean is that parents need to determine ways in which they limit themselves as human beings not out of personal choice but because of gender stereotyping. Also, women need to try to do more "guy stuff," and men need to do more "women's work" in order to support and affirm each other in their relationship as well as in their roles as mothers and fathers. When this happens, fathers often discover that nurturing their children nurtures something within themselves too, while mothers are often pleasantly pleased at the mechanical and financial skills they find they possess.

Thus, breaking out of traditional gender roles can provide a wonderful, exciting, and challenging journey for each parent as well as display for children capable, confident, and creatively expressive role models who convey that what is most important is expressing yourself in ways that are vital to who you are as an individual human being. When a family is made up of such unique individuals who can look to themselves for affirmation and support, rather than depend upon others to give them such things, the family as a whole becomes more emotionally—and soulfully—complete.

NOTES

1. Curran, Dolores. *Traits of a Healthy Family.* HarperSanFrancisco, San Francisco, 1983, p. 62.
2. Walsh, David. *Selling Out America's Children: How America Puts Profits Before Values—and What Parents Can Do.* Deaconess Press, Minneapolis, 1994, p. 89.
3. Schwartz, Pepper. "The Silent Family: Together, But Apart," *New York Times,* February 16, 1995.
4. Curran, p. 231.
5. *Ibid.,* p. 242.
6. Hendryx, William M. "Make Your Child a Self-Starter," *Reader's Digest,* June 1995.
7. *Ibid.*
8. Gallagher, John. "Gay . . . with children," *The Advocate,* May 30, 1995.
9. Hudson, Gail E. "Art for the Soul's Sake," *New Age Journal,* January/February 1995.
10. Lakshmanan, Indira A. R. "Windows on children's worlds," *Boston Globe,* June 5, 1995.
11. Kallen, Ben. "Freeing Your Inner Artist," *New Age Journal,* January/February 1995.
12. Curran, p. 130.
13. *Ibid.*
14. Rowe, Mary Budd. "Teach Your Child to Wonder," *Reader's Digest,* February 1995.
15. Baridon, Andrea. *Working Together: The New Rules and Realities for Managing Men and Women at Work.* McGraw Hill, New York (page unknown; quoted in *Bottom Line Personal,* Boardroom Reports, Inc. April 1, 1995).
16. Blau, Melinda. *Families Apart: Ten Keys to Successful Co-Parenting.* The Berkley Publishing Group, New York, 1993, p. 236.
17. *Ibid.,* p. 237.

CHAPTER 7

⋙

Fostering "The Three Rs": Responsibility, Respect, and Right and Wrong

When things go wrong in a society, the immediate reaction is often to look at families and blame them for the particularly "bad" state of affairs. There are many who believe that the family is merely a microcosm that reflects the nature of the world and thus, in this reflection, seems to support current trends and serious problems. There are others who adhere to the philosophy that "As the family goes, so goes the world." There are still others who believe that the very fabric of society is being torn apart because most of today's families have become dysfunctional in some way.

Those who believe that the direction a family takes greatly influences the course society follows neglect to pay attention to the distinction between the behavior of an individual or a small group of individuals, such as a family, and the behavior of a much larger group, such as society. The distinction is that an individual's behaviors and actions can be more readily observed and assessed in the context of a small group. This creates the potential to influence future occurrences of such behaviors and actions and to enable individuals to become more responsible to themselves and others. In a larger setting, such as society, this dynamic is absent:

For instance, if I steal money from you, I may be able to directly observe and empathize with the impact of my actions on a personal level. If I steal money from a large financial institution, on the other hand, I need not be aware of the impact on any individual. . . .

This dynamic explains how individuals often act in ways as part of a large group that they never would alone. The sense of responsibility gets weaker as the group gets larger. . . . Consequently, large groups sometimes act in ways that individuals within the group might find morally objectionable in another setting.[1]

So those who believe that the family is merely a microcosm that reflects the nature of the world and supports current trends and serious problems need to recognize the dichotomy between societal and parental messages. Families simply do not tell their members, "Please go out and buy a gun so you can shoot someone," "Your mother and I would like you to start snorting cocaine," "I support your decision not to look for work so you can hang out on the street corner with your buddies and drink all day," or "There's no reason why you shouldn't have unprotected sex in junior high school." Parents, educators, religious leaders, and many others today are, for the most part, trying to pass on good, sound, moral, responsible, respectful values to children and, as well, encouraging couples to be positive role models for each other and their children.

Their voices are often not heard, however, above the "thunderous, anonymous voices of our society [that] include television, radio, print media, computers and video games."[2]—all of which promote values that in the name of profit deemphasize right and wrong. Violence, for example, is something families are trying to teach their members is wrong, as they stress cooperation and nonviolent conflict resolution to work through disagreement, discord, and disconnection. But society is actually promoting violent behavior and targeting it not only to adults, but also to children through a multitude of media. Yet violent entertainment is only one facet of the violence in today's society. A 1993 survey of sixteen thousand students in grades nine through twelve re-

vealed that violence in schools had become a major problem for
teenagers:

- 11.8 percent of those surveyed carried weapons on cam-
  pus in the previous month.
- 24 percent said they were offered, sold, or given an illegal
  drug in school in the previous year.
- 16.2 percent said they had been in a fight at school in the
  previous year.
- 7.3 percent were threatened or injured with a weapon
  while at school.
- 4.4 percent of students skipped school at least one day in
  the previous month because they felt unsafe.[3]

Thus, it can be seen that the theory of the family making
today's society immoral or in decline is false. The reality is that,
for the most part, family members are not engaging in or perpetuating society's problems. The majority of family members are
receiving instruction in sound moral values and responsible and
respectful behavior. The majority of family members are doing
their best to build "the nest in which soul is born, nurtured, and
released into life."[4] And, for the most part, family members are
doing this at a time when their teachings are not reinforced by society and the louder, more enticing voices of society often over-
power theirs.

In former generations, the voices of the extended family, village, or tribe would reinforce that of the parents in ways that preserved rather than destroyed or contradicted their teachings. But
today the voice of society often contradicts and undermines the
messages of parents. This can overwhelm families to such an extent that they either willingly or begrudgingly compromise the
notions of right and wrong they wish to impart to their members
or give over the basic tasks of promoting responsibility and teaching respect to schools, churches, coaches, organizations, and institutions.

To care for the soul of the family, it is necessary to shift fostering "The Three Rs"—responsibility, respect, and right and wrong—back to families so they can establish and experience happiness and normalcy together while still functioning in the midst of the reality of a sometimes crazy, abusive, and violent society.

Teaching and Practicing Responsibility

Responsibility depends upon the development and integration of two components: responsibility to oneself, and responsibility toward others. Responsibility to others translates into family members being sensitive to the feelings, moods, and attitudes of other family members (such as when a parent is too tired to cook dinner or when a partner loses a job) as well as being aware of the things that are important to others (such as a test, a prom date, a competitive event, and so on). This enables family members to be tuned into the feelings of others and to be there to provide sympathy, support, nurturing, praise, and celebration.

Family members who have developed this sense of responsibility to others are also able to recognize the role they play in ensuring a reasonably harmonious household. They know that this means that no matter what is going on for them, they may or may not choose to share it with family members but they ought never to allow what is going on for them to dominate other family members or to negatively shift the family's mood or attitude. In a family where one child is allowed to whine and complain throughout a meal or where a parent's angry moods make the entire family on edge, family members do not learn how to be responsible to others, for allowing such behaviors means condoning irresponsible, insensitive selfishness and self-centeredness.

Yet in a family where the whining, complaining child is told to go to his or her room until he or she can return to the dinner table with improved behavior or where the angry parent is encouraged to set aside a "cooling off" space in which to work through the intensity of his or her feelings without impacting on the rest of the family's "turf," family members learn that their behaviors can affect others and that they need to be more responsibly sensitive to those around them. Developing this healthy sense of responsibility toward other family members contributes to family harmony, promotes compromise and reconciliation, and fosters individual growth and independence. This facet of responsibility usually evolves as individual family members learn first how to be responsible to themselves.

Responsibility to oneself—or the belief in one's own abilities—is directly linked to self-esteem. First and foremost, the primary value of developing responsibility in family members is not in benefiting the family, but in benefiting the individual. Requiring family members to help in family chores as well as in their own caretaking, the organization of which can sometimes be more time consuming than a family member simply going ahead and taking care of a task such as baking a cake or cleaning out the garage, can make each individual feel as if they are a valued, contributing member of the family unit. As well, the more responsible a family member can be to himself or herself, the more confident and competent that individual can feel.

Some people might say that today the sense of responsibility exhibited by younger family members is developed out of necessity rather than choice and that far too many demands are being made because of the need for two working parents who have much less time to perform household duties. But oftentimes it is *because* a full-time parent or parents cannot be at home that children are given the opportunity to learn to do the things they need to or ought to do for themselves. As long as family members are given reasonable responsibilities, where the demands are not too high and the balance between responsible time and leisure or play time is still maintained; as long as family members learn responsibility not by being angrily coerced but from being treated with respect and courtesy; and as long as achievement of the responsibilities, even if they fall short of perfection, is recognized through praise, appreciation, commendation, or even a reward, then family members will often display a willingness to become responsible and essential parts of the family. Many children today are even becoming as responsible as their counterparts from years ago, when the family function was based on economic survival; more teens have part-time jobs and use the money they earn not only for themselves, but also for the household. This, in turn, enhances how they feel about themselves.

Simply understanding that a relationship between responsibility and self-esteem exists, however, is not enough; a family needs to be able to develop this relationship actively, as in the following ways:

- **Have family members practice responsibility every day.**

Whether a family member is three or four years old or thirty-four years old, doing chores and performing household duties without pay or reward ought to become part of everyday life. There is simply no good reason why working mothers and fathers should work as hard inside the home as they do outside the home, no matter what the expectations or demands placed upon them, no matter how strong their feelings of guilt are, and no matter how much they want their child or children to have "a good life." Such self-sacrifice does not teach or display responsibility; rather, it stifles the development in family members of the sense of self-respect that comes from assuming responsibilities for themselves. From having younger family members pick up their toys to having older family members pick up food for dinner, such responsibilities can include any aspect of household duties that helps the individual as well as the family as a whole.

- **Allow family members to experience independence.**

Whenever possible, try not to solve problems that individuals can solve or ought to be able to solve on their own, such as finding things to do after school or work, seeking out or creating projects that will hold interest, making friends, and resolving conflicts. Instead, provide adequate support and guidance that encourages family members to stand on their own two feet. Only intervene when struggles go beyond the point of frustration, for those who are "constantly rescued from their frustrations may never develop the ability to persevere in the face of it."[5]

As well, nurture opportunities that support the growth of imagination, creativity, and resourcefulness. This enables family members to explore their capacity for achievement so they can learn how to reach their potential in any undertaking. One father, who allowed his son access to tools and lumber and had to fight the urge to step in and take over the boy's woodworking project, remarked, "My son was ten feet high when he finished that bird house. He worked on it three days. It was crooked as hell and expensive. But it was his."[6]

- **Provide a sense of challenge.**

Rather than question how much responsibility is enough, not enough, or too little, ask instead what opportunities family members can be given that will provide them with a sense of challenge. This sense of challenge ought not to come in the form of achieving perfection or attaining some form of success, but in teaching family members that succeeding is less important than trying— and that what is *most* important is trying and sometimes failing, and then trying again.

Entrepreneur and public speaker Wilson Harrell remembers the challenge his father gave him that taught him responsibility when he was eleven years old. At that time, his father made him a cotton buyer at his gin. Wilson's job was to cut a bale, pull out a wad, examine the sample, identify the grade, and set the price. The first farmer who heard the price young Wilson had set for his cotton turned to Wilson's father and said that he had worked too hard to have his price determined by a boy. "His grade stands," Wilson's father answered and walked away. Wilson recalls that

> over the years my father never publicly changed my grade. However, when we were alone, he'd check my work. If I'd undergraded (and paid too little), I'd have to go tell the farmer I'd made a mistake and pay him the difference. If I'd

overgraded, my father wouldn't say a word—he'd just look at me. . . .

I'm not sure my father knew anything about entrepreneurship, but he understood an awful lot about making a man out of a boy. He gave me responsibility and then backed my hand.[7]

• **Be a positive role model.**

The most significant way family members can influence the development of one another's sense of responsibility is to model the behavior that is expected or desired of one another.

Irresponsibility can breed irresponsibility; the irresponsible words and actions of even one family member can affect the ability of all members to be responsible and to take responsibility for themselves. Thus, the parent who is always tardy for work ought not be surprised with a child who is always tardy to school; the father who routinely beats or berates his wife ought not be surprised when his daughter marries an abusive or violent man; the older sibling who does the chores and "covers up" the mistakes and misbehaviors of a younger sibling ought not be surprised to find that the younger sibling is still looking for protection and help in adulthood.

Yet just as one irresponsible family member can affect other family members in negative ways, one super-responsible family member can do an equal amount of damage. This is true of a parent who constantly "serves" a partner or the children. Assuming the responsibilities of other family members actually does them a disservice, for it paralyzes their desire to learn to do for themselves, as well as blinds their perception of their own capabilities.

As a role model, fostering responsibility in family members in many ways involves making appropriate decisions about when to assume activities and when to delegate them:

One of my children once wrote "Dust me" on top of the TV set and it was a signal that he was old enough to take on the responsibility for dusting the living room after that. Another time, one of ours in junior high became angry over a dental appointment I had scheduled at an inconvenient time. Since then, he schedules his own appointments. It's now his responsibility to make sure I'm available to drive him, not mine to make sure he keeps the day clear.

Sure, there are times we all slip up. . . . But the day-to-day responsibilities must be their own or they will never grow up into responsible adults. Our real responsibility as parents is to offer them the opportunity to grow in responsibility, not assume their responsibilities because they are our children.[8]

Parents who deny the right of their children to learn how to do for themselves and others, as well as a partner who assumes the responsibilities of the other partner, are not only damaging the other person's self-image, but also inhibiting the formation of a high level of self-esteem. People feel good about themselves not when others are doing for them, but when they can do for themselves. Unless a healthy sense of responsibility can be exhibited for family members—one that provides an equal balance of give and take as well as one that sets appropriate boundaries—growing into a responsible person can be difficult and painful. Sometimes irresponsible children or an irresponsible adult are given the opportunity to develop a sense of responsibility outside the family, through a teacher, mentor, boss, therapist, drill sergeant, or responsible partner, but more often than not those family members who are not given an opportunity within the family to develop their own sense of responsibility remain immature throughout childhood, dependent upon the caretaking of others throughout adolescence, and needy in adulthood, constantly searching for someone to "mother" them or for someone or something to blame (the government, a boss, and so on) when they do not get this mothering.

In effect, family members *owe* it to one another to understand that certain boundaries need to be established to distinguish "this is your responsibility" from "this is my responsibility." As well, responsible role modeling involves sharing in household duties and fulfilling personal obligations within the family in equal ways, no matter the gender. This means that in traditional families, mothers need to let go of some of the child care and household duties and pick up some of the financial responsibilities, and fathers need to let go of some of the breadwinning responsibilities and assume more household and child care duties. In the past, it was not unusual for a father to brag that he had never changed his child's diaper; today's responsible dads are often proud to admit that they have changed hundreds of diapers, cooked countless meals, tucked in their children night after night, read and reread bedtime stories, and helped their wives keep the house neat and tidy.

Family members who see active involvement, participation, nurturing, and support between their parents are able to observe how each contributes to the other's self-esteem through co-responsibility.

• **Expect family members to live with the consequences of their irresponsibility.**

Even the most loving and nurturing family members who, for all good intentions, try to remove the unpleasant effects of irresponsible actions from the lives of other family members do nothing to foster more responsible behavior in those they are trying to protect. Rather, they perpetuate irresponsible behavior by shielding family members from the effects of their irresponsible actions. Allowing family members to grow up without making even the simplest amends for their irresponsible actions—for example, paying a library fine for an overdue book, explaining to a teacher why homework was late, or apologizing to a newspaper route customer for late delivery—blinds them to the differences between responsibility and irresponsibility and, in so doing, protects them from the effects of their bad judgment, their lack of discipline or commitment, their neglect of rules, and their mistakes. Nothing is learned from such protection, and their blindness keeps them in the dark as they reach adulthood and oftentimes become irresponsible adults.

But a family that expects its members to live with the consequences of irresponsibility forces them to focus on responsible behavior and, with this expectation, creates learning situations in which irresponsible actions are rarely repeated.

While each of the two parts of responsibility—responsibility to oneself and responsibility to others—can exist without the other, the most responsible individuals are those who can be responsible to themselves *and* to others.

Being Respectful

There is a pressing need for developing respect in *all* families—both nontraditional and traditional—for any family is made up of individuals who have their own personalities, interests, behaviors, feelings, talents, and other differences that make them unique. Individuality is prized in a respectful family, yet frowned upon in a family that values conformity. Those families that devalue individuality do not teach respect; members who are "different" become the "black sheep" of the family—the outcasts, the rejected, the disowned, the embarrassments, and the "problems." Families that crave such conformity reject diversity and, in so doing, undermine the development of self-respect. As well, they lose out on the enriching experience the diversity of individuals and their interests can bring to a family. "We're so lucky," said a mother at a family reunion, "because we get to be part of a lot of different things like soccer, drama, and jazz band. If all of us were alike, think what we'd be missing."[9]

Although many families, in their desire to promote family unity and family pride, might like to consider themselves members of the same team, who wear the same uniforms and who share the same common purpose, a quick glance at any team on any field or in any arena reveals a common purpose and the same uniform, but a variety of differences in individual team members. The same holds true for every family; respect has many faces, and that means all the individual family members need to be respected. If such individuality is not respected in a family early on, then chances are family members will grow resentful and rebellious at all the pressures and expectations placed upon them to be like other family members. They will be confused, insecure, and depressed because their individual values are in conflict with the values of those who provide them with love and nurturing. Worse, they will become and then remain unhappy, disenchanted, and disinterested in the life they are living—a life filled with activities, a career, a home, and a spouse that may have all been chosen in order to conform to the desires of others. As hard as it may be for family members to refrain from "enforcing compliance" with activities, interests, career paths, and beliefs that may have long been part of family tradition or that may have gone into creating the cornerstone of the family's foundation, the development of respect means allowing each family member to be himself or herself—even if that means he or she must be at odds with the family as a whole.

So what happens in a family of musicians when one of the family members expresses an interest in sports? How should a parent deal with a child who wants to pierce a body part? What happens when the behavior of one family member clashes with the behavior of the rest of the family? Accommodating different personal styles and individual desires within a family can be, in the best of circumstances, a minor annoyance and, in the worst-case scenarios, an ongoing clash that disrupts the harmony of family living. Yet in order to teach family members respect, differences of opinion, individual styles, diverse interests, and differing behavior styles need to be tolerated—to some degree. For example, the family member who usually takes some time to wake up in the morning does not have to be talkative at the breakfast table; on the other hand, grumpiness directed at other family members probably would not be tolerated. Likewise, the family member who likes to sleep in on weekends can be given a little extra time in bed on the Saturday when the family is leaving on a vacation, but should not be allowed to keep the family waiting.

Inclinations toward areas of interest outside those of the majority of the family, wearing fashions that do not conform, making second career choices that stress job satisfaction rather than success, and a multitude of other personal preferences are just some of the choices that are a normal part of the growth process, as well as indicators of the thoughts, attitudes, and behaviors of individual family members. A family that has a respectful soul sees these differences as valuable parts of the whole unique family unit rather than as shameful, traumatic traits that undermine the family unit.

Respect is not an innate or automatic outcome of living together with others under one roof, where time, space, food, and a multitude of other things must be shared, because respect is not about sharing. Rather, respect is about embracing individual differences, no matter what those differences may be. As well, respect is not just about how family members treat one another, but also about how they treat others outside the family. Families either teach self-respect and respect for others, or they do not. For multicultural families, single-parent families, families with a gay or lesbian parent or parents, and families in which the two parents are from different cultures, races, or religious backgrounds, respecting the family's own differences from the majority of the population can provide a solid foundation for embracing the differences in all others—or it cannot. It is not enough for family members to be tolerant of the differences among themselves; they need to be tolerant of all racial, religious, cultural, and lifestyle differences.

The family needs to teach its members to accord respect to all groups, not just to specifically approved ones and not just to the ones that are most like the family. The family does this when adults model appropriate behavior toward other minority groups even when they may not approve of the beliefs, attitudes, or lifestyles of that group. A family can teach tolerance of gay men and lesbians, for example, even if they disapprove of elements of the homosexual lifestyle. The family does this when its members are discouraged from using derogatory terms when referring to gay men or lesbians, when its members do not promote discrimination against gay men or lesbians on the job or in the neighborhood, and by wholeheartedly condemning those who would use threats and violence against gay men and lesbians.

Teaching respect for all individuals, regardless of how they differ from one another—in visible as well as in invisible ways—provides a sound basis for being respectful of others.

Recognizing Right from Wrong

Not too long ago, two young boys were observed throwing rocks onto the Kennedy Expressway in the Albany Park section of Chicago. One of the rocks hit a truck and could have killed the driver and his passenger. When the truck driver had safely pulled his vehicle to the side of the road, he chased the boys on foot until he caught up with one of them—a ten-year-old. He held him until the boy gave the driver his name and address and the name and address of his companion—a thirteen-year-old.

Minutes later, as the truck driver was helping a responding police officer fill out her report, the ten-year-old returned to the scene accompanied by an angry adult male. This man, who happened to be the boy's father, told the driver that he was going to sue him for grabbing his boy's arm. The police officer was astounded:

> "You want your son doing that to people?" Officer Peggy asked. "He admitted he threw the rocks."
> And the father said: "Well, my son didn't know what he was doing. He's an innocent victim, and he says he didn't do it. Besides, nobody read him his rights."
> "So I read the kid his rights," Officer Peggy said. "The first time I ever did that for a ten-year-old . . . the father . . . carried on about how he was not only suing the driver for as-

saulting his kid, he was suing the city for false arrest, he was suing the police and just about everybody else. When a youth officer and I told him that if he wouldn't pay the truck damages, he'd have to go to court, he said he'd sue the court too.

"It was one of the worst things I've seen in all my years on the force. If parents don't teach right from wrong, who's going to do it?"[10]

This, unfortunately, is not an isolated case. Families today are raising children in a culture that is beginning to question its own morality. It is a culture that is wallowing in graphic sexual images and violence, in which "heroes" maim and murder, rape and ruin, pillage and plunder, use and abuse. It is a culture in which musical lyrics trumpet and encourage such behaviors, in which toys, games, and play activities replicate the behaviors children see on movie and television screens and hear on their radios and headphones. It is an in-your-face culture that is proud to offend and continually hones its sharp edges, vigilantly searching for the next way it can stun and shock the masses. Is it any wonder, then, that the friends of a fifteen-year-old boy who was arraigned for murder in Cambridge, Massachusetts, cried not for his victim but for the incredibly high bail that had been set for him? They sobbed and told reporters that they did not understand "what the big deal was all about" and that "people die every day."[11]

But it is not just the young who are clearly becoming more and more impacted by the deranged events in their culture. Witness the large number of adults who lined a Los Angeles freeway and cheered on the prime suspect in two brutal murders, as he led authorities on a slow-speed chase. Or the amateur videotape that showed adults who were hired to fulfill positions of trusted authority—trained to protect and uphold moral values—beat a black man senseless. Every day, the media shows that adults riot. Adults kill. Adults rape. Adults abuse. And adults create some very graphic sexual and violent material and then offer it like candy to children.

Has today's world become an "X-rated" world, one in which, as William Kilpatrick, education professor at Boston College opines, "we are raising . . . a nation of 'moral illiterates' "?[12] Has it become an amoral world, one that cannot distinguish between what is right and wrong? The answer to both questions is a resounding yes. But is it fair to blame the overall decline in moral maturation—the ability of society's members to distinguish right from wrong—on an X-rated or amoral world?

Clearly, modern culture is showing that families are coming up short on moral instruction. This is not to say that parents are to blame for the current state of today's society. The state of today's American society, like the state of every society that has preceded it in this country, has its good and its bad influences. Take, for example, the state of society during the time of Prohibition, which promoted bootlegging, extolled more relaxed sexual mores, glorified the rise in organized crime, and made heroes out of gangsters like Al Capone. To think that the government or any form of government censorship or regulation, required record labeling, a more delineated movie rating system, or any act of voluntary self-restraint on the part of the entertainment industry could make society as a whole more moral as well as create an environment in which families could finally "reach" their kids is not confronting the problem.

Families today cannot be like the father of the ten-year-old boy who would prefer to pass off the responsibility of his child's immoral behavior to others, to sue everyone else rather than let his child know in no uncertain terms that what he did was wrong, that such behavior will not be tolerated again, that he needs to apologize to the truck driver and the police officer, that it is his responsibility to earn the money to compensate the truck driver for damages, and that, further, he will be punished for what he did. *This type of moral instruction must rest with the parents.*

Although cultural value messages have always impacted upon families—there have always been negative, evil, law-breaking, or immoral forces at work in society—it has been (and always should be) the family's obligation to instruct its members in standards of

right and wrong and to model for them acceptable and unacceptable behaviors. A child's parent or parents, or other responsible family members, ought to be the earliest and longest
tenured teachers that child has. Even though some of the first
lessons a family member might learn will run contrary to messages that family member receives in school, from his or her
peers, through watching television, or by listening to music, the
need for parental involvement in establishing, and then helping
family members to maintain, moral values has never been greater.
For as long as society continues to extol selfishness and cutthroat
competition as well as to glorify instant gratification, violence,
and a "win-at-all-costs" attitude, moral messages of discipline and
self-restraint need to be continually promoted by family members.

Yet this can be difficult to do today, when parental absence
from the lives of children has a profound psychosocial as well as
moral impact. With more and more time to themselves, children
are making their own decisions with very little adult input; being
baby-sat by television, one of the great promoters of immoral behavior; engaging in sexual activity during times when they are on
their own; and either living in constant fear in crime-ridden
neighborhoods or eventually joining in the action on the streets.
But even though this has had an impact that may lead children,
out of boredom and isolation, to experiment with or do things
they might not normally do if a parent or parents were home:

> The solution, however, is not to return to the days where
> Dad went off to work and Mom looked after the children.
> Even if that were possible in today's economy, it would not
> be advisable. The solutions require joint participation in-
> volving both parents in a two-parent home, and for that
> matter, the extended community as well.[13]

Even though today's parents may have much less time to volunteer for their children's activities or to be involved in their
schools, through the option of sharing responsibilities with other

parents, today's parents are able to maintain either a direct or indirect contact with their children, as well as to establish contact with another parent or parents so parenting styles and experiences can be shared. And, in this way, younger family members are able to receive the guidance and support necessary to the formation and ongoing strengthening of their moral values.

There are other solutions as well that families can use to provide instruction in moral values that can help family members learn to recognize right from wrong. Clear and specific guidelines need to be taught about what is right and wrong outside the home as well as inside (for example, for Orthodox Jews, not eating bacon or ham) and then enforced, even when such guidelines may be at odds with society. Family members need to be held responsible for their own moral behavior; excuses, rationalizations, blaming, and other similar responses should not be allowed to deflect an individual from taking responsibility for his or her inappropriate or unacceptable behavior. Family members need to be taught the difference between good and bad motives; for example, the dog should not be punished for accidentally knocking over a lamp while playing but a child can take responsibility for pushing a lamp off a table in anger.

Finally, children cannot be expected to be moral without help. Ignoring drug use or sexual activity teaches a child that such things may be okay. Dismissing or belittling a child's problems or concerns, which may be related to a decision about right and wrong (such as whether to remain the only virgin in a peer group) shows little support, compassion, or desire to engage in a dialogue that could promote moral behavior. And not taking the time to monitor a child's environment or the people with whom he or she hangs out can place a child's moral values in jeopardy through interactions with a "wrong" crowd.

To improve such moral instruction for family members, specific values need to be given and then continually reinforced. As well, reasons for moral rules need to be shared. Support for such rules can be provided by facts, such as information on the dangers of cigarette smoking for a no smoking rule. To build empathy and create compassion, ask family members to consider how they would feel if they had been on the receiving end of an inappropriate action. Or encourage family members to "check in" on the feelings of someone who has been affected by an inappropriate action in order to become more empathetic and compassionate in the future. Recognize that guilt can play a valuable role in cultivating the ability to learn right and wrong. Because guilt can be a nagging voice of conscience, some of the most valuable and enduring lessons in moral behavior are ones in which the child is left to "live with" a situation (such as telling a lie or stealing money from a sibling's piggy bank) in the hopes that guilt can make an effective impact.

While these suggestions—and countless others—can aid parents in helping family members of all ages learn to recognize right from wrong so their thoughts and behaviors can reflect a moral upbringing, perhaps the most effective teaching tool for instruction in moral behavior is discipline. Members of older generations know all too well how effective authoritarian parents were in ensuring instruction in what was right and what was wrong. Just the simple statement "Wait till your father gets home" was enough to strike terror into the hearts of children who had misbehaved. Sometimes the father used physical punishment, but more often than not the punishment came in the form of more household responsibilities, no dessert after dinner for a week, the loss of the coveted weekly allowance, being grounded for a weekend, or being sent to one's room, which was as bad as being locked in a jail cell, because there was no television or computer for amusement and no compact disc player and large CD collection to listen to—just a bed, a desk, and some books.

This does not mean that any child ought to be beaten or punished whenever he or she does something morally wrong; the most effective disciplinarians rarely punish their children. Rather, they communicate in firm terms exactly where they stand on issues and where they want their children to stand.

So today families do well when they establish and communicate beforehand a suitable consequence that will fit a misbehavior—

for example, "If you're not home by 10 P.M., you'll be grounded for the weekend"—so that expectations about behaviors, as well as consequences for not abiding by them, are made clear. This more disciplined, consequential approach can be used to show the gravity of moral choices as well as to reestablish some of the authoritarian role that parents used to fulfill but now delegate to or expect of others (such as day-care providers or older siblings).

Becoming more authoritarian and, at times, more rigid about compliance with the right and wrong rules that have been established within the family returns instruction in moral values to the family, where it belongs. This ensures, even in the midst of a society that is sending its members mixed messages, that the family can have definite ideas about what is moral and what is not. This establishes clear reprimands for inappropriate behaviors, even in a society where meaningful punishment is rarely doled out even to the most immoral individuals. And this secures punishments that will best ensure that there is no recidivism in immoral behavior, even in a society known for excusing immorality or forgiving repeated misbehavior.

While the adage "Spare the rod and spoil the child" had its place in history, in the formation and reformation of moral family members, today "Determine limits, set consequences, reward good behavior, but discipline when necessary" ought to be the beacon statement that can guide parents as they promote responsible, respectful, and moral behavior in family members.

NOTES

1. Walsh, David. *Selling Out America's Children*. Deaconess Press, Minneapolis, 1994, pp. 9–10.
2. *Ibid.,* p. 12.
3. Hostetler, A. J., "More than 1 in 10 report going to high school armed, CDC says," *Boston Globe,* March 31, 1995.
4. Moore, Thomas. *Soul Mates: Honoring the Mysteries of Love and Relationship.* HarperPerennial, New York, 1994, p. 28.
5. Rosemond, John. "Your Child's Bill of Rights: 10 things you owe your kids," *Better Homes and Gardens,* January 1993.
6. Curran, Dolores. *Traits of a Healthy Family.* HarperSanFrancisco, 1983, p. 170.
7. Harrell, Wilson. "Personal Glimpses: Making the Grade," *Reader's Digest,* February 1995.
8. Curran, pp. 165–166.
9. Curran, p. 80.
10. Royko, Mike. "Another Innocent Victim?" *Reader's Digest,* February 1995.
11. Browder, Sue. "Raising a G-Rated Child in an X-Rated World," *Reader's Digest,* April 1995.
12. *Ibid.*
13. Walsh, David. *Selling Out America's Children.* Deaconess Press, Minneapolis, 1994, p. 20.

CHAPTER 8

⤫

Creating and Honoring Rituals and Traditions

A family that treasures its traditions and rituals seems automatically to have a sense of family soul, a firm foundation of family that symbolizes its uniqueness as well as its unity:

> The great value of traditions . . . is that they give a family a sense of identity, of belongingness. And everybody needs this in this harried day in which we live. That we're not just a cluster of people living together in a house, but we're a family that's conscious of its uniqueness, of its personality, of its character, and its heritage. And the special relationship within the family of love and companionship makes us a unit that has an identity, that has . . . a personality.[1]

A family ritual or tradition can be something that has existed for generations within a family, such as a particular story that has been told and retold throughout the years. It can be a blessing given at the dinner table every Sunday. It can be a unique way of celebrating the life of a deceased family member rather than mourning his or her death. It can be based on a religious activity or belief. It can occur during a holiday period or at the same time every year—for example, a family vacation that is always taken the first week in August. It can be an annual event (a Fourth of July fishing trip), a weekly event (a Friday dinner of leftovers), or a daily event (a morning telephone call to a grandparent). It can be something that is adored—staying at the same cabin in the woods every summer—as well as something that is abhorred—preparing a dish that must be served during Passover even though no family member wants to eat it. It can be something that is done so automatically that no one knows the reason why it exists or ever questions whether there is a "better" way of doing it, or something that has to be taught to family members in order to preserve the ritual or tradition. When a new member joins the family, the rituals and traditions of the family are often passed on; as well, sometimes a new member introduces rituals and traditions that may be incorporated into the family's already established traditions. Thus, in this way, family traditions and rituals are constant as well as ever-changing.

Traditions and rituals are so important to a family because the family is a social unit; the very nature of socialization encompasses learning the values, attitudes, knowledge, skills, and techniques that a society possesses—in short, it involves learning the culture.[2] Thus, traditions and rituals make up the culture of a family. As such, they are often treated as necessities—essential components of a family that its members cannot do without. Comments *Boston Globe* writer Christina Robb, "I need rituals as much as I need money or food or praise or even love."[3] This strong need for family rituals and traditions becomes strikingly evident in some of the conflicts experienced by new couples, when they often are at odds with each other over their own particular family's rituals and traditions:

> It's not coincidental that the most emotional conflict occurring between many young couples . . . arises not from money, in-laws, or chore division but from issues surrounding the celebration of Christmas; whether the tree should be real or artificial; which parents should be invited at what time; and other fundamental issues. . . . Each partner is emotionally invested in passing on Christmas traditions, his or her own traditions. . . . The couple, by a gradual selection and adaptation process, begins to develop its own set of

Christmas traditions and rituals, which then mark them as a unique family and which they ultimately pass on to their own children.[4]

This strong need for rituals and traditions is particularly evident in ethnic families, multicultural families, religious families, gay and lesbian families, and single-parent families. These groups often need to seek ways to develop and foster pride in each family member's ancestry or lifestyle so their children can learn and benefit from rich, unique experiences they can take with them into adulthood and, as well, so the adults can enjoy the depth and value of establishing and sharing such experiences with others as a family. Rituals and traditions may be created to honor the heritage of one or more family members, special foods might be prepared, faith-ritualizing may be practiced, and ethnic traditions and rituals that have been kept hidden may be searched out and reestablished.

Because of their importance, family traditions and rituals often become events that are treasured more than the family jewels because they give each member hope—hope for the future that is nurtured on a firm foundation of rituals and traditions, which connects the past with the present. In effect, family traditions and rituals are the cement that firmly holds family members together, linking them from generation to generation, and thus providing them with a sense of community and continuity. Traditions are, according to Edward C. Sellner, "inheritances of the soul . . . links between the ages, containing past and present expectations, sacred memories and future promise."[5] Because traditions and rituals provide a link that joins the past and the future, they are integral in ensuring the longevity of the family as well as holding its place in history. Today's families exist because of yesterday's families; today's adults were once yesterday's children. Traditions and rituals signify a family's link with time and therefore emphasize the need to pass on the story of ancestors, to listen to elder family members, and to keep in touch with the roots of the family through ways of doing things or histories that have been handed down from previous generations.

Families that have rituals and traditions and whose members maintain and value their presence in their lives are better equipped to withstand separations, losses, and many other stresses that can impact upon them, because they can use the rituals and traditions to draw support from a lifelong base of support and love. Rituals and traditions also provide a sense of stability during even the most stressful times, such as a job change, relocation, or the illness or death of a family member. As well, rituals and traditions travel with each family member when he or she is away from home, and even when they are rejected by family members, who may pull away from them as a natural result of their "leaving the nest" process, or as part of a rebellion, they are still there whenever family members feel their loss and need to welcome them back into their lives.

The comfort and security provided by family rituals and traditions has been known and felt for thousands of years; traditions and rituals can be traced back to a time in the history of families when people were members of clans. Clans would embrace their legends and history, their heroes and characters of renown, their conquests and achievements, and their deceased and newborn, as well as celebrate and commemorate special events. Family meant longevity to them and, because of this, traditions and rituals emphasized "preserving the family" through its established customs. This created an emotional kinship among family members, a tie of uniqueness as well as permanance that bound family members together.

Florentine patrician Leon Battista Alberti explored this kinship in *Della famiglia,* written in the early fifteenth century, in which he sought "to investigate carefully what exalts and ennobles families." In exploring his own family, he discovered that the traditions and rituals he had been taught led to his intense feeling of familial pride and a deep sense of family obligation:

> Members of our family always returned [from tournaments] with great honors and praise. . . . Just think how pleased I was to see the favor our Alberti family justly enjoyed. . . . [I want] to go forth with the others and be admired and praised. . . . It is my duty to do everything within

my power, even risk my own life, for the honor of our house and our family.[6]

Early in American history, families as well as their communities participated in the creation of rituals and traditions, with the oldest and most familiar being the celebration of Thanksgiving. But, over time, with the gradual demise of many of the family functions that focused on survival, the growth of educational institutions, and the emphasis on many forms of learning that could take place outside the home, family rituals and traditions were viewed less and less as the primary tools for socialization of family members. Family rituals and traditions became more private and personal and, quite often, at odds with the concerns of American society as a whole. Ethnic traditions and rituals in particular were often shunned by emigrating families in order to fit in to their new culture.

As well, family rituals and traditions began to overlap or be overwhelmed by the rituals and traditions emphasized by other institutions. Some family rituals and traditions were created because they were dictated by other institutions—for example, in Catholic families eating fish on Fridays—or as a result of significant events in history, such as a tradition of home-canning fruits and vegetables that started in the Depression era as a means of survival. In the 1950s, as families became more contained and less community-based, oftentimes rituals and traditions died out.

Later on, the conflict between clanship as a means of belonging and clanship as a means of suppressing individual expression frequently created families in which people preferred to live together without the bonding provided by rituals and traditions and then leave, to return to the childhood home or gather together with family only for obligatory holidays or because of an illness or death in the family. In such families—and in families today in which there are few rituals and traditions that provide the family with a sense of the unit's importance as a link in the chain of family history—any return to the family is done out of duty rather than out of a sense of connection and belonging.

While such individual family members may feel a strong sense of self, the scarcity of traditions and rituals deprives them of a historical perspective, a sense of their connection and place in community, a rich sense of kinship that can take them through hard times, established events that can enrich and enliven their lives, and the knowledge of what unconditional love is:

> Rituals and traditions are much more than words. They give those who participate in them an opportunity to say nonverbally, "I love you. I like being with you. I want to reenact what's important in life with you because you are important to me."[7]

Traditions and rituals do not need to be complex in order for their positive impact to be felt; they do, however, need to be focused on a central part of a family's life, whether they determine how a meal is to be shared together or how a major event is to be commemorated. Yet many people do not realize how simple a family tradition can be or how routine a ritual may have become in their lives. Because of this, you might not realize that your family, which you may have thought gave you no traditions or rituals, actually abounds with a strong basis of rituals and traditions that has been passed along to you and may now even be part of your own family. These may include such seemingly mundane activities as the ones below, which were drawn up by one family at a seminar in which each family was given five minutes to think of and write down their family traditions and rituals:

—Youngest child always blows out the candles.
—Dad gives kids "dutch rubs" on the crown of their heads when he says goodnight.
—When a child is twelve, he or she becomes responsible for washing the car.
—Wednesday is leftover night.
—Waffles every Sunday morning.
—Mom hides the family valentines.

—We dye Easter eggs on Good Friday night.

—We have a taking-down-the-tree party on January 1.

—Once a year we go family ice skating—no friends allowed.

—We celebrate our cat's birthday.

—Togther we clean out the basement the first day of summer vacation. (We always end with hot dogs cooked outside.)

—We leave notes on the refrigerator.

—We pretend to avoid Mom's goodnight kiss.

—Dad and the boys go fishing on Memorial Day weekend. Mom and the girls go shopping and out to lunch. Each girl gets one day to pick where lunch will be.

—Each child gets to talk alone to Grandma on long distance without anybody else listening.

—We make our own Mother's and Father's Day cards.

—We visit Aunt Ellen in the nursing home after church on holidays.[8]

Making your own list of family rituals and traditions can help you to see the presence of rituals and traditions in your family as well as to acknowledge just how valuable such routines may be to you. Such a listing can also give you a "historical" perspective on why you need to do some things in particular ways or at particular times or why you may sometimes find yourself saying, "My family has always done this in this way." As well, it is important to your soul and to your family's soul to create and honor rituals and traditions that provide a sense of historical family, that strive to make the most of the legends and characters in your families by preserving them in family storytelling, and that encourage you to regularly gather together as a family.

Family History

When Alex Haley was in the process of writing his best-selling autobiographical saga *Roots,* he probably had no idea of the pow-

erful emotional impact his book would have not only upon black
Americans as they strived to link their African heritage and American slave history with their families in the present, but also upon
all Americans who longed for a sense of historical family. For, to
be part of a family "is to understand what it means to be 'stuck
with' a history and a people."⁹ His book and the resulting minis-
eries encouraged people to look more closely at their sense of
family, to explore their lineage so family members could become
more aware of their ancestors, and to honor their "griots"—their
family "legendkeepers," who keep track of all living and dead
family members and research and answer questions put to them
regarding family matters.

Traditions and rituals that focus on preserving this sense of
family history ensure that there will be no breaks in the long
chain of family heritage, thereby strengthening the thread of continuity that joins each successive family generation together. As
well, such historically supportive traditions and rituals provide
family members with a rich sense of kinship that shows them that
they are not alone, assures family members that they are cared for
not because of who they are or what they do but simply because
they are a member of a family, and gives each family member a
valuable sense of belonging and connection that cannot be du-
plicated as profoundly in work, friendships, civic or social afflia-
tions, team sports, political offices, or church memberships.

Such generational linking can not only provide a family with a
reminder of its place in and throughout history, but can also serve
as a valuable chronicle of family generations who have lived
through remarkable times in this country's history. Clancy
Strock, contributing editor of *Reminisce* magazine, writes of how
today's sons and daughters are the grandchildren, great-grand-
children, great-great-grandchildren (and so on) of family members whose lives were affected by wars, plagues, famines,
epidemics, droughts, and floods, and that much of who family
members are today was shaped by those generations that lived before them. The strength, vision, and courage that enabled an entire generation to endure the hardships of the Depression, for

example, created a new generation that was influenced in many ways by the older generation's personal experiences—by the trials of the Depression and also the joys.

As well, the generation of family members who, as their lives progressed, experienced incredible changes evolving about them—"The first automobile they had ever seen, a telephone in the house, electricity, the radio, running water and refrigerators, the extermination of diphtheria and polio and several other killer diseases. Heart transplants. Travel by air. Television. The list goes on and on."[10]—are priceless storehouses of memories for younger family members, who can learn the profound influence history has had upon humanity through their particular family members who lived through it—who *knew* firsthand all about it, because they were there.

One way to maintain evidence of a family history today is to begin to search out and preserve what has been left behind by past generations. Birth certificates, old passports, newspaper clippings, handwritten recipe cards, handmade quilts and other stitchery, photographs, diaries, letters, furniture, jewelery, and other possessions may easily be found in attics and basements. But, more often than not, much is scattered about among personal possessions of geographically distant (and sometimes rarely seen) relatives, in a town's historical records, in museum collections, or in old records—to name but a few possible places to begin a search for family artifacts. Embarking on such a search-for-history adventure can become a family ritual—an activity that is done individually or as a group on a regular basis or prior to a family event such as a reunion—or can become part of a revered tradition where an older family member presents a treasured item from his or her past to a younger member in order to commemorate a birthday, wedding, or other special event. When such family history items are discovered through diligent searching, uncovered as a surprising "find," or given as a gift, they can be made accessible to all family members or displayed during family get-togethers in order to share such pieces of family history with everyone in the family.

As well, families today can participate in the creation of an on-going family history that can be enjoyed by future generations, by taking pictures and/or videotaping family members and special events, saving mementos from family gatherings, making investments or purchases that can be enjoyed now and then passed on to others in the family, such as a cabin on a lake, shares of stock, or ownership of a business.

Another way to preserve family history is to recognize or identify a family locus—the person who will serve as the family historian. This may be the family matriarch or patriarch—a grandparent who brings the family together on holidays or for special gatherings. Sometimes the family locus is a younger family member who volunteers to create a family tree, who compiles and adds to family photo albums, or who composes the seasonal "what's up in the family" greeting. Or the locus can be the one who is chosen by an older family member to be a "locus-in-training," entrusted in the present with learning a multitude of family traditions and rituals—from how to make a favorite family recipe to how best to seat family members during the holiday meal—in order to effectively assume the "official" role when the current locus is no longer available to provide such instruction and guidance.

Because kinship and history are linked, everyone in the family is responsible for creating and maintaining rituals and traditions for the family's history: the elders, who have started traditions and rituals themselves and from whom family members today owe their heritage; and younger members, who are all potential resources for ensuring that traditions and rituals remain in place so the family history can be conveyed to successive generations. This "passing on" aspect of family history can be facilitated through material possessions of the past or treasured family photos that capture a memory or a moment that can be savored again and again and then passed from generation to generation. But more often than not—and because, in the past, cameras were a luxury and photographs were taken only rarely—such family history is conveyed orally, through storytelling.

Family Storytelling

Throughout history, one of the more important ongoing family traditions or rituals has been storytelling about the family and its members, both living and dead. The primary purpose such family storytelling has is providing the genesis of the family or a family member; for example, "Our grandparents immigrated from Sweden at the turn of the century," or "Your birth mother was born in Haiti, and that's where you were born too." After that, family stories define the family and provide the family as a whole, as well as its individual members, with a sense of identity; that is, they hold the spirit and meaning of a family. Family stories convey not only what family members have done and perhaps what they should do, but also who they are and perhaps who they ought to be.

It is through such storytelling that each family member learns the ways in which he or she is special in relationship to the family and becomes adept at recognizing the characteristics that distinguish his or her particular family from others so the family can be seen in relation to the world; for example, "Being a Brown means being strong, being tough, and being able to survive." This "specialness" can build a loyalty in family members so the family can be assured of its survival through shared sensibilities and the sensitivity of its members to one another, both individually and collectively:

> Everyone in the family knows the story about how immigration officials misspelled the original family name, thereby starting a new family name. Or how Uncle Leo tricked Aunt Ellen into marrying him. Or how they didn't find Aunt Maggie's false teeth in the oatmeal box until long after the funeral. . . . These stories are told and retold at family gatherings. . . . These stories are important to the sense of family.
> Why? Because they tell the story. They gather up the past for present family members, who know they must preserve and pass them on to future generations. . . . Stories aren't

icing; they're basic ingredients in any group that claims to be family. [11]

Or, as one family member comments about what meaning his family stories have for him: "I'm Dan Vernale who has this history. . . . I know that I'm bigger than I am by having this background. I have many more people, I have a gang, I have a group, I have a family."[12]

Almost any bit of information about a family or a family member can qualify as a family story as long as it is in some way significant to the family, its history, and/or its members, and has been so accepted into the family history that it has been told and retold—sometimes to the delight and sometimes to the dismay of family members. Thus, the realms family storytelling enters are often the same from family to family. They include the following:

- *Ancestral stories,* or stories that provide a genealogical identity for blood as well as nonblood family members
- *Teaching stories,* or the telling of experiences the family elders have had that can instruct family members in the ways of the world
- *Moral stories,* or stories that make known the family's values, norms, and mores on a variety of issues, from religion to the expression of feelings
- *Family myths,* or unverifiable accounts of family history as well as "family secrets" that can be scandalous but may be, more often than not, based on fiction rather than fact
- *Connecting stories,* which are sometimes augmented by photographs, old letters, 8-mm movie reels, and other illustrative articles that display similarities in appearance as well as in behavior between generations
- *Character stories,* or bits of lore or casually delivered statements about a living or deceased family member (for example, "Your great-grandfather used to play that same song on the piano")
- *Comprehension stories,* or stories that avoid intricate analysis of a complex family occurrence and instead reduce the

cause of the occurrence to a simple and easily understood cause (for example, "Your aunt killed herself because she was very ill.")

- *Family tales,* or stories that, like fairy tales, have two meanings—one more obvious and easily comprehended, and the other more hidden and harder to figure out
- *Red Badge of Courage* stories, which portray acts of bravery, dexterity, or the sheer courage of a family member and are often told to instill confidence and build self-esteem in other family members
- *Bad stories,* or tales about "black sheep" family members or tragic things the family or a family member may have done ("Your cousin Arthur played with matches, and his baby sister died in the fire he started.")
- *Tell-me-again stories,* often shared between an adult and a child, such as a grandparent and a grandchild or a parent and child, the most familiar and most often told of all the family stories because they are the ones a child repeatedly requests to hear—"Tell me again about the time you fell down the well" or "Did you really ride a train all the way to California when you were little?"—and therefore the ones that attract the most attentive audience for the teller of the tale.

Very often, however, family stories are not of just one type but seem to have a bit of each type within them.

While family storytelling goes on in families everywhere, the stories' sustenance comes from the ability of family members to pay attention to as well as remember them. Not listening to them, not paying deliberate attention to their telling and retelling, not repeating them to others, or never alluding to them slowly starves them, silencing them, so that eventually family members become soulless "rootless nomads who travel light, uninstructed by memory and family ties."[13]

Even if you loathe your family, it is vitally important to pay attention to family stories, if not for the purpose of sustaining them, at least to learn more about yourself through your collective family experience:

> All of us, long after we've left our original families, keep at least some of the stories with us, and they continue to matter, but sometimes in new ways. At moments of major life transitions, we may claim certain of the stories, take them over, shape them, reshape them, put our own stamp on them, make them part of us instead of making ourselves part of them. We are always in conversation with them, one way or another. The ancestral figures in them—especially grandparents or great-grandparents of the same sex as us—often become a major part of our imaginative life. They can . . . serve as our role models and our guides. [14]

Unfortunately today much of family storytelling is viewed as entertainment rather than appreciated for its moral value—a value that portrays the family's history as well as its internal and external relationships. Yet, as entertaining as some family stories may be, a closer look at the most enjoyable may reveal that, in some small way, either good or bad, they matter to the family or to one or more individuals in a profound or influential way:

> They provide the family with esteem because they often show family members in an attractive light or define the family in a flattering way. They also give messages and instructions; they offer blueprints and ideals; they issue warnings and prohibitions. And when they no longer serve, they disappear. [15]

The Hawaiians commonly get together and share family tales, or participate in "talking story," an activity in which family and extended family members talk about the legends, characters, and circumstances that make the family unique. In effect, everyone needs to "talk story" in order to nurture his or her family's soul. Talking story means sharing past tales about family and family members in ways that help to preserve a family's legends, share family members' experiences, provide insights into what adults were like when they were children, satisfy curiosity about the family and/or its members, provide valuable perspective, preserve the unique and influential characters in a family (those who were conventional as well as those who may have been highly unconventional), and open up the world to family members rather than shut it down.

John Shea, storytelling theologian, offers this simple advice for families on developing their storytelling abilities: "Gather the people. Tell the story. Break the bread."[16] Thus, besides paying attention to your family's oral histories for your own benefit, and recounting them to others for their benefit (and to keep the tradition and ritual of family storytelling alive), it is vitally important to gather family together so everyone can share the tales that support the family as a viable and valuable unit of society.

Family Gatherings

Most often families gather together when it is expected of them—at funerals, weddings and wedding anniversaries, Mother's Day and Father's Day, birthdays, bar mitzvahs, graduations, communions, holidays, and so on. But the family that is striving to create, cultivate, and nurture a strong soul that honors its traditions and rituals needs to make a conscious effort to gather together as a people *at any time,* for no significant reason. In the past, with family members living under the same roof or within close geographical distance to one another, it was much easier to gather together as a family. Such events as country fairs, weekly dances, spelling bees, quilting parties, concerts in the town park, trips to town, or family outings readily drew family members together; as well, board games, baking bread or making ice cream, and—before the invention of television—the broadcast of a favorite radio show would easily bring family members together. Such activities kept a family close and encouraged "talking story," as well as sharing other traditions and rituals.

But in today's scattered families, with members who attend school or set up their own homes thousands of miles from one another, an increasingly mobile culture in which family members no longer have a childhood home or one specific place to return to for special occasions, and relationships among family members that are less inclusive and personal, combined with family expectations to get together that can feel oppressive and demanding with all the other obligations that need to be met, family gatherings rarely hold a top priority. As well, the dichotomy between freedom (a sense of self) and belonging (a sense of family) can create a tension in family members that drives them away from the family, from any attempt to foster traditions, rituals, or even a family history "because they might impinge upon individual freedom in daily life."[17]

But in those families that have a strong sense of clanship—whose members consider the family to be their lifelong foundation of love and support, a source of their sustenance, a link to the past, and a bridge to the future—the desire to get together is strong. The family enjoys being together; members plan reunions and/or get together whenever possible. This is not to say that the members always get along well with one another or that the planned reunions are stress free. But the family members know that such reunions—big or small, spontaneous or planned, frequent or infrequent, inclusive of all family members (a true family reunion) or just some (a "mini" family reunion)—serve a useful purpose in cementing generations together and confirming a sense of belonging. As Alex Haley comments, "Reunions are the conveyor belts of our individual histories. They reaffirm the thread of continuity, establish pride in self and kin, and transmit a family's awareness of itself, from the youngest to the oldest."[18]

In families where geographical distances, time constraints, or other reasons make it impossible to physically get together, family members can use the telephone, write letters, or exchange audiocassettes as ways to "reunite" with one another. One family even went so far as to set up a tape recorder during their Sunday night dinner to record the reciting of grace, the sounds of food being served, and the dinner conversation for their eldest daughter, who was attending college a thousand miles from home, so she could still feel as if she were part of the family's traditional meal. In other families that are deprived of the opportunity of frequent or ritual get-togethers, a conscious effort needs to be made to stay in touch with one another in order to keep from becoming strangers. Photos of children can be updated often, along with the events in family member's lives; in this way, even the most distant cousins in a family get to know one another not just as a name in passing but as a person who shares their same history and sense of connection.

The important point to remember in striving to gather together as a family is to not simply wait for the "right" time when everyone can gather together or to create some sort of grand or complicated affair to commemorate a significant event such as a fiftieth wedding anniversary. While such reunions ought to be created whenever possible, it is also vital to create the feeling within the family and among its members that anyone can get together at any time, in any place, without an invitation. In particular, regularly dropping in on elderly relatives or taking them out for a lunch or dinner, as well as spontaneously sharing in the care of the very young, can establish traditions and rituals to be cherished and maintained by all family members.

It is also important to keep in mind that while most family traditions and rituals are shared with and within a family of origin, extended families—neighbors, friends, friends of friends, business partners, and others—can also participate in established family traditions and rituals. Most often, extended family members are included in a multitude of traditional or ritual family gatherings, from birthdays to holiday celebrations to family outings. One such extended family picnic, which has taken place every year for over two-and-a-half centuries in Salem, Massachusetts, is known as the Black Picnic. Many of the annual picnic's more than one thousand participants have called the historic extended family gathering a tradition that has survived slavery. According to Salem records, the first African-American picnic took place in Salem in 1741. Twenty-six slaves from Lynn spent their one day off during the year to gather along a riverbank:

> The Black Picnic, referred to in the past as the "Colored People's Picnic" or as the "Union of Colored Peoples," evolved into a church event in the 1920s. Churches from Lynn, Malden, Everett and other areas would charter trolley cars and buses to take thousands of children and parents to Salem Willows.
>
> The picnic's purpose, however, has never changed.
>
> "You come here to see old friends and make new ones," said Rod Chavous, 30, of Lynn. "Friends you haven't seen in years, you'll see here today."[19]

In 1995 the organizers of the Black Picnic dedicated the gathering to Gladys Haywood of Lynn, a loyal picnic-goer of ninety years, who passed away that year. "She just loved coming and seeing all of the family," explained her son-in-law. Amelia Sparrow, a sixty-five-year-old grandmother, arrived at the picnic dedicated to Haywood just before 6 A.M. so she could claim her traditional spot under a particular tree. "When I was a child," she said, "my dad would load up the car and we'd head out to this exact same spot under this tree." Although time has passed on and so has Sparrow's father, the once-a-year tradition endures generation after generation. "Now the grandchildren will be able to carry on this tradition for us once we're gone," she proudly proclaims.[20]

Family Symbols

Family traditions and rituals are usually based on a physical, emotional, or spiritual symbol. The display of a family crest in a home or flying the flag of the family's country of origin are examples of a physical symbol. As well, giving the same type of birthday gift every year to a family member (such as a collectible), preparing the same dish for a family gathering, hanging the same Christmas ornaments, wearing a piece of jewelry that displays the family crest or the birthstones of each child or grandchild, or playing a family game of touch football every Thanksgiving are physical symbols of family traditions and rituals. All of these are also examples of emotional traditions or rituals that can be established within a family. Emotional traditions and rituals can be joyful celebrations (such as decorating the Christmas tree or caroling together in the neighborhood with extended family), acts of commemoration (such as placing an American flag at the grave marker of a family member who was a war veteran), bittersweet reminders (such as viewing a family photo album or rereading letters from a loved one who has passed away), or times of sadness and reflection (such as mourning the loss of a family member).

As family gathers together at a table to share a holiday meal, the time for grace is often considered to be not only a time for reflection and thanksgiving, but also one of the best times to create or honor a family's spiritual tradition. While grace may often be delivered in the old, reliable form of a well-known prayer, such as "God is great, God is good, let us thank Him for this food," it can also consist of a poem, nonreligious prayer, or other sentiment.

As well, traditions or rituals based on the family's religion or ways in which the family experiences faith and hope together—worshipping as a family every Sunday, preparing food for a family booth at a church's annual bake sale, attending a family weekend spiritual retreat, meditating together, lighting a candle on the anniversary of a family member's passing, and so on—create spiritual traditions and rituals that connect a family together in comforting and cherished ways.

Nontraditional Family Rituals

Families that are "different" from the majority of American families or those who are living with them or around them (for example, an African-American family that lives in a predominantly white neighborhood, a single mother who resides in an apartment complex filled with two-parent households, or a gay or lesbian couple that shares a household with a heterosexual couple) often benefit from traditions and rituals that are created because of such differences, in order to make family members aware of their diversity, to help them in accepting and embracing such differences, and to encourage them to take pride in and honor the qualities that make them unique. So, for example, an adopted child's date of birth as well as the day he or she was adopted can be celebrated; the "rainbow flag," a symbol of gay pride, can be displayed every year during Pride Week in June; African-American families, along with their extended families, can plan to share special activities during Martin Luther King, Jr., Day; and families that share Christian as well as Jewish religious beliefs can celebrate Hanukkah as well as Christmas, Passover as well as Easter, Rosh Hashana, and Yom Kippur.

While it is important to keep in mind that awareness of differences in a family or among family members, such as a multicultural adopted child's culture and customs, ought to be made a routine part of family life rather than a special ritual, it is still worthwhile to make some aspects of a family's or a child's heritage or circumstances part of the family's traditions or rituals. Families do not need to have a multitude of such traditions and rituals in order to benefit from them as a family. Perhaps only one, two, or a few are all that is needed to honor an aspect of the family's or a family member's diversity.

As well, the family needs to honor and cherish its already established traditions and rituals and blend them with new ones. This blending of established with newly created traditions and rituals is particularly needed in two-household families, where a historical foundation and traditions and rituals from a family of origin or previous family can be added to the current family's traditions and rituals. The children in such coparenting situations can benefit greatly from this blending of traditions and rituals, for such a mix allows them to hold on to and cherish positive memories from a different time in their lives as they move through the transition to another time. As a widowed mother who raised a two-year-old daughter once commented about the need for traditions and rituals for her small family:

Even with just my daughter and me, we established rich events within our life-style, and we loved them and looked forward to living them together. And if a single parent with an only child can become such a ritualizing family, no one need live without such rich experiences to take into adulthood.[21]

Yet any family can benefit from such a blending of the old traditions and rituals with the creation of new ones. Doing such things, as well as creating and honoring family traditions and rituals that focus on family history, family storytelling, family gatherings, and family symbols—and then eagerly participating in them—helps build a family that nurtures the soul of each member, and enhances a supportive soul for the family as a whole.

NOTES

1. Curran, Dolores. *Traits of a Healthy Family.* HarperSanFrancisco, 1983, p. 210.
2. Leslie, Gerald R. *The Family in Social Context,* 4th Edition. Oxford University Press, Inc., New York, 1979, pp. 12–18.
3. Curran, p. 211.
4. *Ibid.,* pp. 210–211.
5. Brussat, Frederic and Mary Ann. *100 Ways to Keep Your Soul Alive: Living Deeply and Fully Every Day.* HarperSanFrancisco, 1994, p. 60.
6. Alberti, Leon Battista. *The Albertis of Florence,* trans. (of *Della famiglia*). Guido A. Guarino, Lewisburg, PA, 1971, p. 249.
7. Curran, p. 212.
8. *Ibid.,* p. 213.
9. *Ibid.,* p. 199.
10. Strock, Clancy. *'We Had Everything But Money.'* Reminisce Books, Greendale, WI, 1992, p. 8.
11. Curran, p. 202.
12. Stone, Elizabeth. *Black Sheep & Kissing Cousins: How Our Family Stories Shape Us.* Times Books, New York, 1988, p. 13.
13. *Ibid.,* p. 6.
14. *Ibid.,* p. 8.
15. *Ibid.,* p. 5.
16. Curran, p. 203.
17. *Ibid.,* pp. 200–201.
18. *Ibid.,* p. 200.
19. Martinez, Anne. "History is marked in Salem with picnic," *Boston Sunday Globe,* July 16, 1995.
20. *Ibid.*
21. Curran, p. 211.

CHAPTER 9

⌒∞⌒

Valuing Spirituality and Service to Others

How important is spirituality to a family—spirituality that embodies faith in the teachings of an organized religion, so the family has a religious core, and/or spirituality that embodies faith in some transcendent belief, so the family has a sense of reverence that comes from a deep place?

"The soul suffers when we lack reverence," says D. Stephenson Bond in *Living Myth*. "We live in an age that understands rights, obligations, and sets of commitments. But we have difficulty experiencing reverence because it comes from a deeper place."[1] Author Robert Bellah, a professor of sociology at the University of California, Berkeley, and his colleagues conclude in their book *Habits of the Heart* that "late twentieth century Americans' preoccupation with personal ambition and consumerism is . . . rendering much of the country's middle class incapable of a commitment to their most basic institutions: marriage, family, religion, and politics."[2] And Harvard psychologist Dr. Robert Coles validates both sentiments, explaining that "Many of the kids I've looked at don't have faith. That's the problem. They don't have religious faith or the kind of human faith that can be called natural religion as St. Augustine talks about it."[3]

Society, with its skewed cultural value messages, has done its part in creating a powerful influence that has decreased the role religion and spirituality play in today's family life. Schools now outrank churches as the institution that has the greatest influence on children, but not because most teachers are great spiritual and moral role models. Rather, a great many teachers have become society's preachers, whose gospel is "Winning isn't everything—it's the only thing." Many school systems feel that the best way to overcome a student's complacency or contentment with mediocrity is to instill competition and increase the pressure to excel.

Society's message, often reinforced by the schools through academic as well as athletic programs, is that if you are not the best, then what you do, what you try for, or how much time you put into studying or training does not matter. The fixation on being the best, the top, the number one is critical for kids as well as their coaches. Witness the number of high school athletic coaches who lose their jobs not because they are poor coaches or because their teams have not enjoyed their share of success, but because their teams do not always win championships. When winning becomes the dominant value, moral and ethnical values, as well as faith and belief, inevitably suffer.

Today children as well as adults hero-worship some sports figures and pop stars despite their criminal actions, their outrageous behavior, the abusive or degrading remarks they make, or their excesses. Even noncelebrities can become overnight sensations—people who make it to that coveted place at the top of the hero-worship mountain—not because of their good deeds or righteous behaviors but because they kill a lot of people (Jeffrey Dahmer), provide sexual contacts for clients (Heidi Fleiss), murder their parents (the Menendez brothers), drown their children (Susan Smith), cut off a sexual organ (Lorena Bobbitt), have their sexual organ cut off (John Wayne Bobbitt), or happen to be the houseguest of a celebrity (Kato Kaelin), to cite but a few examples. Society's obsession with the sensationally horrifying rather than the spiritually uplifting is most defiantly at odds with religious teachings of doing good deeds and living by moral guidelines in order to achieve "greatness." Society rather enjoys what is bad (in fact, the worse, the better) and makes heroes and heroines out of the perpetrators of disgusting and dastardly do-ings. Society has become the Pied Piper of Hamlin's evil twin, who now leads all the rats through town so the adults and children can admire them.

While children live in this society in which they are taught to win at all costs, to get all they can, and to view violence and abusive behavior as entertaining, many adults oftentimes set themselves up as godlike figures within their families, striving to do it all, to achieve it all, and to get it all—all the while setting high expectations for a similar drive to achieve in family members from very early ages. Many other adults who are trying to raise their children in this marketplace-mentality society, which "educates" its members to live by the values of the "In God We Trust" dollar rather than by the values that come from a sense of purpose and as a more altruistic and generous way of living, feel that things have gotten so far out of their control and so far away from the values that encouraged families to say a simple grace before shared meals or to respect others, that they have no idea where to begin to restore experiences of reverence. Many other adults have simply given up trying to contradict the messages society is giving to its members and have adopted the attitude "If you can't beat 'em, join 'em."

The evolution of cultural value messages regarding religion and spirituality from a historic past in America, in which faith in God played a foundational role in daily family life and a spiritual core strengthened the family and its support system, can even be seen symbolically in today's urban planning and architecture. The landscape of the towns and cities of the Middle Ages was dominated by magnificent cathedrals. In the American colonies, towns and villages sprang up around the familiar church and its spire that reached toward the heavens. And, in the American cities of the 1900s that grew by leaps and bounds, churches were still some of the most central, accessible, majestic, and massive structures, dwarfing surrounding buildings. But what does America's late-twentieth-century architecture and urban planning reveal of its cultural values?

Contemporary landscapes are dominated by gleaming towers of steel and glass, dedicated to the endeavors of business and finance. More recently, architects and developers have entered into fierce competition to create the largest entertainment complexes and shopping malls. Each new structure is designed to be the biggest and most splendid of all, and visitors from all over the world are traveling by the millions to places like Disney World in Florida and the Mall of America in Minnesota.[4]

So, to return to the original question—How important is a religious core or deeply felt spirituality to a family? Studies on families reveal that there is a strong correlation between religion and happiness and success not just in family life, but in all phases of an individual's life. A sense of spirituality that is valued and shared in a family and among its members provides a base of values (a sense of right and wrong, respect, responsibility, trust, moral actions, and so on), a sense of purpose, a source of strength, a belief in a power or being greater than the family, and the feeling of connection outside the family. But too often families and churches have presented religion as a subject to be taught or as a responsibility to be fulfilled once a week rather than a belief that can be relied upon in daily life.

Learning how to share religion/spirituality within a family is essential to helping a family reclaim its sense of intimacy with itself so it can become more unified. In reuniting a family with itself, the family soul becomes restored so that oneness with the family group can be sealed with the bond of a shared faith. Through this bonding—this sense of healthy "oneness"—the family can then look toward fostering an ability to experience "otherness," or a sense of connection and responsibility outside of the family, to a community, an organization, a global cause, a civic concern, the neighborhood in which the family resides, other families, or individuals in need.

How important is it that a family value such service to others? Many families today are focused on their possessions, their power, their success, and making it for themselves. They believe in the adage "You can't fight city hall," and thus instill in family members a sense of hopelessness and powerlessness. They blame their personal problems on the world around them. They take as much as they can for themselves and think of themselves first. They get tied into competition. They strive to rear the smartest, prettiest, most popular—*the best*—children. Their home life is filled with stress. Their intense and constant pursuit of wealth and power dominates their time and attention and thus isolates them from others.

Many other families, however, are making a real effort to go beyond themselves, to enlarge their focus to include the people around them, in their communities and the world, as validated by the slogan "Think locally; act globally." They have and act on the belief that "City hall can be improved, and we can help to make this happen." They have a sense of national purpose, one that was fostered years ago and which helped take this country through some difficult times. They are able to look beyond themselves and their own individual family life. They want to live less for themselves only. They are more relaxed about life. They strive to raise kids who care about others as well as about themselves. The difference between the two families is that because the first is identified according to its possessions, its primary consideration is to itself, while the second is capable of looking beyond itself and its own family life.

Every family needs to develop its own soul in regards to how it will value spirituality and service to others. It does not matter whether your family is part of the Christian Coalition or an ashram or whether your family displays its service to others through its checkbook or by dishing out meals in a homeless shelter. What matters is that your family focus on its spiritual health through creating, cultivating, and nurturing ways of giving to its own soul as well as to the soul of others.

Family Religious/Spiritual Values

"Like family life, religion is in essence intimate,"[5] writes Arthur L. Swift. Yet as personal as religion or spirituality may be, it often reflects the standards of the broader social environment. Long ago, the worship of ancestors reflected the belief held in the clan or tribe that since the ancestral spirits loved and lived by the old accustomed ways, changing from such ways would be viewed as a mark of disrespect and would anger the spirits. Prayers, sacrifices, and celebrations made to wildlife, nature, or "supernatural" events signified the important role such things played in the community in which families gathered. In ancient Egypt there was the religion of the peasant and the religion of the prince, reflective of a society that was based upon a division between royalty and commoner; as well, there was the religion of the "Nile-flooded earth and that of the sky-borne sun,"[6] which were indicative of the importance living off the land had in the lives of ancient Egyptians. The religion of pagan Rome was expressed as that of the people as well as the state, signifying the beginning of a culture in which state religion was valued.

As organized religion began to gain strength, the attitudes and values it imparted upon family life often took precedence over the authority of the parents. At first such regulations helped to create unity within a culture so marriages, births, deaths, and other events could be commemorated in the same ways. But, over time, as families that immigrated to America brought with them their own religions and religious beliefs, ethnic cultures returned to their religious roots, and families strived to observe strict adherence to religious codes in the midst of changing social values, more and more families began to feel conflicted. Parental beliefs and teachings often contradicted the tenets of the church. As well, youths began to question the benefit of holding fast to the faith of generations before them without essential compromise with the changes that were occurring around them. For instance—both then and now—the sanctions that the Catholic Church has placed upon marriage and sexual relations are at direct odds with social changes that have occurred in those areas for decades. In addition, religion's ever-growing focus and influence upon government policy and the political future of America has forced many family members to make choices to relinquish their participation in family religious practices or has created schisms within families.

Throughout all the shifts that have occurred in organized religion—or, in some cases, nonshifts—folk religion, or family religion, has always been present, throughout America's history. This is the religion that has been concerned with

> birth and marriage and death; with planting and harvesting, hunting and fishing; with eating and sleeping and waking with friendship and enmity; with illness and health. Religion . . . in these terms, ceases to be entirely a matter of creeds and hierarchies of institutions and agencies, and reveals itself simply as man's belief in spiritual powers and his efforts to deal with them so as to have their help and not their hindrance in all the business of life.[7]

Folk religion touches families intimately, constantly, and in a great variety of ways because it is the spirituality that connects the family through sharing its particular beliefs, attitudes, and methods of devotion. It is this quality that enables the family to hold fast to its own spiritual practices and language as a minority group—a family—within a majority group—society. It is also this quality upon which the family can depend during private times of difficulty. And it is this quality that maintains the family "altar," where customs such as offering thanks for food at the family table or hearing children say their prayers at bedtime are practiced.

Folk religion is also a family's spiritual "repository," which holds fast to traditions and rituals that are cherished by the family as a unit, preserves relics of significant symbolic value to family members, and treasures its "family tales," which impart wisdom and guidance to all family members. Finally, folk religion represents the moral code of the family unit, where values such as honesty, truthfulness, parental obedience, respect, and other small requirements of individual goodness are taught and modeled both within the family and without.

Therefore, *which* religion a family believes in is not as important as the need for some kind of spiritual core—most likely developed from the family's folk religion—to be present in a family in order to develop the family's soul. That means that a family need not attend or even belong to a church in order to be spiritual. It also means that externalizing beliefs outside the family to a wider faith community such as in a church or synagogue will not replace the need for the experience of folk religion within the family. Too it means that a faith that is different from other family members will not create a negative impact on the family's ability as a group to develop and share its spirituality, for the folk religion that a family shares is nondenominational.

The spiritual core provided by a family's folk religion can help the family find a deep meaning to life, teach its members right from wrong, develop trust, teach respect for others, foster a strong sense of family, and encourage service to others. Families can rediscover or create their own religion and sense of spirituality through the use of one, more, or all of the following Ten Family "Commandments."

The Ten Family "Commandments"

1. Recognize that religious/spiritual values, which are vital to the health of the family, are ultimately the responsibility of the family.

It is not the responsibility of American society or of organized religion to provide religious/spiritual guidance for a particular family; their concerns are for the general population or their particular congregation. More importantly, the norms that either society or organized religion have set may not necessarily establish or reinforce values that will benefit or strengthen a particular family. For example, at present individual parents and families often find themselves teaching a set of spiritual values—justice, fairness, honesty, respect, patience, generosity, and peaceful resolution to conflict—that are constantly being undermined by society through its own "values education" that urges winning at all costs, equates happiness with wealth, rewards self-focus, encourages instant gratification, approves of a "me-first" attitude, and entertains through violence.[8]

While many families might readily support a movement to restore the simple but profound religious/spiritual family values that were part of the American culture before the Industrial Revolution—religious and spiritual values that were inherent in the structure of the family as well as in the neighborhood before suburbanization and modernization occurred—it is unrealistic to think that anyone can turn back the clock of time. It is also unrealistic to think that religious beliefs or spiritual values can work well universally, in a large group. Historically this has been proven so; "primitive tribalism, to which all others' gods are by definition demons, breaks the unity of true neighborliness and at times invades and divides the family."[9] Sometimes churches, through their own pettiness and lack of vision or the revision of some of the very values that united their believers, create schisms within their congregations. And the very existence in cities and towns of a variety of churches or spiritual centers is, in itself, divisive because each promotes its own form of prayer, worship, or other spiritual expression, focused on sustaining values that apply only to particular sects or groups.

Religion or spirituality best functions through a small group; thus, a small community such as a family can do more to create and preserve its spiritual values, use these values to create strong unity within the family, and find its greatest service and fulfillment through them. Setting such religious and spiritual norms needs to be done within a family.

2. Never let science or technology replace or become more important than a family's religion or spirituality.

Science and technology, with their "magical gifts," variety of wonders, and astounding improvements that impact everyday life, may sometimes be seen as competitors to religion and/or spirituality. After all, family members spend more time in front of computers or in classrooms than they do in front of an altar or meditating at a quiet spot in a forest; as well, they spend more time searching and "surfing" for information than they do exploring and practicing a faith of their own.

But science and technology are not focused on spiritual growth. They do not speak to an individual's deep yearning to belong. They play no role in establishing faith or faith-related experiences. They do not strengthen a family's spiritual support system. They do not present themselves as a moral, righteous authority. They do not provide the lessons that are needed to teach love and respect, compassion, wisdom, and peaceful resolution to conflict. They do not help develop important attributes of kindness, warmth, common sense, and discipline. They do not help a family to pass on its religious and spiritual lessons to younger members or weave religious customs, prayer, and other spiritual traditions and rituals into the fabric of family life.

Rather, science and technology impart information and deal in a reality of specifics that no religion or spirituality can ever vie with; science and technology often provide concrete, irrefutable answers, while spirituality asks for blind faith and trust. In those families where religion or some form of spirituality has not been emphasized or practiced, it becomes much easier not to believe in the "one Reality, great beyond all words and formulae" and to desire to be liberated "from the obscurantism of a naive faith."[10] It becomes much easier to believe more in textbook learning than testament learning, to challenge religious attitudes and values, to express wonder at an impressive new computer game or program, rather than to be impressed by the wonder of a beautiful sunset, the song of the whale, the smile of a baby, the simple play of children at a playground, or the beauty of sexual intimacy.

But a core of faith within a family does not come from science or technology. Rather, it comes from

> parents—with their sense of humility and awe in the face of the world's mysteries. It comes from church and from going to church and understanding that one worships something outside one's self and one's desires. It comes from a

sense of mystery in this world that is cultivated at home and in schools. It comes from experiences with teachers who have the good sense to tell students they don't have all the answers, that this is a puzzling world which we must bow down to as well as try to take over and manipulate.[11]

Religion need not be apologized for or ignored in the face of science and technology. It can coexist with science and technology and be used to impart its own sense of wisdom and wonder.

3. Keep religion and politics separate.

Positions on school prayer, abortion, homosexual adoptions and government-sanctioned gay marriages, sex education and condom distribution in schools, the morality of Hollywood, welfare reform, deregulation, federal funding for the National Endowment for the Arts and the Corporation for Public Broadcasting, and tax cuts are just a few of the issues that have helped to make at least one religious group—the Christian Coalition—one of the most powerful grassroots organizations in American politics. With its 1.6 million active supporters and $25 million annual budget, the Coalition exerts an extraordinary influence over the occupant of the Oval Office and Washington's decision-makers.[12]

Today, churches have become places of worship as well as "spiritual precincts," as millions of congregation members can locate their hymnals as well as their voter guides in their pews. Religious organizations have attained the power to "preach" their gospel as well as to set forth their governmental guidelines via a "satellite-Internet-and-fax-machine juggernaut."[13] Religious denominations have become as powerful and preemptive as political parties.

To many families, such infiltration of government by religion harkens back to a not-so-pleasant time in American history in which seventeenth-century New England theocracies invaded families that taught or practiced beliefs that diverged from what was commonly accepted. Today the "spiritual imperative" of some religious organizations has delegated the use of money they raise not for the sick and needy or even to make necessary repairs on a church or rectory, but for advertising, direct mail, and phone-bank work in response to government amendments that come up for vote. Rather than promote Sunday school, religious outings, couples counseling seminars, and spiritual workshops, churches and their leaders provide specific instruction on political organizing and call to order high-tech meetings for forming rapid-response networks.

What does this say to American families and their right to freedom of religious expression as well as their right to vote? When parents give up their authority to establish and maintain the family's folk religion and its spirituality or are forced to expand their teachings and beliefs to include organizations outside the realm of spirituality, such as the United States government, then faith in God or a belief in something or someone larger than themselves no longer plays a foundational role in that family's daily life. It is the rule of the land—the platforms of those who are running for office as well as the voting records of those who hold office—that become the spoken or taught faith in a family, rather than a search for the meaning to life—the spiritual process, or "pilgrimage," in which individuals seek an understanding of, as well as a way of connecting to, life.

Family faith is not a legal issue, an educational issue, or a governmental issue; family faith is a personal and private issue that needs to be delineated from having any affiliation and outside influences, unless such influences support celebrations that reinforce the family and encourage couples to grow in loving and life-fulfilling relationships, seek to strengthen family relations, create programs for mutual support in times of need, and extend outreach services to others.

4. Recognize that each family member needs to go through various levels of building and rebuilding faith.

Theologian John Westerhoff, in his book *Will Our Children Have Faith?*, provides valuable insight into what he identifies as three levels of faith through which family members usually proceed in their quest to reach the fourth level, or the level at which an "owned faith," or a meaningful, personal idea of faith in adulthood, is attained.[14] There is no set pattern for movement through any or all of these levels; some family members stay in one level all their lives, while some move back and forth among the levels depending on circumstances in their lives, the maturation process, and the need for periodic self-exploration and reexamination of spiritual values.

Level one is "the experiential level," or the level of childhood faith in which younger family members begin to experience the faith of those around them. It is at this level that children are capable of understanding God or the concept of an "all powerful" something or someone, through attending church or synagogue with family members as well as through participating at home in religious and spiritual traditions and rituals, such as giving a blessing before an evening meal, saying prayers before bedtime, and so on.

Level two, "the affiliative level," begins in adolescence. This is the point in family members' search for faith and meaning in their lives in which members seek a sense of belonging. If this sense of connection and belonging has been established within the family, then family members may not wish to look elsewhere for it, in cults, gangs, or other groups that have their own set of personalized traditions and rituals for instilling group connection.

Level three, "the searching level," is the stage at which serious religious questioning occurs. In some cases this can be seen as a logical step out of adolescence and into adulthood. A young adult will search with peers, test the validity of parental beliefs with others, and doubt, examine, and study other faiths and/or his or her own in an attempt to establish an "owned faith." In other cases this level may be the site at which an adult will stay, conducting an ongoing or even lifelong process of religious and/or spiritual searching.

The final level, or "the owned faith," is "the prize" that families as well as individual family members seek, for it is at this level that religious and spiritual fulfillment is often attained.

5. Provide space in the home for meditation and renewal.

Dr. Benjamin Spock has said, "The best upbringing that children can receive is to observe their parents taking excellent care of themselves—mind, body, spirit. Children, being the world's greatest mimics, naturally and automatically model their parents' behavior."[15] Each day family members may display to one another that they can meet the needs of the body—physical needs—by doing such things as eating and sleeping at regular intervals. Each day family members may display to one another that they can meet the needs of the mind—mental needs—by doing things such as reading for learning as well as for pleasure and talking about how they feel. But each day family members may neglect to display to one another that they can meet the needs of the spirit—religious and spiritual needs—by doing such things as taking time for reflection (meditating), cultivating a sense of inner peace (relaxing), and seeking out periods of silence (for spiritual "listening" and prayer).

For meeting such needs of the spirit, family members do not need to retreat to a monastary or relocate to the forest or seashore. Very simply, a space in the home can be set aside or regularly used by all family members—young and old—for taking spiritual time-outs to restore inner harmony and peace. Having this space and then using it is necessary in the everyday world of crisis and conflict both inside and outside the home, which makes demands upon the head and the heart, but ignores the spirit. As well, establishing a space in which there can be a sense of stillness within the family living space can head off any crisis and conflict that could potentially be brought into the home from the outside world.

A clutter-free room, a space within a room in which to be quiet and peaceful, or simply a comfortable chair in a corner of the family living space for everyone to use when he or she needs time for spiritual renewal can work well. The regular use of such a space can help each family member to build inner strength, release tension, and become more at peace with him or herself, the family, and the world.

6. Pass on valuable spiritual lessons in positive and meaningful ways.

The most meaningful way to pass on religious and/or spiritual lessons to other family members so they will have long-lasting value is not through requiring memorization of Bible passages or catechisms, urging attendance at Sunday school or membership in a religious youth group, or enforcing attention to the family's "sermons" or religious beliefs. Rather, the most enduring spiritual lessons are those family members learn through shared life experiences that help them connect in a meaningful way to themselves, to others, and to life.

As well, a family's enduring sense of spirituality—one that can be passed on to future generations—comes not from verbal instruction but from the teaching provided by positive and meaningful examples—the hugs and kisses freely given to family members, the discipline used to enforce and reinforce right from wrong, the respect and courtesy shown to family members, the compassion and understanding expressed during times of need, and so on.

7. Remember that the essential component of religion and spirituality is love.

The power of love has united people for centuries, connecting souls in ways that often take them beyond personal limits, bring them to greater levels of consciousness, illuminate a sometimes dark and confusing world with the light of new awareness, and enable people to reach out and give of themselves. Carl Jung recognized the power of love to expand consciousness in a way that brings people into "a reunion with the laws of life." Plato described love as the union of two souls with divinity itself. Dante's love for Beatrice led him to the gates of paradise, where he sang of "the love that moves the sun and the other stars." Chuang-Tzu taught that it is through love that people experience the "inherent connections between ourselves and others, seeing all creation as one." Eastern religion says that "the Way of Love" is a "path of compassion that enables us to see beneath apparent discord into the underlying unity of all creation."[16]

Like love, religion and spirituality can hold an equally intimate relationship with family life, for they impact and shape each family member's lives and give them the courage to go on. They can be relied upon by family members who are intimately associated with one another in the essential tasks of living, who are confronting risks together, who are attempting to satisfy their own needs as well as the needs of others, and who are together thrilling to a success or nursing the wounds of a setback to a family member.

Because of this, religion and spirituality thrive best in a family environment that is lived through the love its members have for one another, their ability to express this love, and the desire each member has to actively share in the process of nurturing the family. Through the establishment of family intimacy that is founded on love, those who gather together as a family can more readily acknowledge the presence of a power greater than themselves and to commune with this power in order to attain true peace of mind.

To find this true peace of mind, resolve to give, live, play, pray, and love another family member every day. Do something kind for your partner. Enjoy the natural beauty of the day. Play a game with your kids. Pray for riches in your life that no amount of money can buy. And express your love to a family member. Do this, and it will be easy to believe that "God has given each one of us approximatley 25,000 to 26,000 days on this earth. I truly believe He (or She) has something very specific in mind: 8,300 days to sleep, 8,300 to work, and 8,300 to give, live, play, pray, and love one another."[17]

8. Support peaceful resolution to conflict and nonviolent action.

One of the cornerstones of any civilized society is the ability of its members to get along; one of the cornerstones of any religious/spiritual family life is living together in peace and harmony.

Yet the rate of reported crime in the United States is the highest in the industrialized world and, on a daily basis, quarrels between those who know each other as well as perfect strangers erupt into damage to property, minor injury, permanent scarring, or even death. Outside the home as well as inside, America's families are being fed a steady diet of increasingly graphic and violent entertainment. Although this country has rarely been immune to violence throughout its history—from skirmishes with Indians to hand-to-hand combat between brothers and fellow Americans in the Civil War—in the past more nonviolent action was promoted and pursued. The Quakers, with their tradition of "witnessing" (which upheld that once an injustice is recognized, that knowledge becomes part of a person's life, and he or she cannot turn away in ignorance, but must do something about the injustice), have influenced centuries of letter writers, speech makers, and peaceful demonstrators. In addition, Quaker philosophy has helped modern organizations such as Greenpeace and Amnesty International find more peaceful ways to resolve the injustices they have witnessed toward whales, seals, and other endangered animals and prisoners of conscience being held in foreign countries.

As well, those today who practice nonviolent action through civil disobedience—from taking direct action through boycotts, work slowdowns, and strikes to immobilize the opposition, to organizing and participating in symbolic protests, vigils, and peaceful demonstrations—take a historical cue from Henry David Thoreau, who was jailed for refusing to pay taxes that supported slavery and the Mexican War. Moral leaders from Gandhi to Martin Luther King, Jr., have also been role models for today's nonviolent action; in their lifetimes, they sought to affirm oneness in cause and protest against unjust laws, by investigating facts, negotiating with opponents, and preparing themselves to act in ways that promoted the spirit of nonviolence in tandem with spiritual beliefs.

While it may be hard to practice and preach nonviolence, compromise, and peace to family members in the overwhelming presence of the aggression, anger, abuse, and confrontation they may face on a daily basis in today's schools, workplaces, and society, religious and spiritual lessons can be used to encourage family members to take personal responsibility and personal action as well as to follow a path of peace.

Inside the home, family members learn that conflict between people is normal because each person, more often than not, has a different set of needs and desires. Therefore, it is not the conflict itself but how it is responded to that may or may not produce violence. Seen in this way, assessing blame, focusing on which person is right and which person is wrong, or taking an adversarial position that creates a "me-against-you" attitude only serves to escalate conflict and keep those in conflict entrenched in their own particular way of thinking. Facing conflict in healthy ways is how people learn and develop; facing conflict is the basis of all thinking, problem-solving, creativity, and personal development. Thus, it is important that each family member model how to "make harmony" with the others, by not engaging in name calling, slamming doors, throwing objects, or resorting to physical violence. Instead, family members need to learn and then practice steps they can take to resolve their conflicts with one another, such as first separating from one another when their emotions are high, so they can get their emotions under control, and then coming back together to sit down and clarify their positions for one another. This position-clarification discussion is integral in conflict resolution, for it teaches each family member to look at the world not only from his or her viewpoint but also from the other's point of view.

Once family members are able to let go of the intensity of their emotional response to a conflict and open up a dialogue, then they can work toward generating solutions or alternatives to resolve the present conflict, which may require that one or both members revise their needs and interests at that time so harmony between them can be restored. As well, families need to be supportive of church and school programs and workshops that deal with conflict resolution.

To deal with the violence and violent behaviors in today's society, families need to band together in their neighborhoods to fight crime and work together to support and create parks, playgrounds, picnic areas, and other spaces in the community so family members have alternatives to watching inappropriately violent television shows and movies or engaging in criminal activities not out of desire but out of boredom. Families need to organize boycotts of corporations, such as toy and game manufacturers, that advocate violent behavior through the products they sell, and purchase toys and games for family members that encourage imaginative and creative fun play. Families need to pay attention to the ratings of movies, music, video games, and television shows. Families need to ask their religious or spiritual leaders to provide education about what unhealthy conflict resolution and violent entertainment is doing to America's families. Families need to make and enforce curfews. And families need to take personal responsibility for instilling peace and harmony in the home and within each family member by becoming more actively involved in the family's life:

> If a company was selling food to children that was tainted with disease and making them sick, we'd take action in a second. But over time, little by little, parts of our society have been rewarded for poisoning our children with violence. The effects are just as serious, and it is just as vital that we take action.[18]

Just as all religions teach to play fair and not to hit or kill or steal or cheat, so too do families have to teach and model the same things.

9. Foster simplicity.
American society encourages accumulating material possessions. Every day manufacturers announce new and improved products, the latest must-have gadgets and "in" fashions. As a result, family homes have become department stores. Dresser draw-

ers and closets are jam-packed, living rooms are filled with wall-to-wall electronic equipment, kids' rooms are complete with computer and clutter, the family cars are loaded with the best options, and garages and attics are piled high with possessions.

As well, America has become a "throw-away society"—"Fast food wrappers, grocery bags, bottles, cans, paper napkins, plastic packaging, high fashion clothing, disposable razors, cameras, even relationships are quickly discarded when their usefulness is gone."[19] Planned obsolescence in consumable goods has spilled over into family life, precipitating attitudes that lean toward expendability rather than dependability, foster short-term interest rather than long-term commitment, and cast a sense of impermanence over daily living rather than give a sense of hope for the future.

Every day family life is also stressfully frittered away in dozens of details, obligations, meetings, errands, and obligations. Calendars are impossibly cluttered, the pace is rushed. People race off in a dozen directions at once thinking ten different thoughts and harboring the nagging feeling that there are countless other things they ought to be doing. It is not unusual for two parents to rush out of the house at the same time, only to stop and look at each other and realize that they have left a child behind.

Twenty-five centuries ago, Eastern spiritualist Lao Tzu realized the dangers of such excesses, warning that great personal as well as social conflict arises from wanting too much. Student of Eastern philosophy Henry David Thoreau praised the silent reveries and joy of contemplation he enjoyed during his unrushed days at Walden Pond and called for other Americans as well to "simplify, simplify." In the 1950s a woman who called herself Peace Pilgrim applied the spiritual principle to "seek simplicity" in her walk across America on a pilgrimage for peace: "Paring down her possessions to the clothes on her back and a few items in her pockets, she chose to live at what she called 'need-level,' rejoicing in the freedom she found."[20]

Religious tenets value simplicity. Those who are spiritually wise are capable of sweeping away the clutter in their lives so they can discover life's essentials: serenity, harmony, balance, beauty, patience, the joy of silence, stability, and peace. One way of seeking such simplicity in the family home and with family members is to pare down personal possessions. Ask each family member to consider his or her "need-level" in regard to possessions and personal "things" already owned and to get rid of things that are no longer used, have been forgotten about, have long since been outgrown, or have not been fixed since they were broken. Then, as a family, work together to recycle what your family no longer needs by cleaning out one area of the house a month. Give duplicate or surplus items to younger family members who are starting out on their own or to neighbors; donate discarded items to a favorite charity or church bazaar. By giving away what you no longer need or use, you are bringing greater order to the family's living space and shifting the family's value focus from things to people.

Then individuals as well as the entire family can work together to limit future purchases to "need-level" items, perhaps instituting a voting system for "big ticket" items (such as anything over $100). As well, the family can work independently and as a group to create more free time in overcrowded calendars, set aside time to volunteer at a local charity, and engage in hobbies that entail activities rather than collecting or accumulating material items. Through such simplifying, family members gain greater power over their own lives and create a simpler but more spiritually rewarding family life.

Living simply is a liberating, empowering, and soul-restoring method of discerning what is materially useless but spiritually beneficial.

10. Teach family members that they are part of everything and everyone around them.

All religions teach love. All religions encourage helping others. All religions urge forgiveness. All religions preach respect. Thus, all religions strive to "teach the same right way to live."[21]

In families, this "same right way to live" can be seen as a reaching out by family members and families themselves to others—to individuals, to the family, to the extended family, to the neighborhood, to a county, to a state, and even farther, to a more global community. Such a reaching out is nurtured by a spiritual heart that beats a steady cadence of cooperation and consideration toward others so that peaceful growth and caring can occur within a large community.

In colonial and frontier times, Americans recognized and cherished this ideal of giving to others, through their sense of belonging to a "whole" community that was made up of many smaller, interdependent parts. Families at that time knew that although they needed to be self-sufficient in order to survive, they also faced the same obstacles as other families; thus, lending a hand to help a neighbor, bartering for necessities, and looking out for other's safety were part of their "community of heart." And up until the advent of the automobile, most people grew up, worked, and raised families in places where such communities had already been established and where it was only natural for them to reach out to others.

But increased mobility and new technologies slowly began to undermine such communities of the heart. Businesses ripped communities apart through relocation of employees. Suburban housing eliminated intimate neighborhood gathering places. Television destroyed the need to look outside of the home for interaction. And the push toward individualism emphasized independence from one another rather than interdependence. (Peter Yarrow, of the singing group Peter, Paul, and Mary, once told a concert audience that such a shift in values could easily be noted from the evolving titles of popular magazines. "First there was *Life*. Then there was *People*. And now there is *Self*."[22])

Life without others, without a community of some sort, is completely contrary to religious teachings and spiritual values. Both honor those who make sacrifices for others, who transcend their own desires and put the needs of others ahead of their own. Both teach that while an experience of growing closer to oneself is important, what is equally—if not more—important is an experience of "otherness," or the connection to one or more communities outside of family, friends, neighbors, coworkers, and social circles.

Families can foster this desire to experience "otherness" by modeling and encouraging values that support generosity, cooperation, and sacrifice to others—from altruistic behaviors (helping others without being asked or making an effort to do a special favor for someone) to volunteering time and sharing resources with others.

Valuing Service to Others

When President John F. Kennedy issued his famous inaugural challenge to Americans—"Ask not what your country can do for you; ask what you can do for your country"—he was inviting Americans to reach out and create for themselves a better society rather than wait for or expect the government to do so. In effect, he was reminding Americans not only of the importance of service to others, but also of the history of interdependency that had been fostered at a much earlier time in the country, when individuals were part of families who were part of extended families who were part of communities who were part of the colonies that were part of the "New World" that was part of the whole world. Such communities, and the interdependency created within them, were central to human life; the health and welfare of each member of the community was the responsibility of the entire community. So each individual had support—and gave support—in ensuring emotional, spiritual, and physical needs were met.

But as society became more mobile, communities broke down into smaller and more isolated units. Nuclear families dissolved into individual members who lived separately and who, for the most part, valued power and acquisition rather than going beyond themselves in ways that enlarged their focus to include people around them, in their communities and world.

Yet during times of social crisis in this country—the Depression, for instance, or World War II—Americans maintained communities in order to create stability, promote a common cause, and survive as a group. As well, individuals reached out at such times to others, and to other causes and concerns, less for their own good than for the good of something or someone outside them. But service to others has not always been in response to a difficult time. During the 1950s, a variety of nonprofit organizations benefited from volunteerism provided by suburban housewives: the PTA, Girl Scouts, the American Red Cross, horticultural and historical societies, charities, hospitals, nursing homes, and so on. And many of the children who grew up in those homes went on to create grassroots organizations, civil rights groups, and political platforms that flourished from the energy and effort the individuals put into working together on a specific cause or problem.

The problems in society today—social injustice, crime, environmental issues, homelessness, and countless others—require that people leave their lives of isolation and band together, acting communally to find solutions that extend beyond the scope of such problems. Families, in particular, need to do this in order to reunite family members with one another and to divert them from their own solo journeys so they can participate in (and receive the benefits from) the spiritual healing process that comes from caring for others. Then the family can work toward developing the soul of a giving spirit—a spirit filled with vitality and energy that comes from a common sense of purpose, of reaching out to another or others, and which, as an added benefit, unites all family members.

For as long as individual family members or the family itself is focused on success and pursuit of "the good life," however, service to others will most likely not happen. The family may talk about such service or even make an occasional financial or material donation to a cause, but rarely will it actually reach out to others. Such an all-talk-and-no-action stance has become quite acceptable in today's society; it is often rhetoric, nor righteousness, that determines who gets the votes, the money, the time, and the attention.

Thus, families need to actively serve others in concrete ways so each member can take part in revitalizing an altruistic, caring, concern-for-others family soul. Families can do this in a variety of ways:

> Some join voluntary organizations, such as those dedicated to fighting leukemia, to developing youth programs, or to carrying out special community or church projects. . . .
>
> Some families help single-parent families by offering to absorb their children into after-school car pools or by inviting them to go along on such things as fishing expeditions. . . .
>
> Other families help with emergency housing during blizzards, floods, occurrences of child abuse. Some families open their doors to youths who are thrown out of their own homes or to hard-to-place foster children or to babies waiting for adoption.[23]

Service to others does not have to be done on a grand scale; it can be a simple gesture of kindness. Sometimes a simple act of kindness or a desire to "fix" or make better a social condition can blossom into something that teaches others to value such reaching out and, as well, encourages them to participate. For example, when a young Catholic priest named Patrick Hughes started the Walk for Hunger in Boston in 1969, he began a Massachusetts tradition that today enlists over half a million sponsors of nearly fifty thousand people who walk all or part of the twenty-mile course to raise millions of dollars to fund hundreds of soup kitchens and food pantries in Massachusetts. As well, his Walk for Hunger unites families and communities for a few hours on a Sunday afternoon in the spring.[24]

Valuing service to others comes from the heart—a heart that yearns to give to a community; a heart that yearns to be part of a community; a heart that strives to create that community. A family that is basically caring, basically empathetic, and basically altruistic toward its members and to others more often than not provides a sound religious and spiritual base for its members. And it is from this base that the family's soul can be preserved in ways that make a world of difference both within the family and without.

NOTES

1. Brussat, Frederic and Mary Ann. *100 Ways to Keep Your Soul Alive: Living Deeply and Fully Every Day.* HarperSanFrancisco, San Francisco, 1994, p. 93.
2. Walsh, David. *Selling Out America's Children: How America Puts Profits Before Values—and What Parents Can Do.* Deaconess Press, Minneapolis, 1994, p. 108.
3. Curran, Dolores. *Traits of a Healthy Family.* HarperSanFrancisco, San Francisco, 1983, p. 218.
4. Walsh, p. 15.
5. Anshen, Ruth Nanda. *The Family: Its Function and Destiny.* Harper & Brothers Publishers, New York, 1949, p. 393.
6. *Ibid.,* p. 396.
7. *Ibid.*
8. Walsh, p. 117.
9. Anshen, p. 402.
10. *Ibid.,* p. 398.
11. Curran, p. 224.
12. Birnbaum, Jeffrey H. "The Gospel According to Ralph," *Time,* May 15, 1995.
13. *Ibid.*
14. Curran, pp. 220–221.
15. "Points to Ponder," *Reader's Digest,* April 1995.
16. *Ibid.,* pp. 201–202.
17. Dean, Amy E. *Pleasant Dreams: Nighttime Meditations for Peace of Mind.* Hay House, 1993, November 6.
18. Walsh, pp. 60–61, 66.
19. Dreher, Diane. *The Tao of Inner Peace.* HarperPerennial, New York, 1990, p. 78.
20. *Ibid.,* p. 82.
21. "Points to Ponder," *Reader's Digest,* August 1995.
22. Walsh, p. 105.
23. Curran, pp. 249–250.
24. Carroll, James. "The people's marathon," *Boston Globe,* May 2, 1995.

CHAPTER 10

⌘

Cultivating a Future

If you and your family could be transported back in time to any period in American history in which you could all live and grow together as a family—in effect, in which you could reexperience your own childhood, fall in love and get married or join with your partner, raise children, and grow old, in which time period would you choose? During the settling of the colonies? During the Civil War? During industrialization? Perhaps during the Depression? In the forties, fifties, sixties, seventies, or eighties?

There are many people today who claim that the decade of the 1950s was the best for American families. In fact, there are many who raised families during that time period who claim that it was the best time of their lives. What made it such a great and memorable time for families?

> The depression of the 1930s and World War II laid the foundation for a commitment to a stable home life. . . . [Then Vice President Richard] Nixon insisted that American superiority in the cold war rested not on weapons, but on the secure, abundant family life of modern suburban homes. In these structures, adorned and worshiped by their inhabitants, women would achieve glory and men would display their success. Consumerism was not an end in itself; it was the means for achieving individuality, leisure, and upward mobility.[1]

But yet, at the same time, the explosion of the first atomic bombs on Hiroshima and Nagasaki in 1945, which hastened the end of World War II, marked the beginning of the Cold War, a time in which world peace suddenly became problematic and international tensions soared. In 1949 the USSR detonated its first atomic bomb. The Korean War erupted in 1950, making World War III an imminent possibility in many people's minds. In 1951 the United States exploded its first hydrogen bomb. The next year, the first British nuclear explosion occurred; the following year, the Soviets exploded their first hydrogen bomb. Americans began to live in fear and dread of the supposedly "peaceful atom." Bomb shelters were built and stocked; civil defense drills were held in schools. Pop culture captured the fear of instant death and mass trauma with a proliferation of science fiction movies that focused on accidents or misuse of atomic radiation. The terror of annihilation was prevalent, even though most Americans had a strong faith that their country was going to be their savior, their protector from all the evil forces of the world. Thus, a "home filled with children would create a feeling of warmth and security against the cold forces of disruption and alienation. . . . The family seemed to be the one place where people could control their destinies and perhaps even shape their future."[2]

Now imagine that you and your family could be transported forward in time to a period in which you could live and grow together, in which you could realize your ideals, desires, and goals as a family. What in this future time period would be different from today? From your chosen time period of the past?

Alan Ehrenhalt, executive editor of *Governing* magazine and author of *The Lost City: Discovering the Forgotten Virtues of Community in the Chicago of the 1950s,* probed life in a working-class Catholic neighborhood on the Southwest Side of Chicago in the 1950s. What he discovered were people who today regret the loss of spirit, identity, and community among "people who would rather stay indoors with the remote control than get to know their neighbors."[3] What he also discovered was that there are lessons to be learned in the nineties from family life in the fifties: "We don't want the fifties back. What we want is to edit them . . . a more ordered world, in which people have fewer choices, authority is clear and people have more of a sense of right and wrong, is a decent world to live in."[4]

At the beginning of Part III of this book, Alex Haley's words lent credence to the need to "grow" a family's soul: "The family is our refuge and springboard; nourished on it, we can advance to new horizons. In every conceivable manner, the family is link to our past, bridge to our future."[5] In this book, the past influences on families have been explored, along with recommendations of things to do in the present—things that families can do right now to begin to care for their family soul.

But what of tomorrow? And of the tomorrows of future generations of families? Can families today do more not only for themselves, but also for future generations, in order to advance to new horizons and build a bridge to what lies ahead? Just as you have explored the requirements to "farm the soul" and plant the "soul seeds" that are needed to create, cultivate, and nurture your experience of family, so too can you explore the ways to "harvest" the family soul—to gather the product of the "soul crop" you are tending so you can reap the benefits of the soul-enriching experience of family you are creating now for years to come.

Harvesting the family soul is a soul-strengthening experience. The more you do it, the stronger the family becomes, the healthier the family can be, and the more capable the family will be of surviving its own life crises, as well as the crises, challenges, and pressures presented by society. Harvesting the family soul involves five actions that families and their members need to make on a regular basis—actions that can be considered integral to investing in the family's future:

1. Put the family first—*no matter what*.
2. Focus on positive family influences; insist on seeing the good in your family despite what statistics or the media might convey.

3. Forge the family's version of the "American Dream" rather than pursue an idealistic and unattainable American Dream.
4. Promote family services on all levels—in your neighborhood, in your state, in the country.
5. Embrace *all* families no matter what their race, ethnicity, religion, or lifestyle.

Harvesting the Family Soul: Putting the Family First

Crucial to a family's future is the willingness on the part of each family member to be committed to the family—to invest time, energy, and attention in ensuring that the family comes first. Such a commitment needs to be active—that is, shown not stated—and obvious—from actual investment of time rather than from talk about the desire for time together. As well, such a commitment needs to be made in spite of the continual sense of urgency in everyday life, the financial tension that can cascade into emotional squabbles and arguments, the constant feeling of never being able to catch up or get things done, the pressure of being pulled in several directions at one time, and the nagging desire that any minute not spent working or focused on achieving a goal is wasted.

Granted, the gradual shift in American life over the years from an agrarian to a computer society is the main reason why Americans have become "speed demons" who have individually lost control of their time and who have collectively created "speed-demon families" who are continually rushing to and fro, each individual in hot pursuit of his or her own agenda and clearly incapable of spending quality time with others. American families began to lose this battle with time in the 1950s, when, along with "the good life" of living in the suburbs, came afterschool athletic leagues, lessons designed to enhance the competitiveness between families to have the most gifted children, and long, mind-numbing commutes to work.

For many male and female Americans who find that they must work not only to afford all the lessons and leagues, but also just to make ends meet, "work is now the emotional and spiritual center of life . . . an end in itself, a way to escape from family, the inner life, the world."[6] Thus, putting the family first means not sacrificing the family on the altar of career and other obligations, but sacrificing career and other obligations so the family can be honored.

A 1991 public opinion poll done for Hilton Hotels Corporation revealed that "65 percent of American workers would take a salary reduction to get more time off."[7] Which is perhaps why the politically progressive, Manhattan-based New Party advocated in its 1996 campaign longer vacation time as part of its new social contract with American workers, who rank far below the average lengths of vacation time offered in Western European countries, where vacation policy is usually government mandated. In the United States, just because vacation time is not on the public agenda does not mean that the idea could not become popular. Working mothers and fathers need to advocate with their congresspeople and/or employers to be able to get more time away from work to spend with their families.

As well, from time to time family members need to take stock of the amount of time they are spending at work (or at school, or in pursuit of other obligations) and with the family and then make conscious choices about where to spend their time: on the job at the office, or on the "job" as a father, mother, partner, or sibling. As one father comments:

> Sometimes I feel that the time I spend with my sons could be better spent at the office. Then I remind myself that the productivity report will affect life for a few days or a few weeks. I must do it and it's important, but my job as a father is more important.
>
> If I'm a good father to my sons, they're likely to be good parents too. Someday—after I'm gone, and certainly after that report has rotted—my grandchild or grandchildren will have a good father because *I* was a good father.[8]

This is not to say that work, school, and other obligations can never depose the family from being top priority. There are always going to be "crunch times" that require more time than usual spent away from the family and some family activities being temporarily put on hold or postponed. During such times, however, the family can offer physical and emotional support in order to maintain family spirit and the sense of "we are all in this together." So long as work is not portrayed as coming first and does not routinely affect the family's time together, then a healthy balance between work and family can be established and maintained.

"When 1500 children were asked, 'What do you think makes a happy family?'" wrote Nick Stinnett and John DeFrain in their book *Secrets of Strong Families,* "they didn't list money, cars, or fine homes. They replied: doing things together."[9] When family members want the family to endure, they need to be dedicated to the family in ways that involve routinely—not sporadically or catch-as-catch-can—spending time together. A regular night out for pizza or another regularly scheduled activity (such as a weekend shopping outing or a camping or fishing trip) is one way of showing family members that they come first. Or setting aside a certain time period—Sunday morning or afternoon, for instance—as family time and then not letting anything impact on this time can convey the importance such time together has for the family and its members.

What happens in this time is not as significant as the fact that time has been set aside that is completely and wholly family time. This can be time spent doing fun things together—playing ball in the backyard, going on vacation, taking in a first-run movie—or working together on a home project or sharing in a responsibility—raking leaves, doing the dishes, walking the dog. Keep in mind, however, the difference between quality time and quantity time. A family that spends night after night clumped together like mashed potatoes on the living room couch in front of the television may be spending time together, but they are not spending quality time together. As well, the family that drives a member to his or her soccer game and then stands around on the sidelines watching the game is not enjoying quality time together as a family. Quantity time is measured in terms of accumulated minutes, while quality time is thought of in terms of interaction. When family members interact with one another through playful activities, in conversation, and while sharing an interest, they can enjoy one another's company as well as learn more about one another as individuals. This helps to create family unity as well as positive connections among family members that show that they appreciate and respect one another—from each member of a couple honoring sexual fidelity, to parents frequently conveying messages of praise and love, to children giving thanks for rewards and gifts.

Initiating casual conversations to discuss such topics as sports, clothing, music, and so on also helps family members to develop an appreciation for one another, through learning about their likes and dislikes. As well, such casual conversations can sometimes evolve into discussions of more important and profound issues such as sex, drugs, love, and a multitude of other subjects, so family members can express their feelings and values and thus learn to respect and appreciate the opinions of others.

Additionally, appreciation and respect for the family is shown when each member takes the time to weigh options and make choices about participating in activities outside the family that may affect the time the family and its members can spend together. For example, allowing only one child to sign up for activities he or she would like to do and then expecting the rest of the family to be tolerant or supportive of these activities does not respect the feelings or appreciate the opinions other family members may have about such an imbalanced situation. As well, parents who sacrifice everything so their children can do whatever they want to do are not conveying a healthy message about appreciation and respect for others. Instead, what the children learn is that other people are always going to give them what they want.

To assist family members in learning how to balance their time spent in pursuits outside the family, guidelines can be used for weighing and choosing outside activities that make appreciation and respect for the family and its members a priority. Such guidelines can include asking and answering the following questions, and then basing decisions upon the responses:

• How will participating in this activity (taking a course, joining an athletic team, becoming a Girl Scout or Boy Scout, etc.) affect our family life? Both the negative as well as the positive impacts need to be explored.

If there are negative impacts, can these be overcome without taking away from the family or any member? For example, a family member who wishes to play basketball may not be able to complete after-school chores because of practice, but another family member may volunteer to assume this job and trade one of his or her own, such as collecting and taking out the trash every other night.

If there are positive impacts, can the family or any other member also benefit from the activity? For example, a father who wishes to get out of the house on weekends and exercise more and a daughter who is training for the school's running team can appreciate and respect each other's needs when the father bicycles alongside his daughter on a Saturday morning, carrying her water and any other supplies she might need during her long training run.

• How important is doing the activity? A final decision needs to be based ultimately on the amount of time, energy, and attention that it is necessary to give to the family and the impact participating in the activity will make on this essential family time.

• What activity can this replace? Neither the family nor its members are shown appreciation and respect when one or more members are participating in a multitude of activities that take up all or the majority of their afternoons, nights, and weekends. As part of the decision-making process, family members need to learn that sometimes taking on a new interest or activity means letting go of something else, even if it is something they enjoy just as much.

Finally, family members show respect and appreciation for one another when they show that the family and its members are far more important than some arbitrary standard that no one can quite measure up to (for example, expecting each room in the home to be always like a picture out of *House Beautiful* rather than having its usual lived-in look) and when they cease fault-finding with one another or belittling one another in sarcastic, biting, and negative ways. Couples in particular can improve their relationships with each other—and thus become role models for a healthy intimate relationship—by accentuating the positive.

Thus, families who wish to cultivate a future for the family's soul need to be committed to the family group, spend quality time together, limit activities that take them away from the family, and support one another by showing appreciation and respect.

Harvesting the Family Soul: Focusing on the Good in the Family

Child psychologist Bruno Bettelheim tells a story about a conversation he had when he was four years old with his grandmother, who reared eleven children in Vienna. He knew one of the children was schizophrenic, and so he asked her what she thought of the son of hers "who acted funny":

> She said—and I translate roughly—"One out of eleven is a good batting average."
> He added, "How come my 84-year-old grandmother with a seventh-grade education knew that not everyone can be perfect, and accepted with equanimity that one of her sons was crazy? It didn't hurt her, upset her, or shake her confi-

dence in herself. Yet modern, well-educated parents who know all the laws of statistics cannot accept this . . . and they ruin their own life and their child's life by completely unreasonable expectations."[10]

American society today is adept at focusing on the negative in families, searching out all sorts of dysfunctions—big and small—and then focusing on them, citing them as the causes for the weaknesses and failures in today's families. Tune into any talk show, read any newspaper, study any self-help book, listen to professionals who study families, and what you will learn is that families are considered the creators of problems. As well, families have been so frequently told that they and their members need help that they tend to be conscious much more of what is wrong with their families than of what is right. Or they have become so painfully sensitive to being labeled dysfunctional that they are ready to obtain professional help for thoughts, feelings, and behaviors which, for the most part, are a normal part of an individual's or a family's development.

Then, to add further injury to an already sore wound, families of the past are held up to today's families as role models of how families ought to be or could be. These families in the past are made out to be happy, selfless, wonderful, healthy, wholesome, and trouble-free. Society teaches families today that Ozzie and Harriet and the rest of the Nelson family, as well as the Brady Bunch, could have landed at Plymouth Rock, while Edith and Archie and the rest of the Bunkers or Walter, Maude, and Carol Finley would have never even been allowed to disembark from the *Mayflower*. The reasoning behind this is that the Finleys and the Bunkers are perceived to have PROBLEMS and are therefore not very much like "real-life" historical families, while the Bradys and the Nelsons deal with teeny-tiny situations that never tarnish the golden glow that surrounds the family.

It is pure bunk, however, the notion that families of the past were without their problems, troubles, embarrassing situations, or tragic circumstances. Families of the past have, indeed, always had their fair share of marital problems, sexual and verbal abuse, violence, murder, criminal members, ne'er-do-wells, children born out of wedlock, abortions, alcoholics and drug addicts, suicides, deformities, handicaps, and mental illnesses—surprisingly, all the things that families today have. But what makes the families of the past appear to be "good" and "pure" and "perfect" in comparison to today's families is that they were adept at hiding their problems. In fact, culture dictated that the families claim they had no problems:

> They wrote off the people owning the problem as different. . . . The spouse who was unfaithful or alcoholic was labeled "ne'er-do-well" by the community, thus sparing the family the responsibility and shame for his or her behavior. The depressed woman was "going through her time" or "in the change," and her family was thus alleviated from blaming itself for her problem. The teenage boy who wanted a slice of life bigger than his local community had to offer had "itchy feet," and if he decided to go off for a year or two to find himself, his parents weren't castigated for pushing him out. . . . . Old people got "ornery," children who were heard as well as seen were dismissed as "young upstarts," and women who asked for more out of marriage than cooking and children were considered suspect. A child with an emotional or learning problem was "not quite right," and those who questioned approved mores and customs were "just plain crazy." In sum, the problems in the family of the past were attributed solely to the individual, never to the family.[11]

For years family professionals went along with this focus, treating troubled family members outside their homes in institutional settings until their difficulties were overcome. But what they found was that when the family members returned to their homes, their problems oftentimes eventually resurfaced. Families began to be studied to uncover what was causing children and adults to become less healthy individuals upon their return home, which eventually led professionals to conclude that individuals were part of a family system. Or, as more succinctly stated by Dr. Charles Figley, director of the Family Research Institute at Purdue University: "The family is a system like a spiderweb. When you pluck one strand, the entire web is affected."[12]

Thus, today's families need to see that admitting to and then getting help for their problems, whether that help be from a self-help group, a professional, a family member, or a member of the extended family, is a positive step in caring for the future of the entire family and focusing on the good in the family.

Focusing on the good in the family also involves dealing with family crises. A Chinese proverb wisely states, "Nobody's family can hang out the sign, 'Nothing the matter here.'" A family today that admits when it needs help and then readily seeks help ensures a stronger and healthier tomorrow for its future generations than does a family that strives to be trouble-free, for the family that strives to be trouble-free is not capable of looking at its problems and solving them; rather, that family's goal is to eliminate the problems instead of deal with them. As a result, while the trouble-free family may appear to be more joyful and free of conflict, when faced with a crisis that is too big to sweep under the carpet, the members may not be capable of pulling together to face the crisis and handle it effectively. As well, individuals from such families who have been trained to ignore, deny, or hide problems may have a hard time dealing with problems they must face in their everyday lives outside of the family.

But the family that rejects the expectation of being trouble-free and instead expects to have its share of joys as well as its share of problems—both a normal part of family life—can learn to approach problems and resolve them with a positive attitude. This means that the family is able to join together to work through their troubles and face crises head-on without feeling that the problems in any way reflect negatively upon the family or its members. They do this by employing any one of a number of problem-solving support systems that are available:

- *In the family itself,* through airing and resolving issues and conflicts in one-on-one family meetings or in a family group discussion
- *In the family circle,* by relying upon the experience and wisdom of the family elders to provide guidance or present options to work through a tough time or toward resolution
- *In supportive family organizations,* such as churches, schools, and social groups
- *In "gatherings at the well,"* or informal discussions with a network of friends and relatives with whom the family and its members can talk and receive support
- *In support groups* made up of like-minded individuals, such as bereavement groups, divorce groups, young mothers' groups, single parents groups, and so on
- *In counseling and therapy sessions*
- *In twelve-step support groups,* such as Alcoholics Anonymous, Overeaters Anonymous, Al-Anon, Codependents Anonymous, Adult Children of Alcoholics, and so on.

A family that is unafraid to admit that it has bad times as well as good ones and can show its members its willingness to use any one of a number of tools available within and without the family to work through the bad times is conveying a very positive message to its members.

Focusing on the good in the family also means providing perspective for family members on society's issues. In her book *Life, Liberty and the Pursuit of Happiness,* author Peggy Noonan recounted what goes through the minds of children when "we go through one of our national seizures on an issue":

A dozen years ago, Hollywood fell in love with the environmental issue and put enviro messages in all their shows. The messages made their way into the funnies and magazines, and parents went to school officials and said, "We'd like our children to be better educated on environmental concerns."

The schools came through with a vengeance. Now I have a little son who thinks he's going to die from pollution.

We do not educate our children; we traumatize them. We are not giving them a vision of a better world; we are giving them nightmares.[13]

Although life is meant to be a challenge, the psychological impact created by daily doses of "bad news," persistent warnings of imminent or future danger or distress, or constant reminders of what is wrong with the world can instill fear, discouragement, depression, isolation, stress, and doubt in children as well as adults. In a world where security devices are installed in homes to protect families from their neighbors, where walls are built around playgrounds to protect against stray bullets fired by gangs, where day-care centers and airplanes carrying family members from faraway places are blown up, where hard-earned material possessions cannot be displayed with pride for fear of theft, families need to work hard to teach their members to seek out good, positive cultural messages.

They can do this in many ways. They can help their members to distinguish between celebrities and heroes and encourage them to read biographies and history books to discover the heroes of the world. They can make decisions based on positive values—values that have endured and held societies together over time, such as reaching out to others and living by the Golden Rule. They can fight against stress and develop the family's peace of mind by encouraging exercise, relaxation and play, hobbies, and raising pets. They can balance the serious with the humorous. They can devote some of the family's time to a cause or concern that is bigger than the family—the homeless population, for example, or the reduction of neighborhood crime—and work together on this as a family. They can reinforce positive behaviors—for example, "I like it when you clear the table after dinner without me having to ask"—and look for the good in one another. They can eliminate all forms of violence in the home by disciplining without slapping or spanking, by arguing without pushing and shoving, by expressing thoughts and feelings without shouting, by seeking assistance without threats. And they can protect family members, to the best of their ability, from the horrors of the world in ways that teach them to learn from such horrors, not run from them; to triumph over such horrors, not be defeated by them; and to appreciate that while everything and everybody in this world may not be all good, everything and everyone also is not all bad.

Finally, focusing on the good in the family is facilitated by reaching out to other families in the community. But this cannot happen without recognizing how each family member is responsible to other families, how intertwined families are, and how dependent they are upon one another.

When Michael Pollen decided to hire excavators to create a backyard pond behind his house in October 1993, he was amazed at how quickly the pond filled with water and life began to teem in and around it. In March, algae began to drift through the water. By the end of the month, the song of the spring peepers came from the pond, soon joined by a chorus of bullfrogs. In May backswimmers sought meals of insect larvae and whirligig beetles zoomed across the surface. Water striders, aquatic plants, cattails, spiders, and waterfowl used the pond during the warm months, while the tracks of fox, wild turkeys, deer, raccoons, woodchucks, and various species of birds were visible in the snow.

Elated at the success of his pond, Pollen "was happy now to let nature take its course, pleased to have had a hand in the making of this thriving new ecosystem."[14] He brought a jar of its water to a local biology teacher to gain a deeper knowledge of the life his pond was sustaining. As the teacher viewed the water, he informed Pollan that his man-made pond would not remain a pond for very long. Left untended, the algae and weeds would continue to grow, die, and then settle to the bottom. This would make the water shallower which, in turn, would let more light into the bottom of the pond so the weeds would redouble. The pond would gradually turn into a swamp, then a wet spot, and then return to its original state—woodland—unless Pollan intervened and began a rigorous program of pond maintenance. As he listened to the teacher, Pollan thought:

> I had naively assumed that, the digging done, I could step back and let my pond take care of itself. Not so. Digging this hole, I took on a responsibility—sharing, for better or worse, in the life and death of a pond. No longer a spectator standing on the shore, I'm now in deep.[15]

A family community can be likened to a pond. It is made up of a variety of different families, each with its own lifestyles, backgrounds, cultures, ethnicities, religions, beliefs, and so on. Yet all the diverse families in the community must learn to share in ensuring each family's survival, in order to ensure the survival of the entire "pond" community. Remove one family from the community "pond," and the impact is felt in each of the remaining families; thus, each must exist in order to sustain the others. Yet, on the other hand, each, if allowed to proliferate uncontrollably, will strangle the others, leading to the ultimate destruction of the whole community. So family communities work best when the individual families are committed to the survival not only of themselves, but also of the others in their community.

Service to other families in a community can take many forms: individual (such as helping neighbors paint their house, offering child-care assistance, or taking food to a family that has lost a member) or through outside organizations (such as coaching a softball team, volunteering to take a scouting group on a camping trip, or starting a neighborhood crime watch campaign). Supporting the positive development of other families in the community can bring joy and self-esteem to all who are involved—those being helped as well those who are helping. And each experience of reaching out to other families is an investment in the family's community—an investment in the community's future and well as the family's own future—so the family can look ahead to forging and attaining its American Dream.

Harvesting the Family Soul: Forging the Family's "American Dream"

The American Dream began as a "shimmering vision of freedom and democracy, a vision not so much about coming here as leaving somewhere else."[16] The Pilgrims escaped religious oppression and King George III. Immigrants left famine, civil war and conflict, poverty, and pogroms. While the original American Dream was about freedom *from* something rather than freedom *to be* something, gradually everything and anything seemed possible in America. After all, the Pilgrims could arrive in America sick and starving, land by mistake on a freezing Cape Cod beach rather than on the shores of Virginia, and still plant the seeds to grow a powerful nation. As well, immigrants could leave their homelands with very little, pack themselves like cattle in steerage, endure incredible hardship, arrive at Ellis Island, and go on to earn diplomas and degrees, build businesses, buy homes, and prosper. The story of America being a great land of opportunity turned out to be reality rather than myth; thus, the American Dream was filled with great opportunities and possibilities.

But gradually the American Dream, which began with a vision of freedom and democracy and which promised its citizens fulfillment of such basic and simple needs as life, liberty, and the pursuit of happiness, shifted. To have a job, adequate food, comfortable shelter, and a place to gather and worship were not enough. America determined to do more for her citizens, which initiated a process of granting and giving that subconsciously established a historical trend of each succeeding generation desiring to live better than the one before it. This historical trend soon distinguished America not just as the land of the free, but also as "the land of the freebie":

Freed slaves were promised 40 acres and a mule. Herbert Hoover offered a chicken in every pot. Huey Long said he'd make every man a king in Louisiana. In America, a free lunch—and free land—came with the citizenship papers. The Homestead Act in 1862 offered 160 acres of Midwestern land to anyone who would settle on them.

In Oklahoma, they fired a pistol in 1889 and let settlers stake their claim to whatever land they could grab. When the winds came in the '30s and blew the topsoil away, the dispossessed farmers and ranchers crammed their belongings into jalopies and headed for the next Eden. . . . [17]

Yet even when the "Okies" ended up living in shacks picking fruit for pennies a bushel, when blacks left the South only to end up working in northern factories for "slave" wages and living in big-city ghettos, and when laid-off workers surged to Texas only to find that the oil industry had gone bust, Americans still believed that a newspaper boy could become a millionaire. Because they lived in a relatively young nation that had done nothing to dissuade them from believing that anything was possible, they invested hard-earned dollars in the stock market and then watched it crash. But before the impact of bankruptcy, joblessness, and hunger could be felt, President Franklin Roosevelt gave Americans back their dream and led them to believe that they could expect entitlements without taxation.

As federal benefits kept growing, the American Dream became firmly and irrevocably linked to prosperity, instilling the expectation that everyone could have anything he or she wanted; if Americans could not provide it themselves, someone else would. Americans went credit-crazy. They pumped cash into speculative investments and real estate and continued to live as they had, even though inflation ran into the double digits, the economy grew stagnant, and fistfights were a common occurrence in long gas lines. At the time, President Carter stated that buying had become more valued than being and that Americans were looking for happiness in the wrong places; he lost his bid for reelection.

In many ways the 1950s were most probably the best times—and the last times—for Americans to attain an American Dream that linked the freedom to live an independent life with unexpected and great economic prosperity. It was a time in which young Americans could buy a home, own a car, and purchase a color television on one blue-collar worker's salary. It was a time in which a child who had grown up in the Depression and survived World War II could live in relative peace, prosperity, and harmony. It was a time in which Americans gave to their country without question or hesitation because the country had given to them in ways that honored the trust and faith its citizens had in it. And it was a time in which Americans expected relatively little and received much.

For American families today, however, much has changed. Most Americans are barely treading water, most are not better off than their parents were (nor do they expect to be), most realize that where they are now is most likely where they will be for an unknown period of time. Rather than a time in which people think that things will get better, the 1990s has become a time in which layoffs, furloughs, pay freezes, real estate downswings, "academic gypsies" (people with PhDs who go from place to place, wherever there is a teaching job), temp services, six-figure private college tabs, decreasing child-care services, health-care restructuring, threats to Social Security, and little chance of advancement have led Americans into a time of adjustment in which the American Dream as it was known to previous generations no longer exists, cannot be achieved in the same way again, and thus must be rethought.

This means that families today need to forge their own version of the American Dream for their present and for their future. Rather than remain disillusioned over what cannot be, families must begin to restore a sense of optimism within their families from what can be: a newfound freedom, a new possibility, a new hope, a new opportunity—all of the things that the American Dream has provided for families in the past. To live without any dream in this time of diminished expectations is to give up hope for the future. To instead forge a new dream within the family unit means to create and believe in a collective vision of a way to best live with devotion, pride, and faith in the future of the individual, the family, the nation, and the world.

The family's own version of the American Dream ought not to be based on material possessions and their attainment—these are financial goals and budgetary considerations—but needs to be based on something more directly beneficial over the long term to the family and its members. The family's own version of the American Dream, like the dream of the country's earliest settlers, needs to be simple and devoid of expectations. The family's own version of the American Dream needs to use the wisdom of the past to provide a foundation for a future that is based on the heritage of the country and its peoples.

The family's own version of the American Dream needs to be based on meaningful relationships and respect for the community of land, animals, plants, and other people. The family's own version of the American Dream needs to restore those things promised in the Declaration of Independence and the Bill of Rights. And the family's own version of the American Dream needs to be about service and giving so it can retreat from its materialistic focus and move closer to emotional and spiritual matters.

To make a most profound effect, the family's own version of the American Dream ought to flow from the original vision of the founding mothers and fathers of this country, a vision that materialized from a naive faith that "spurred Americans to defy King George III . . . helped them patch their country together after the Civil War and gave them the grit and ingenuity to get through the Depression."[18] In order to best do this, families need to fashion an American Dream that requires them to expect more from themselves—to promote greater self-reliance and autonomy within the family. And they need to do this on their own, without expecting the government or society to provide it for them. Then, and only then, can families begin to issue calls of action to other families, to their communities, and to the nation that promote politics, economics, and services that value the family and its American Dream.

Harvesting the Family Soul: Promoting Family Services

A family's future is greatly influenced by what society decides to do for the family—by how it treats the family, by the messages it conveys to the family, by how well it responds to the family, and by the support it provides for the family. Because the family is a fundamental and vital social institution, its survival needs to be assured by society; society needs to do for the family, and so the family needs to take an active role in making sure that this happens.

But society does not always make it easy for the family. For more than two hundred years, the development of this nation first as an industrial society and then as a technological society has had a major influence on family life—from courtship to marriage to child-rearing to personal lifestyles. The family has had to adapt to its society; in fact, the major changes that have occurred in family life even in the past few decades have been in response to economic, political, and social changes that are not only shaping the future of the country, but also the futures of families and their members.

But just how well does American society make its choices to protect the family, to ensure its survival, and to respect and honor its value to society? For families that wish to develop their potential, the task is made much more difficult when they are threatened with conflict (such as war) or national and international problems. For most Americans, who desire that their families be free from poverty, want, and hunger, the national economy has created an unprecedented combination of economic woes that have been evidenced by a steady decline in the standard of living and a gradual deterioration in the quality of personal and family life. As well, despite numerous studies and surveys, the government continually places in jeopardy the very programs designed to ease some of the fallout created by this financial strain on families. One program in particular, the 1946 National School Lunch Act, has been threatened with cuts since the Reagan Administration attempted to reclassify catsup and pickles as vegetables—cuts that are seriously considered despite evidence of frighteningly high percentages of hunger in America's children, nationwide participation by over 14 million children in the program, and studies that reveal that food programs are associated with significant improvements in academic functioning.

For families that wish to safeguard the health of each family member, society has done little to make health care equitably available to all of its citizens, to ease the fear of being wiped out financially by medical expenses in connection with a major illness, or to protect its families from arbitrary, life-threatening, and incomprehensible health care system decisions.

For families in which a parent or parents need to work graveyard shifts, swing shifts, or weekends in order to make ends meet, there is little available child care that corresponds with such hours. As a result, children are sometimes left sleeping in cars parked in company lots, or parents opt to go on welfare or unemployment until they can find suitable arrangements for the children.

Families that are concerned about television and the impact that violent, sexually explicit, ethnically ignorant, and commercially slanted programming has on their children are being ignored. Instead, families are being forced to accept cuts in funding for public broadcasting and educational programming. They are finding only limited regulatory enforcement of the Children's Television Act of 1990, which requires television stations to provide some educational and informational programming for children. They are seeing gradual network abandonment of the "family hour"—between 8 P.M. and 9 P.M.—in which kid-oriented shows have now been replaced by prime-time slots for adult comedies and shows that dramatize many of the horrors and tragedies in the daily news. And they are waging their own private conflicts with their children over major merchandising tie-ins to television characters. What children watch on television does make a difference, but society chooses to ignore studies like the one that showed "those who regularly watched 'Sesame Street' and other educational programs performed signficantly better on standard verbal and math tests than did children who consistently watched adult programs and entertainment cartoons."[19]

For families that are concerned about ensuring their members know the difference between right and wrong, conduct themselves in moral ways, become and remain honest and trustworthy, take initiative and seek to effect change, and assume responsibility for their own lives as well as for the lives of those around them, their most constant and determined detractor is society itself. A culture such as that of the United States, which allows its individuals so much free choice, so many alternatives, and so much freedom is

> asking a great deal of human beings. In social life, as in literature, some of the finest human achievements have been within restrictions as rigid as those of the sonnet form. Our American culture is more like a sprawling novel where every page may deal with a new encounter and with a special choice. We ask a great deal of individuals when we give them such wide latitude and so little respected authority.[20]

All of the previous examples of conflicts between a family's needs and how society chooses to address such needs has led one author of a book on American families to conclude:

> In spite of all our American sentiment about the home and the family, we do not show great concern about buttressing it against catastrophe. Any well-considered national program must have regard for the children; if they are housed and fed below a certain minimum, if their health is not attended to, the nation suffers in the next

generation. The lack of a tolerable economic floor under the family is especially crucial. . . . When factories close, when inflation comes, the family gets little consideration in the United States. Sickness insurance, too, which would provide preventive care as well as relieve the family budget of all expenses in a crisis, needs high priority in a national program. When one reads about families in trouble, it is clear that many of the reefs which are threatening shipwreck are avoidable by intelligent local, state, or national programs.[21]

While this author's observations appear to be timely for the current position of the family in America's social hierarchy, it ought to be pointed out that they were penned in *1949!* The fact that not much has changed in nearly five decades means that American families have not chosen to speak up for themselves, have declined to take an active role in protecting themselves, have been content to live in a vacuum, and have placed the greater part of their efforts into day-to-day survival rather than into the creation of exciting future potential and possibilities for a better life. In effect, some American families have no one to blame but themselves for society's abandonment of them.

It is obvious that family life is affected and shaped by society. Knowing this ought to empower and liberate families, while ignoring this weakens and limits them. Thus, a family can motivate itself as a unit to begin to work together as a family as well as with other families in its community, to rebuild family strengths, to focus on issues of concern, and to get involved from a variety of different perspectives in order to effect changes in society that will create positive impacts on the family. Or, more simply stated, *families need to take action now.*

Families and their members can work through government and the political process to facilitate change and vote for those who propose and promote programs and regulations that benefit the family—and pressure and publicize those who do not. Families can become involved in campaigns to develop and implement family programs on the national, state, and local level. Families can gather together with other families who have similar needs and use public speaking or letter writing skills to activate the group to work together on a common cause that can assist each family. Families can even start businesses that will fill the needs not only of one family, but of many, and support and strengthen the family's community. As well, there are a multitude of societal issues to become involved in as a family that directly affect families: calling for family-oriented personnel policies in the workplace (flex time, leave policies, child care, and so on); seeking ways to prevent alcohol and drug abuse and fighting tobacco companies' insistence on marketing cigarettes to minors; urging that changes be made in tax codes that recognize full-time homemakers, single parents, cohabiting partners, and the infirm; promoting child-care options in the home, in the community, and on a national level; supporting family violence prevention programs; encouraging regulation of cable television; and many, many others. By focusing on what society can do for families in the broad sense and by not getting bogged down in emotional issues such as abortion, teen pregnancy, feminism, gay and lesbian issues, and racial inequities, families can learn to embrace their own needs as well as the needs of all families.

Harvesting the Family Soul: Embracing All Families

Because many families are needed to create and nurture a society, it is vital to the future of the society as well as to the future of each family that families support one another. It is simply not enough to care about what goes on within the four walls of your family's home, within your extended family, in your family's neighborhood, or in your community. Your family is part of the human family, and that means that you are linked with many other families that may be physically, emotionally, and spiritually different from yours. Thus, what goes on in the black community goes on in the white community;

what goes on in the Christian community goes on in the Jewish community; what goes on in the single-parent community goes on in the two-parent community; what goes on in the gay and lesbian community goes on in the straight community; what goes on in the adopted-adoptee community goes on in the birth child–birth parent community; and so on. All of these communities make up the entire human community, and every family is part of that community.

This modern desire for a more universal reaching out to other families regardless of differences was most recently and profoundly evidenced by the National Association of Black Social Workers, a coalition which has, since its formation in the 1970s, condemned interracial adoption and at one point vehemently termed such placements "cultural genocide." But in 1994 the NABSW "softened its stance to make transracial adoption a third option behind preservation of biological African-American families and placement of black children in black homes."[22] In revising its decades-old prejudice against transracial placements, the coalition went a step further and began to press for new federal guidelines to make the adoption process color-blind, leading First Lady Hillary Clinton to write in her syndicated newspaper column that "skin color [should] not outweigh the more important gift of love that adoptive parents want to offer."[23]

The action of embracing all families signifies that the most important consideration is families, not their differences, and that, because of this, the needs of all families are, in the broadest and most meaningful sense, very much alike. The need to care for your family's soul, for example, is just as significant as the need for other families to care for theirs. Every other family too must create, cultivate, and nurture an experience of family that connects them not only to themselves, but also to society and nature, to the nation and its history, to the world and its mysteries, to the families that have preceded them, and to the families that will succeed them.

Thus, through the simple act of embracing all families—

through extending compassion and assistance when needed; through educating your family about other backgrounds, religions, and lifestyles; through enjoying festivals, celebrations, music, dance, and art of other cultures; and through supporting the causes that concern others—you are touching the heart and the soul of the "world" of family. In doing this, you are embracing a culture of family which, in turn, embraces the culture of your family. And this means that you are truly caring for your family's soul.

NOTES

1. May, Elaine Tyler. *Homeward Bound: American Families in the Cold War Era.* Basic Books, Inc., New York, 1988, pp. 17–18, 20.
2. *Ibid.*, pp. 23–24.
3. Oder, Norman. "Back to the Fifties," *Publishers Weekly,* May 29, 1995.
4. *Ibid.*
5. Curran, Dolores. *Traits of a Healthy Family.* HarperSanFrancisco, San Francisco, 1983, p. 199.
6. Salkin, Rabbi Jeffrey K. "Are Americans Working Too Hard?" *Reader's Digest,* July 1995.
7. Lehigh, Scot. "Vacation fax," *Boston Sunday Globe,* July 30, 1995.
8. Stinnett, Nick and DeFrain, John. *Secrets of Strong Families.* Little, Brown and Company, Boston, 1985, (page number unknown).
9. *Ibid.*
10. Curran, pp. 257–258.
11. *Ibid.*, pp. 258–259.
12. *Ibid.*, p. 259.
13. Noonan, Peggy. "Points to Ponder," *Reader's Digest,* August 1995.
14. Pollan, Michael. "Secret World of a Pond," *Reader's Digest,* June 1995.
15. *Ibid.*
16. Powers, John. "Great expectations and how we became so disappointed," *The Boston Globe Magazine,* March 12, 1995.
17. *Ibid.*
18. *Ibid.*
19. Wulf, Steve. "Glued to the Tube," *Time,* June 26, 1995.
20. Anshen, Ruth Nanda. *The Family: Its Function and Destiny.* Harper & Brothers Publishers, New York, 1949, p. 167.
21. *Ibid.*, p. 166.
22. Smolowe, Jill. "Adoption in Black and White," *Time,* August 14, 1995.
23. *Ibid.*

BIBLIOGRAPHY

Abrams, Ray H. *The American Family in World War II*. Arno Press & The New York Times, New York, 1972.

Alexander, Shoshana. *In Praise of Single Parents: Mothers and Fathers Embracing the Challenge*. Houghton Mifflin, Boston, 1994.

Anshen, Ruth Nanda. *The Family: Its Function and Destiny*. Harper & Brothers Publishers, New York, 1949.

Bartholet, Elizabeth. *Family Bonds: Adoption and the Politics of Parenting*. Houghton Mifflin Company, Boston, 1993.

Benkov, Laura. *Reinventing the Family: The Emerging Story of Lesbian and Gay Parents*. Crown Publishers, Inc., New York, 1994.

Beuttler, William. *Family, The Future: A Bill of Rights for Children*. Libra Publishers, Inc., San Diego, CA, 1990.

Blau, Melinda. *Families Apart: Ten Keys to Successful Co-Parenting*. Perigee, New York, 1993.

Bradshaw, John. *Bradshaw On: The Family*. Health Communications, Inc., Deerfield Beach, FL, 1993.

Brussat, Frederic and Mary Ann. *100 Ways to Keep Your Soul Alive: Living Deeply and Fully Every Day*. HarperSanFrancisco, San Francisco, 1994.

Burke, Phyllis. *Family Values: Two Moms and Their Son*. Random House, New York, 1993.

Calhoun, Arthur W. *A Social History of the American Family from Colonial Times to Present*. Barnes & Noble, Inc., New York, 1945.

Caplow, Theodore, Bahr, Howard M., Chadwick, Bruce A., Hill, Reuben, and Williamson, Margaret Holmes. *Middletown Families: Fifty Years of Change and Continuity*. University of Minnesota Press, Minneapolis, 1982.

Carter, Richard B. *Nurturing Evolution: The Family as a Social Womb*. University Press of America, Lanham, MD, 1993.

Coontz, Stephanie. *The Way We Never Were: American Families and the Nostalgia Trap*. Basic Books, New York, 1992.

Curran, Dolores. *Traits of a Healthy Family: Fifteen Traits Commonly Found in Healthy Families by Those Who Work with Them.* HarperSanFrancisco, San Francisco, 1983.

Demos, John. *Past, Present, and Personal: The Family and the Life Course in American History.* Oxford University Press, New York, 1986.

Finney, Jack. *Time and Again.* Simon and Schuster, New York, 1970.

Gilman, Lois. *The Adoption Resource Book.* Harper & Row Publishers, New York, 1987.

Gottlieb, Beatrice. *The Family in the Western World: From the Black Death to the Industrial Age.* Oxford University Press, New York, 1993.

Hirshey, Gerri. *Nowhere to Run: The Story of Soul Music.* Times Books, New York, 1984.

Hultkrantz, Åke. *Conceptions of the Soul Among North American Indians.* Caslon Press, Stockholm, Sweden, 1953.

Ingerman, Sandra. *Soul Retrieval: Mending the Fragmented Self.* HarperSanFrancisco, San Francisco, 1991.

Kirkendall, Lester A., and Gravatt, Arthur E., eds. *Marriage and the Family in the Year 2020.* Prometheus Books, Buffalo, NY, 1984.

Jenness, Aylette. *Families: A Celebration of Diversity, Commitment, and Love.* Houghton Mifflin Company, Boston, 1990.

Leslie, Gerald. *The Family in Social Context,* 4th ed. Oxford University Press, Inc., New York, 1979.

Lindsey, Karen. *Friends As Family: New Kinds of Families and What They Could Mean For You.* Beacon Press, Boston, 1981.

Lockridge, Frances. *Adopting a Child: Where, When and How to Obtain a Happy, Healthy Youngster.* Greenberg: Publisher, New York, 1947.

Martin, April. *The Lesbian and Gay Parenting Book: Creating and Raising Our Families.* Harper Perennial, New York, 1993.

Mathabane, Mark and Mathabane, Gail. *Love in Black and White: The Triumph of Love Over Prejudice and Taboo.* HarperCollins, New York, 1992.

May, Elaine Tyler. *Homeward Bound: American Families in the Cold War Era.* Basic Books, Inc., New York, 1988.

Mead, Margaret, and Heyman, Ken. *Family.* MacMillan, New York, 1965.

Melina, Lois Ruskai. *Making Sense of Adoption.* Harper & Row Publishers, Inc., 1989.

Melina, Lois Ruskai. *Raising Adopted Children: A Manual for Adoptive Parents.* Harper & Row Publishers, Inc., New York, 1986.

Moore, Thomas. *Soul Mates: Honoring the Mysteries of Love and Relationship.* HarperPerennial, New York, 1994.

Queen, Stuart, and Habenstein, Robert W. *The Family in Various Cultures,* 3rd ed. J. B. Lippincott Company, Philadelphia, 1967.

Reinhardt, Adina M., and Quinn, Mildred D. *Family-Centered Community Nursing: A Socio-cultural Framework.* The C. V. Mosby Community, St. Louis, 1973.

Salk, Dr. Lee. *Familyhood: Nuturing the Values That Matter.* Simon & Schuster, New York, 1992.

Schiffman, Jack. *Harlem Heyday: A Pictorial History of Modern Black Show Business and the Apollo Theatre.* Prometheus Books, Buffalo, NY, 1984.

SOUL An Archaeology: Readings from Socrates to Ray Charles. Cousineau, Phil, ed. HarperSanFrancisco, San Francisco, 1994.

Stinnett, Nick, and Birdsong, Craig Wayne. *The Family and Alternate Life Styles.* Nelson-Hall Inc., Chicago, 1978.

Stinnett, Nick, and DeFrain, John. *Secrets of Strong Families.* Little, Brown and Company, Boston, 1985.

Stone, Elizabeth. *Black Sheep and Kissing Cousins: How Our Family Stories Shape Us.* Times Books, New York, 1988.

Straus, Murray A., Gelles, Richard J., and Steinmetz, Suzanne K. *Behind Closed Doors: Violence in the American Family.* Anchor Press/Doubleday, New York, 1980.

Swinburne, Richard. *The Evolution of the Soul.* Clarendon Press, Oxford, 1986.

Thomas, Marlo & Friends. *Free To Be . . . A Family: A Book About All Kinds of Belonging.* Bantam Books, New York, 1987.

Tilby, Angela. *Soul: God, Self and The New Cosmology.* Doubleday, New York, 1992.

Vannoy, Steven W. *The 10 Greatest Gifts I Give My Children: Parenting from the Heart.* Simon & Schuster, New York, 1994.

Walsh, David. *Selling Out America's Children: How America Puts Profits Before Values—and What Parents Can Do.* Deaconess Press, Minneapolis, 1994.

"We Had Everything But Money." Reminisce Books, Greendale, WI, 1992.